THE BOOK OF POOLE

Harbour and Town

RODNEY LEGG

HALSGROVE

First published in Great Britain in 2005

British Library Cataloguing-in-Publication Data
A CIP record for this title is available from the British Library

ISBN 1 84114 411 8

HALSGROVE

Halsgrove House
Lower Moor Way
Tiverton, Devon EX16 6SS
Tel: 01884 243242
Fax: 01884 243325
Email: sales@halsgrove.com
Website: www.halsgrove.com

Frontispiece photograph: *The Parish Church of St James, seen from the corner of Thames Street and Church Street, was rebuilt in 1820.*

Printed and bound in Great Britain by CPI Bath

Contents

Introduction

Maritime Poole, the biggest of Dorset's historic towns, spreads across three peninsulas. The outer one, consisting now of the most valuable real estate this side of Tokyo, is Sandbanks. The next is the industrial salient of Hamworthy. Thirdly, central to the story, comes the Old Town itself.

The local coastline is as relatively recent as any in these days. Post-glacial rises in sea level, between 100,000 and 60,000 years ago and then from 10,000 to 7,000BC, caused the rapid coastal retreats that resulted in the shapes of Poole Bay and Poole Harbour almost as we know them today. Heathland sands were rapidly eroded, as far back as the ironstone beds of Hengistbury Head, in a landform setting held at the outer edges by a triangle of bayside 'fixed points' on the harder beds of stone and chalk that are represented by Durlston Head, Handfast Point and the Needles of the Isle of Wight. The mouldings to this frame are still in a state of flux, with Little Sea and the eastern side of South Haven peninsula having developed since 1700, through the dynamics of deposition that delivered a succession of Bournemouth beaches. Inside the harbour, the marshes of *Spartina* cord-grass – a South American immigrant – date from the twentieth century.

The first thing I learned about Poole Harbour when, as a teenager, I walked around its succession of inlets and marshes that encircle between 50 miles in theory and 100 miles in practice – straight-line progress is impossible – is that it experiences double tides. The phenomenon is caused by its virtually land-locked nature and the added complication of the mouth of the Solent on the other side of Poole Bay, in which there are eight changes of the tide in a 24-hour period. The standard sequence is four, which you have to take into account in order to realise the difference: 1, flowing for six hours; 2, ebbing for six hours; 3, flowing for six hours; 4, ebbing for six hours.

The tidal sequence in Poole Harbour is as follows, with inward movements being longer and slower than the quicker outward spasms: 1, the tide flows in for six hours; 2, goes out for an hour and a half; 3, comes in for an hour and a half; 4, goes out for three hours; 5, comes in for six hours; 6, goes out for an hour and a half; 7, comes in for an hour and a half; 8, goes out for 3 hours.

In Poole Bay the average tidal range, influenced by the strong flows in and out of the Solent, is one of the smallest on the South Coast. The difference rises to 1.7 metres (spring flood tides) and then drops to only 0.6 metre (near ebb tides).

Out on the water, in rowing parlance, 'Pooleman's jit' is a hunched short stroke. It is characteristic of the handling of the traditional shallow-draught punts on Poole Harbour and was demonstrated to me by retired boatman Benjamin Beaverstock Pond (1898–1982). Many claimed to have recognised the distinctive action in Poole expatriates the world over, such as a member of the Hardy family from Swanage, who spotted a Poole man rowing off Shanghai and shouted an appropriate greeting. Woodes Rogers, who discovered the model for Robinson Crusoe, took it all the way to the Pacific island of Juan Fernandez, down below the tropics towards Cape Horn at latitude 79 degrees south.

Poole Harbour, in winter, is of international importance for black-tailed godwit and shelduck. It is of national importance for several species of wildfowl, including gadwall, goldeneye, pochard, red-breasted merganser and scaup. Waders of equal significance – the cachet applying to an area holding more than one per cent of the national population of a species – are avocet, curlew, dunlin, grey plover and redshank.

Offshore there are four species of grebe and three of diver, plus significant numbers of red-breasted merganser, and Pilot's Point at the south end of Shell Bay is the roosting place at dusk for more than 3,000 birds. Principal species here are bar-tailed godwit, dunlin, grey plover, and ringed plover.

My introduction to the landscape and the setting came from the last of such old-timers as Benjamin Pond, who I have already mentioned. Richard Blomfield also remembered him as being the last of his line, literally, as he was baiting 'trot-lines' with dozens of hooks. Each hook on these hand-lines carried a worm. This was Blomfield writing in 1989 about Pond in *Harbour, Heath and Islands*:

> *Ben Pond looks as if he has grown out of the reeds and saltings of those bird-haunted, fish-haunted waters. He is tall, craggy, sun and wind-burned and looks a little like one of those long-legged gaunt fishermen, like herons, who stand so patiently in the shallows. He has a remarkable understanding of the ways of fish and always knows where to find them.*

I came to feel the same affinity and empathy for the waterscape and its characters. My notes from them have been accumulated over four decades and range from Bernard Short in suburban Parkstone in 1964 to

Geoff Hann, during 2004, wardening the National Trust seaboard across the water from the Sandbanks ferry. Another layer of Poole anecdotes was almost freshly caught from Newfoundland returnees and visitors, with echoes of the Grand Banks which provided the town with its long-distance fishing grounds.

As a boy, with friend Norman Chislett in 1959, I climbed into the pilots' seats of the beached hulks of Empire flying-boats at Hamworthy. Since then I have recorded the experiences of both crew and passengers on the postwar flights from Poole to Australia. On and off, for 500 years, Poole has been at the hub of the British Empire. The town's emblem, symbolising its prosperity from the sixteenth century onwards, is dried cod.

Being a Bournemouth boy, I learned at school that Poole and Christchurch held our birthright, and that as a Victorian new town we had no claim to our own history. Poole was credited with having, after Sydney, the second largest natural harbour in the world. Even our own Bournemouth Bay, cartographically and correctly, is Poole Bay. That says it all.

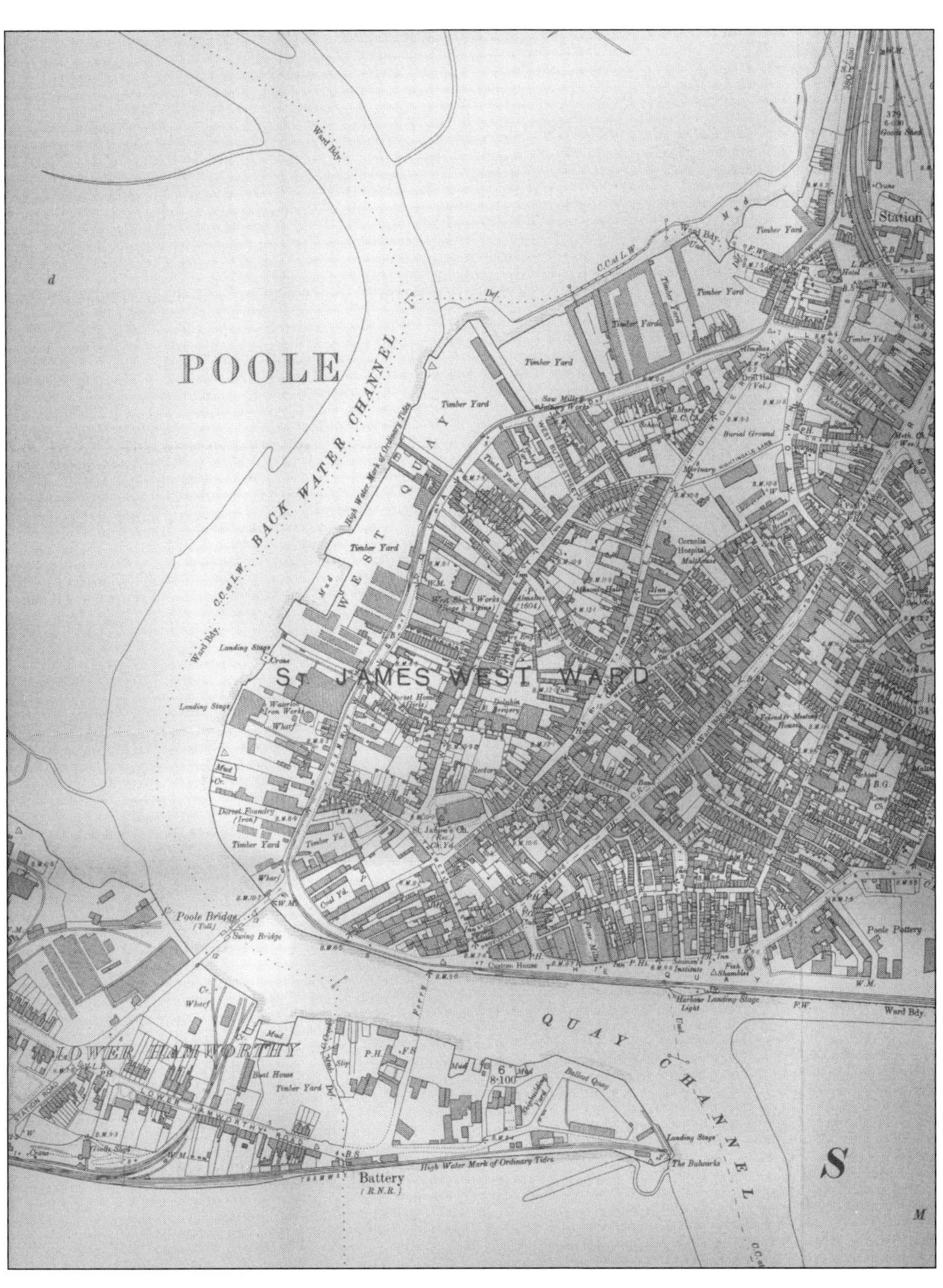

Poole's inner peninsulas of the Old Town (top) *and Hamworthy* (bottom left) *as mapped by the Ordnance Survey in 1900.*

The Poole Bay approach to Poole Harbour, from Canford Cliffs, across the Swash Channel to Old Harry Rocks (top left) *and the Purbeck Hills.*

✦ CHAPTER 1 ✦

Prehistoric People

Palaeolithic hand-axes of the Chellean and Acheulian types, in flints long since stained to match the brown tones of the gravels in which they are discovered, were regularly found at Canford Cliffs, Branksome Park and Corfe Mullen. Cogdean Pit and the Ballast Pit of the Southern Railway Company, both at Corfe Mullen, were particularly productive. Palaeolithic hunters of the Lower Palaeolithic Chellean period date from the second inter-glacial epoch of 350,000BC. The Acheulian period covers the third inter-glacial epoch, from 150,000 to 50,000BC, with Late Acheulian activity continuing into the succeeding glacial epoch, probably until 25,000BC.

This side of the last Ice Age, from 4,000 to 2,500BC, much more prolific quantities of flints and pottery, left by Neolithic herdsmen, have been discovered during development for housing and digging for aggregates. A hoard of five polished flint axes were found at Hamworthy.

For the first physical features left on the landscape, there were a total of 34 surviving Bronze-Age round barrow burial-mounds in Poole's hinterland, as recorded by the Royal Commission on Historical Monuments in 1970. The locations were given of another seven that had been destroyed in the twentieth century.

Mainly dating from 2,500 to 1,500BC, about half of the surviving mounds occur in clusters, with groups on Barrow Hill (six), Broadstone Golf Course and Rose Lawn Coppice (eight), Canford Heath (four) and Knighton Heath (two survive, but there used to be at least six). Knighton was still a 'great heath' in late-Victorian times, when it was recorded that 'on it are Figbury, Hawkesbury, Lush and other barrows.' The majority of these were of the standard bowl barrow shape, except on Barrow Hill where four of the six are Wessex Culture bell barrows with a berm between the ditch and the mound. Fern Barrow, though damaged, just about holds the line where Bourne Valley nature reserve meets Bournemouth suburbia.

Under a tree in the grounds of Branksome Library, covered in grass, is a mystery stone. It is a half-ton sarsen boulder from the downlands of central Dorset, which is a rock alien to the Bagshot Beds of the eastern heaths. It was dug up in 1909 about 8–10ft below Ashley Road, Parkstone, near the top of Constitution Hill. There was conjecture on whether it was a monolith erected by Bronze- Age man or, given its depth, a relic of the strata of hard rock that formerly overlaid the chalk and could have slid down on to the heath in an ancient ice age. Subsequent research has made the latter increasingly implausible. Instead, as with the Devil's Stone on Black Hill above Bere Regis, it seems to have had a relationship with heathland burial-mounds. With the relentless advance of suburbia, these have been disappearing from all over the former heaths of Poole and Bournemouth for the past couple of centuries.

Long after its religious, astronomical or ceremonial significance had been forgotten, the prehistoric monolith became a boundary stone in Anglo-Saxon times. The trackways beside it made the transitions from prehistoric ridgeway to medieval road and then turnpike route into modern highways. The historian and writer Michael Dawney shares my fascination in this remarkable stone and its relationship to both Ringwood Road and Ashley Road. Many such stones, along with distinctive trees and natural landmarks, appear in charters. The stone then took on a name, being the Park Stone of medieval Canford Manor – a reference to its deer park rather than an ornamental landscape – and gave its name to the Parkstone of today.

Poole as a name is equally easy to locate. The 'pool' was a coastal mere surrounded by reed beds. It formed the backwater of the harbour between the ancient but now in-filled and reclaimed Baiter peninsula and the Poole Park lakes.

Ancient Greek and Aegean bronze coins which found their way to Poole Harbour and the Stour Valley were collected by Revd Thomas Rackett, the rector of Spetisbury, who died in 1840. His finds, and those of others, were studied by Dr Joseph Grafton Milne for his *Finds of Greek Coins in the British Isles*, published in 1948. They date from the fourth to the first centuries BC and are compelling evidence of the international nature of activity through the Iron Age port settlements in Poole and Christchurch Harbours. These included Cleavel Point, Hamworthy and Hengistbury Head. The most remarkable relic is one of the contemporary boats, which survives almost intact.

Saturated and sodden, a dug-out oak canoe was dredged up from Brownsea Road anchorage in 1964. It is 5ft wide and had been paddled by a 19-strong crew. The stern section, 23ft long, was found first that August, with a further 10ft of the hull being recovered by skin-divers a few days later. For years these were immersed in a great tank at Scaplen's Court, gently soaking in successive baths of preservatives, as faster treatment would have seen them falling to bits, until polyethylene glycol turned them into a stabilised display item.

The monoxylon (a boat made from a single piece of timber) dates from about 295BC. It has two strengthening transverse ribs carved out of the floor and is significant as the linear predecessor of the harbour's shallow-draught punts. These retained the same basic design for the unusually well protected semi-landlocked waters. Such boats were the mainstay of the harbour's non-seagoing internal transport system for both cargoes and passengers.

The main Iron-Age port for the Isle of Purbeck was on Cleavel Point. At the eastern extremity of the Ower peninsula, reached by the South Deep channel from the far side of Brownsea Island, this vied with Hengistbury in Christchurch Harbour which became a major Durotrigian trading post. The name of the Durotriges means 'water dwellers'. They were mentioned by the astronomer Ptolemy and secured a place in classical history as the last to resist Roman rule in these parts, having built the biggest of the British hill-forts in the century before the invasion.

Early Iron-Age activity at Lower Hamworthy, from 450 to 200BC, included long-distance trading that brought an old bronze torc, a coin from the Greek colony of Tauromenium, in Sicily, four glass beads from Gaul and a glass bracelet. Cross-Channel trade was with the seafaring Veneti tribe from Brittany and the Loire estuary. An anchor, chain and 7-inch nails found at Bulbury Camp, between Lytchett Minster and Morden, in 1881, match the description of the fittings of such ships in Julius Caesar's *The Conquest of Gaul.*

The Quay Channel and boatyards on the Hamworthy side of the water, where Iron-Age traders established the first port of Poole.

✦ CHAPTER 2 ✦

Roman Rulers

Vespasian brought the Second Legion Augusta into Poole Harbour to subdue resistance in the West Country after the Roman landings of AD43. His chosen sea-base at Lower Hamworthy, where he took over the existing Iron-Age settlement, reached from the Backwater Channel into Holes Bay. It had as its haven an oval basin to the east between the present Poole Bridge and Ferry Road. Unlike Hamworthy's shallow southern shore, this not only had deep-water access but was totally protected from waves and the weather.

Vespasian built a road from here, westwards to the shore of Wareham Channel beside what was later to become Hamworthy Station, where smaller boats would have been beached at a hard, which is a nautical term for a slipway. The road goes north-westwards before heading north, inland to Lake Gates at Corfe Mullen, where a major legionary base was established. It may have been named Moriconium or Moriduno to describe its location as a 'fortress by the sea'.

In Lower Hamworthy the course of the Roman road was discovered in 1947 when workmen were laying a water main as they prepared the site for Herbert Carter Secondary Modern School. It crossed Blandford Road north-west of the Old Ropewalk and then passed Blandford Close, Beccles Close and Hinchcliffe Close. From here the Roman road re-crossed Blandford Road between the Hinchcliffe Road junction and that for Burngate Road. It then passed through St Michael's Close, Halter Path and Dean Close, across the main road from St Michael's Church, where Roman remains, including cubes of tesserae, have been found. The owners of new bungalows who found sections of the road in their gardens described its gravel as 'just like concrete'.

The course of the Roman road next passes under Lake Road and Winspit Close. Then it bends north, between Upwey Avenue and Freshwater Road, into the next straight section beside Almer Road (perpetuating the name of Alma bungalow, which carried the correct spelling of the Crimean battle).

There, a visible length of 'agger', or causeway,

One of the Romano-British ovens, uncovered in the 1920s, which were used for salt production. Inset: *Colchester head of Vespasian in his prime, when he brought the Second Legion to Hamworthy.*

was sectioned by Harry Smith. It had been laid on a 4-inch layer of 'clayey sand' laid on a bed of heather. This remains an approved method of road building, which I saw being carried out in Wimborne Road, Kinson, in 1960. Above was 18 inches of beach shingle, topped with sandy gravel, and the width of this causeway was 26ft. Flanking it, 4ft to the west, there was a ditch. The onward course was across Blandford Road, for the third time, and beneath Symes Road on the west side of Vineyard Copse. Here there was 'a gravel streak' of 'sea-shore shingle' 40ft wide and 2.5ft high when the land, still a field, was ploughed in 1946.

The road then goes under the railway line immediately west of the footpath from Symes Road and emerges as a flat scatter of gravel in trees and grass beside and under electricity pylons on the north side of the embankment. From here the course is a straight line northwards, into the ground of the country park, where it passes 425ft west of Upton House.

Beyond here the line of the road forms the borough boundary, crossing the A350 dual carriageway and A35 roundabout, and becoming the Castleman Trailway behind the trees, parallel with Longmeadow Lane. Here, exploring with a trowel in 1942, evacuee Stanley Currens from Henry Harbin Boys' School found a sestertius (ancient coin) of the Emperor Commodus. It came from one of the ditches beside the track which coincide with the Roman side-ditches to the road. The coin dated from AD180 to 192. After this length of bridleway the old Roman road becomes modern Roman Road. The actual 'agger' of the original road then survives as a scrubby earthwork across Corfe Hills, Mount Pleasant and Barrow Hill.

Below here, north of the Chillwater Stream through Happy Bottom, the digging of the old Corfe Mullen gravel pits on either side of Blandford Road at East End frequently revealed first-century Roman pottery. Westwards, these workings became the Ballast Pit for the Southern Railway. A pot dating from the post-invasion period, found in 1865 'in a gravel pit near the Cogdean Elms Inn', preserved with Henry Durden's collection of antiquities from Blandford in the British Museum, contained bones and a coin of the Emperor Claudius no later than AD42. The fabric is so similar to potsherds among rubbish and finds of potters' waste from East End that it may well have been made in the very kiln excavated by J. Bernard Calkin in 1932. More than 200 similar vessels were found among the kiln debris.

The whitish or buff-coloured wares contrast with the later black-burnished wares that were manufactured in even greater quantities around the shore on both sides of Poole Harbour. Another Roman coin find was an 'as' of Caligula, from AD40. Beyond the kiln and its associated settlement, on the other side of former Corfe Mullen Halt and Lambs' Green Farm, the next railway line at Lake Crossing skirted Vespasian's just missed legionary fortress at Lake Gates. An intaglio seal found here, just 16mm (just over half an inch) in length with a gold loop set in an orange gemstone, is engraved with the Pegasus winged-steed emblem of the Second Legion. Its last user could well have been Vespasian himself.

Inland from Lake Gates, the Roman advance to conquer the western Durotrigian hill-forts continued north-westwards up the Stour Valley, via Badbury Rings and Spetisbury Rings, to a fort built by the legion inside existing prehistoric ramparts on Hod Hill. Vespasian also made progress, personally and politically, becoming Emperor after his return to Rome.

Several years of excavations by schoolmaster Harry Smith and his pupils from South Road Boys' School were carried out across 6 acres between Carter's Tile Works and Ivor Road from 1926. These revealed a potter's kiln and thousands of fragments of locally-made Iron-Age and Roman pottery. There were also scores of wine and olive-oil amphorae handles, bases and mouth-pieces of Mediterranean origin; pieces of imported deluxe Samian pottery; bracelets and other ornaments in Kimmeridge shale; beads; coins; and a large number of iron objects. Oysters were a food of choice beloved by archaeologists for leaving such easy evidence.

From the same site, at 'Ham, near Poole', a pole-operated quern from the mid-Victorian Durden collection, acquired by the British Museum, is in imported Niedermendig lava from the Rhine. It was used for grinding grain and was described in *The History of Corn Milling*, in 1898, as 'the largest and most perfect example of Roman type yet discovered in Great Britain'. Another Niedermendig fragment, from East End at Corfe Mullen, is from the 'catillus' of a donkey-mill of the Pompeian type. Sherds of Samian pottery and pieces of salt-boiling briquetage were found in a deep layer when drainage trenches were dug across Turlin Moor in 1963.

Roman pottery kilns and their spoil heaps of 'wasters' have been excavated elsewhere, at Hamworthy and beyond. They date from the second century, when shoreline kilns beside Poole Harbour were providing black-burnished pottery, on contract to the Roman Army, for delivery to the supply depots for Hadrian's Wall. There were also rectangular firing chambers, which seem to have been used for boiling sea water to produce salt, such as the two examples found beside West Quay Road in June 1994. These were accompanied by second-century finds including 120 fragments of salt-making pottery. This doubled the known quantity from Poole. Previous scatterings were located in the Old Town peninsula. David Watson, an archaeologist, explained the significance of the finds:

This has put another piece in the jigsaw as far as ancient Poole is concerned. It could have looked a bit like

Sandbanks with a beach and smoky kilns behind the sand dunes.

A vessel containing a hoard of 978 double-denarii Roman coins, hidden in the third century, were discovered in a shoreline meadow at Sterte in October 1930. Their sequence of dates ends with a single coin of the Emperor Aurelian, who styled himself Britannicus – after recovering Britain and Gaul from the usurper Tetricus – but was assassinated while fortifying Rome in AD275. A similar hoard, of several hundred coins, was said to have come from the same spot in about 1833. Though such hoards show obvious wealth, their burial and subsequent non-recovery is an indication of troubled times.

From the southern shore of Holes Bay, on newly-dug allotments at Hamworthy, the jewelled remains of a leather helmet were found in the summer of 1932 by a father working with his son. The boy was Allan Read. He presented the trophy, sparkling with 12 cornelians, to his teacher the following morning. The master, in South Road Boys' School, was archaeologist Harry Smith, who passed the find to Lieutenant-Colonel Charles Douglas Drew, of Dudsbury House, West Parley, field secretary of Dorset Natural History and Archaeological Society. Jointly they reported the discovery to Christopher Hawkes at the British Museum and Reginald Smith, who was working for the Victoria County Histories. It was tentatively identified as a 'Roman parade helmet'.

Arrangements were made to have the find displayed at the London Museum, in August 1932, where scholars attending the International Prehistoric Conference decided on a date. They placed it a little beyond their period of expertise. It was identified as a Continental Dark-Age treasure, Frankish-made, and treated to the lead article 'with the expense of a colour plate' in volume 54 of the *Proceedings of the Dorset Natural History and Archaeological Society*. Harry Smith went on to claim it for the 'barbarian Frankish tribes' led by Clovis, founder of the Merovingian empire, who died in AD511. Smith rounded off his paper with thoughts on 'the romantic life-story of the warrior who, in this obscure pagan period, proudly wore it'.

Subsequently there was much embarrassment and back-peddling as a different string of experts reclassified the object as a Gypsy bridal belt. Smith conceded it was an 'anti-climax' but was almost inspired by adversity. This was 'a survival in high Albania from antiquity' which provided 'yet another instance of the archaeological fertility of the Hamworthy soil'.

Broadstone from a suburbanised section of the Roman Road.

Viking raiders were the fearsome sight that brought Brownsea Island, Poole Harbour and Wareham into the front line of Anglo-Saxon affairs.

✦ CHAPTER 3 ✦

Vikings and Normans

In 876 a Viking fleet sailed the full width of Poole Harbour and up the estuary of the River Frome, to attack Wareham and sack its rich convent, which made the main news of the year for the *Anglo-Saxon Chronicle*:

> *In this year the enemy army slipped past the army of the West Saxons into Wareham and then the King* [Alfred] *made peace with the enemy and they gave him hostages, who were the most important men next to their King in the army, and swore oaths to him on the holy ring – a thing which they would not do before for any nation – that they would speedily leave his kingdom. And then, under cover of that, they – the mounted army – stole by night away from the English army to Exeter.*

In 1015, two years before being proclaimed King of England, Sweyn's son, the Danish King Cnut, came to Dorset as a Viking raider. He plundered Cerne Abbey along with its tiny hermitage on Brownsea Island. This was dedicated to St Andrew, the patron saint of fishermen, and his name was attached to St Andrew's Bay, which is now the marshy lagoon forming the north-east corner of the island. King Cnut later made reparations to the Abbot of Cerne and died in Dorset, at Shaftesbury, on 12 November 1034. His body was taken to Winchester for burial.

Canford Magna Church incorporates the core of a late Anglo-Saxon Minster, of cruciform shape, dating from c.1040. The walls of its nave form the inner part of the chancel end of the present church, which has no known dedication. This warm, brown heathstone building in the grounds of Canford School became the Parish Church of Canford Magna in 1256. Soft both to the eye and the knife, these stone blocks are much cut with initials and other rub marks, and even enhanced by them.

The ancient, eastern half of the church is visibly

The medieval mother church of Poole, at Canford Magna, seen from the chancel end, which incorporates pre-Norman stonework.

Brownsea Island, stretching for more than a mile from east (left) *to west, from salt marsh on the Lilliput shore.*

Branksea Castle on Brownsea Island (foreground) *and Brownsea Road anchorage* (left centre), *looking south-eastwards across the Main Channel to Sandbanks peninsula and Poole Bay* (top).

out of alignment with the rest, which suggests a previous building on the site dating back to the time of the early Church. Even the existing masonry is of obvious great age, with bulging, cracked and leaning walls, 2½ft thick. Bits of Anglo-Saxon window can be seen in what are now solid walls to the north-west of the altar and on the west side of the old south doorway. Other early features include two plain semicircular arches, facing each other at the east end of the building, with external doorways beyond in the outer wall.

Though much restored, the rest of the building, with distinctive Norman arches, nave, aisle and three-stage north tower, was attached in the twelfth century. The tower is in line with the Anglo-Saxon walls, rather than contemporary Norman additions, and adjoins the north-west corner of the chancel. The thirteenth-century font has an octagonal bowl of Purbeck marble. The outer faces are carved with trefoil panels. Eight perimeter shafts surround the central stem, though only three are original.

Poole, at the time of the Domesday Book, in William the Conqueror's great survey of 1086, does not exist as an identifiable entity but was part of the manor of Canford. This was sizeable, with what has been estimated as 2,160 acres of arable land, 1,600 acres of pasture, 600 acres of woodland and 4,000 acres of open heathland. The latter had its apiaries – as there were several beekeepers – with the closest such survival on the ground being an earthwork at Holt Heath, on the other side of Wimborne, which is known as the Bee Garden. Other estate workers included two carpenters, a mason, two millers, and a smith. Although Poole receives no mention in the Domesday Book there is a reference to 'Hame' (Hamworthy), a small manor which was held by the widow of Hugo fitz Grip, the Sheriff of Dorset, who died in 1084. She let it for a shilling a year to one William, who also held her bigger manors of Wimborne and Bere.

Salt production in shallow iron-pans was a prime product of the Purbeck shore. The output of these salterns, from Arne across to Studland, was exported to the wider world from Ower Quay. In the mid-twelfth century, perhaps because effigies and cathedral columns were monopolising shipping facilities, salt extraction was transferred across the harbour to Sterte, on the eastern shore of Holes Bay.

✦ CHAPTER 4 ✦

Plantagenet Players

Poole's occupation in the mid-twelfth century resulted from the demise of Wareham. The Saxon walled town and Norman castle played their part in the insurrections of King Stephen's strife-torn reign. Robert, Earl of Gloucester, sailed from Wareham for France in 1142. His son, William, lost control of the castle to the King, and the town was torched. Robert recovered them again in 1143. 'Wareham was indeed no place for peaceful traders,' is how Harry Smith put it.

The early medieval merchants of the Old Town peninsula utilised the exposed spit eastwards to Baiter, since reclaimed to the south of the present Poole Park, which is shown as having a windmill in the 1774-printed first edition of John Hutchins's *History and Antiquities of the County of Dorset*. This was the location of the original Poole Quay, which has since moved eastwards.

The scallop shells that are the emblems both of St James's Church and Poole borough date from Norman times and have a direct Canford connection. Patrick, 1st Earl of Salisbury, was Henry II's 'Lieutenant' of the English-owned province of Aquitaine in southern France – its governor, in effect. In 1167 he made a final and fatal pilgrimage across the Pyrenees to the famous shrine of St James at Santiago de Compostella. On his return Earl Patrick was ambushed by Guy de Lusigman on behalf of Aquitaine's discontented barons.

Patrick's son, William, 2nd Earl of Salisbury, inherited Canford. There is circumstantial evidence that he built St James's Chapel (a chapel of ease) as a memorial to his father, who was regarded by the family as a Christian martyr. What is known is that in 1196, Canford Parish Church and St James's Chapel in Poole – 'La Pole', as it was called – were granted by Earl William, as lord of the manor, to Bradenstoke Priory at Lyneham, in Wiltshire. This evidence for the existence of St James's Chapel, indicating a community in the vicinity, also provides the earliest documentary mention of Poole as a place-name, though it would remain a dependency of Greater Canford for centuries to come. Earl William was also powerful nationally and acted as 'verger' to Richard Coeur de Lion by carrying the ceremonial dove-mounted rod at his coronation in Westminster Abbey in 1189.

William de Longespee, also known as William Longswords, or Longespee, 3rd Earl of Salisbury (died 1226), was the illegitimate son of Henry II. When Earl William died in 1198, King Richard granted him, Longespee, both the earldom and the hand of William's widow. Their son, known both as William de Longespee (1212–50) and as Earl of Salisbury – out of courtesy as he never formally assumed the title – was the Crusader who returns to our story in 1247.

King John (1167–1216) took the throne on the death of his brother, Richard I, in 1199. After his initial adventures in France he frequently hunted in Dorset and often stayed at Canford for a night or two. His first recorded visit was on 12 December 1200, and he returned in 1204, and then at least once a year from 1210 to 1214. His final visit was on 1 February 1215, as barons took up arms against them, in the prelude to the conference that sealed Magna Carta at Runnymede on 15 June 1215.

One of the joint inhabitants of Canford and Poole was John of Kaneford (Canford), a freeholder listed in a 'Feet of Fines' dating from 1220. He held land 'in Kaneford and Pola' belonging to Ela, Countess of Salisbury. In 1229 'The Port of La Pole' was given a royal command to dispatch all ships that were large enough to carry 16 horses to Portsmouth by St Michael's Day. Insufficient vessels were sent for an expedition to be mounted.

Four traders or shipowners from 'La Pole' are mentioned in the *Calendar of Patent Rolls* for 1230. They were Peter de la Chaene, William Curneis, Walter Stanherd and Luke Wulwy. William Curneis – a name linked to Cerne Abbas – certainly had a ship, as he escorted Henry III from Portsmouth on 30 April 1230. They sailed via Guernsey and arrived in St Malo on 3 May 1230, where the King was met by the Duke of Brittany. Curneis was discharged and set sail for home as Henry proceeded to Dinant and Nantes.

Poole was regularly being named and recognised as an entity, functioning as a quasi-autonomous part of Canford Manor. William de Longespee – the Crusader grandson of Henry II – then sold the rights to Baiter and its 'Poole', the shallow lake inland from the peninsula, to its traders and fishermen. The price was the sum of 70 marks and the bargain was enshrined in what is called the Longespee Charter. The money was needed to enable the Earl of Salisbury, who had taken part in the crusade of 1240, to set off again on another Anglo–French expedition in 1247. He eventually reached the castle at El Mansûra in Egypt, where the Turks trapped the western leaders and proceeded to hack them to death. Before that misadventure, in 1247, Longespee

Eighteenth-century print of Town Cellars, after Thames Street had been cut through the western end of the medieval building (left), *with the Ship Inn on the other side* (right).

An early photographic view from the waterside of Town Cellars (centre) *with the Harbour Office* (left) *and Ship Inn* (right), *prior to demolition of the tavern in 1871.*

Town Cellars from the cut-off end in Thames Street (left), *towards warehouses* (right) *which replaced the Ship Inn after demolition in 1871, with the hoarding in 1973 advertising Whiteway's Cydrex, Haig's scotch and Wondermash.*

Outstanding medieval roof of the Town Cellars, built as a woolstore when Poole became a Port of the Staple in 1433, seen in the 1960s before its conversion to the Maritime Museum.

Town Cellars following its conversion to Poole Maritime Museum, with the yacht Mistletoe *just fitting into the building, after the floor had been excavated to its original fifteenth-century level.*

Poole's seal of 1325, featuring a trading ship with castles fore and aft – a design weakness that culminated with Henry VIII's flagship Mary Rose *keeling over and sinking off Spithead with the loss of all hands in 1545.*

Medieval Poole also had its Swannery, further west from present-day Poole Park, when a tongue of marshy water gave Longfleet its name.

Fourteenth-century seals of 'Ville de Pole' and 'Villae de Poole ad morem' (right).

signed away his Canford birthright:

> *Know those present and those to come that I, William Longespee, have given and granted and by this my present charter have confirmed for me and mine heirs to the burgesses of Poole and their heirs all manner of liberties and free customs and aquittances, as well as of their bodies as of their goods from toll and all other customs and suits to be done without my borough of Poole, to me or mine heirs belonging as the free citizens or burgesses of the cities or boroughs of the lord the King have throughout all England as fully as to me or my predecessors or heirs in any manner was known to belong through all my land sea ports and passages saving to me and mine heirs for every ship going to foreign parts beyond the seas two shillings.*

Excavations on the site of the car park in Orchard Street have revealed continuous habitation since the mid-thirteenth century. It was about this time that timber buildings gave way to replacements in stone. Much of the older pottery from the middens and beneath later foundations was of European origin and indicates Poole's origins as a port.

By this time, during the long reign of Henry III, Hamworthy Manor became a property of the Turberville family of Bere Regis and Wool. It remained in their hands for three centuries, before

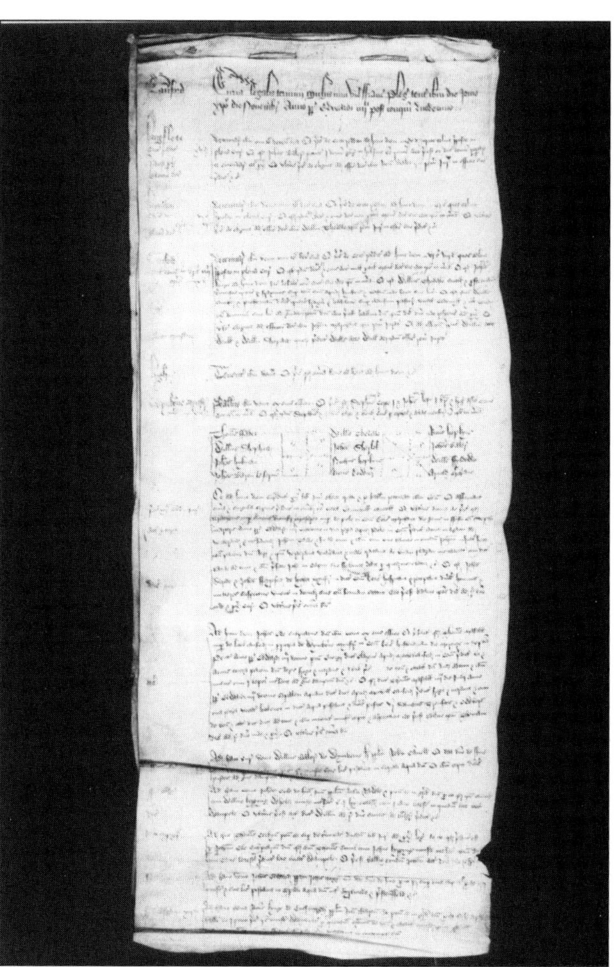

Canford manorial roll, starting with an entry for Langflete (Longfleet), prior to Poole winning its independence with the Longespee Charter of 1248.

joining Canford Manor, in the time of Queen Elizabeth I.

Longfleet (then spelt 'Langflete') was Canford's other maritime tithing and went by the attractive name 'Longfleet-next-the-Sea'. It was notable for its Swannery which, as with that established by monks at Abbotsbury, dated from a century or two before 1393, when swans were given legal protection as 'royal birds'. They would have provided a dependable source of feast-day meat in John of Gaunt's house, named Kitchen, at Canford. Hugh Boys was a 'swan keeper' in the 'long creek', at Longfleet Bay, which is now Holes Bay. The latter name has since been transferred here, westwards, from now largely filled-in marshes and mud-flats between Towngate and Poole Park that used to be known as Holes Bay.

Inland, the manorial estate's rich riparian rights ran along the Stour from 'Steyresmill' in the west – apparently former Lake Mill at Lambs' Green – to Riddlesford in the east, below Redhill Common. There, at an ancient ferry point, the Ensbury tithing of Kinson parish in Dorset met Muscliffe hamlet and Throop tithing in the Holdenhurst parish of Hampshire.

The next call on the emergent port of Poole to do

its royal duty and loan a ship and crew 'for His Majesty's Service' was in 1295. There was no standing navy until Tudor times and the tradition of state requisitions – last seen for gathering the South Atlantic task force in April 1982 – dates back to King Alfred's Wessex. Edward Longshanks, the Plantagenet Edward I, 'arrested' ships from Poole and other 'New Ports' to join the seamen of the Cinque Ports which customarily supplied vessels to the King in return for their prestige and privileges. The King had demanded the use of fortresses in the Scottish Borders until peace had been negotiated with France. The ships were needed to support a 35,000 strong English army, which prepared to attack Berwick upon Tweed. The naval force attacked too soon and lost three vessels, which were burnt, before Berwick was secured in April 1296 with the slaughter of thousands of Scots, 'as was the custom of war'.

By 1322 Poole had eclipsed Wareham, which dropped to the status of a third division port behind both the Cinque Ports and the new leading lights along the South Coast, namely Southampton, Poole, Weymouth and Lyme. The mariners of Hampshire and Dorset frequently indulged in 'disputes and murderous affrays' with their counterparts from

Medieval curving 'batter', the sloping wall of the castle (right), *of Henry VIII's coastal fort, now entombed in the laundry of Branksea Castle.*

'Caesar's coast', as the waters of south-eastern England have been known for as long as there has been classical education in public schools. Such 'outrages' were banned by a royal proclamation and a similar measure was drafted to ease the fraught relationship between West Country seamen and those from Brittany.

There were no warships as such and the seal of Poole, dating from 1325, features a trading vessel of about 105 tons. This armed merchantman had a waterline length which has been estimated by marine architect John Armstrong as 64ft. Castles project fore and aft and would have extended lengthwise to 75ft overall. Even allowing for 'vertical exaggeration' and the stylistic artistry necessary for any logo, there is a look of inherent instability, which reached its catastrophic climax when Henry VIII's flagship *Mary Rose* keeled over and sank off Spithead. The Poole ship has a single mast at its centre, surmounted by a top-castle lookout, which would also have provided a sniping position for archers in time of danger.

The 'anchorage and dockage' facilities of the 'free borough' of Poole were listed by the town's burgesses in a deposition of 1341. This also lists imports and their Customs duties. The fish, in the order in which they are mentioned, are herrings, salmon and codfish. John Armstrong, in his description of *The Poole Ship* of 1325, points out that the inclusion of cod indicates that long-distance Atlantic fisheries were already in business. He links rosin, tar and pitch with the Baltic trade, but notes the omission of wine from the list.

This is easily explained. Edward III had laid claim to the throne of France, declared war on Philip VI, and formed an alliance with Emperor Louis of Bavaria. Edward won a stunning victory over the French fleet at Sluis, in 1340, as a result of which the links between Poole and Bordeaux and Bristol were severed.

The biggest royal call on England and Poole to provide a fleet for the King took place in 1347. The cause was Calais and a total of 784 ships were commandeered and mustered. Poole provided four ships and 94 sailors. Wareham, still a port but in decline as ship sizes increased and the Frome estuary gradually silted up, sent three vessels. Southampton was the biggest local player, fielding 21 ships with 662 men, as Edward III's navy gathered towards the end of what proved to be a year-long siege. Calais was taken on 4 August 1347.

Poole, though granted full port rights by the Winchelsea Certificate of 1346, which was signed by the wardens of the Cinque Ports, did not begin to stage official perambulations of the harbour shores until the early-seventeenth century. By then, in 1626, John Odwell had extended the area of jurisdiction by claiming Redcliffe near Wareham as the 'Rodeclyve Attwelle' of the charter, when Poole men beat their bounds.

Branksea Castle, rebuilt in 1897 after being gutted by fire, stands on the remains of a medieval castle which faced seawards to the harbour entrance.

The limits of jurisdiction of the borough and port of Poole were marked by beating-the-bounds ceremonies which were revived in the 1920s.

Wareham men knew better. With added authority, as Dorset's county historian, Revd John Hutchins wrote in 1774 that 'this is certainly a usurpation', and identified it with the other red-sand cliffs of Rockley Point at the turn of the Hamworthy peninsula into Lytchett Bay.

The Winchelsea Certificate had given the port of Poole jurisdiction over the northern side of the harbour from this 'Redeclyve Attwelle' to the North Haven Point beside the harbour entrance at Sandbanks. Importantly, a translation of its Latin shows that the certificate also gave Poole a width to its waters but that was only midway into the shipping channel – 'in the breadth to the middle of the water between the said port *[Poole]* and Brownsea *[Island]*'. That width, as Paul Randall pointed out to me when he was town clerk of Wareham, must settle the matter in favour of Rockley. For no extended bounds as far upstream as Redcliffe, or indeed any further west than Rockley Sands, could incorporate Brownsea as the geographical limit upon its southern boundary. The island is 6 miles away from Redcliffe, far out of view on the other side of the Arne heaths. Redcliffe lies on the south bank of the River Frome in sight of Wareham's South Bridge.

Poole's historic parish limits also end off Rockley Point, which is further evidence of the extent of the town's influence. In the fourteenth century, to quote John Hutchins, there was a powerful legacy of past supremacy to contain Poole's ambitions:

> *It will not admit of much doubt that Wareham was the only port upon this bay long before Poole existed, but that at least all the bay bordering upon that parish belonged to it.*

By this he means that Poole would have no claim upon anywhere in the anciently ascendant parish of Wareham, which began 50yds off Rockley Point.

The Winchelsea Certificate addresses the mayor and burgesses of Poole as 'dear friends and allies' of the Cinque Port that is now landlocked into obscurity. They were granted equality of status with the privileged ports of East Anglia and Kent. Poole (or 'Pole' as it was often spelt) then had a population of between 1,250 and 1,500.

An age of piracy made its first brush with Poole Harbour in 1371, when Canford Manor was held by William Montacute, Earl of Salisbury, who had presented Poole's burgesses with a charter allowing them to collect fines. There was, however, a problem beyond their control.

The French adventurer John le Vienne looted the town and caused a general panic along the southern coast. Beacons were prepared with fire-buckets and brushwood. Horsemen were mustered and roll calls kept of those responsible for preparing beacons such as that at Werybarrow 'in the time of war'. Werybarrow appears to have been the Anglo-Saxon name for Beacon Hill above Lytchett Minster.

Poole was known across western Europe in the first decade of the fifteenth century as the source of harassment to shipping by the privateer and pirate 'Arripay', as the French and Spanish called Dorset-based Henry (Harry) Paye. The distinction in the mariner's description is between state-endorsed theft (privateering) and that based on purely personal initiative (piracy).

Harry Paye's seal of acceptability came in 1404 with his secondment to an English naval squadron under Lord Berkeley and Sir Thomas Swynburn which put 14 French ships out of action. Then, also with Lord Berkeley, he blocked the fleet which was heading towards Wales where the rebel Owen Glendower had begun his insurrection, in 1405. A total of 15 French ships were sunk or taken. Paye was also responsible for the burning of Gyon and

Finisterre, from where he carried off the crucifix of Santa Maria.

This resulted in retaliation. French and Spanish vessels sailed into Poole Harbour in 1405, setting fire to coastal buildings and taking hostages, as the remainder of the population ran for their lives into Canford Heath. Harry Paye's brother was among those killed but the villain of the piece was elsewhere, as usual, on London-authorised naval attachment.

Harry Paye had made his base on Round Island which, as Richard Blomfield points out in *Poole Town and Harbour* is 'the most remote of those islands in the harbour which have deep water access'. There he had the advantage over approaching vessels, which 'would have a very good chance of running aground, especially at low water or on a falling tide'. The year 1407 must have been a busy one for Paye and his merry men. They are reputed and reported to have brought a total of 120 captured ships into Poole Harbour from Brittany and the Bay of Biscay. Even allowing for an element of exaggeration, Poole Quay must have been virtually awash with oil and wine, and a market-place for iron and salt.

Thomas de Montacute, 4th Earl of Salisbury (1388–1428) owned Canford Manor in 1411. He confirmed the rights granted to Poole's merchants by his predecessors, before leaving for Orleans in July 1428, where his luck and skill as one of the greatest soldiers in Europe finally deserted him. During the siege of Orleans, he suffered a smashed eye and 'a grievous gash' to the face, as a window in nearby Tourelles was shattered by a stone cannon-ball from the forces of Joan of Arc. He was carried to Meung and died there, a week later, on 3 November 1428.

The stone-built almshouses in Church Street are medieval. Despite many later changes, their basic exterior shape dates from before 1429, when they were built by the Guild of St George. The editors of the third edition of John Hutchins's county history, in 1861, were able to claim 'the lower parts of the walls' as 'portions of the first erection' though 'the projecting timber storey *[which]* was afterwards built' had already been 'cut away by modern alterations'. The brethren of St George provided accommodation for the priests of St James's Church, until the Reformation. In 1550 the building was acquired for almshouses by Poole Corporation.

At about this time, the antiquary John Leland recorded a century later, the Baiter peninsula was protected by the cutting of a dyke which effectively turned it into an island: 'It standeth almost as an isle in the haven, and hangeth by north-east to the mainland by the space of almost a flit *[arrow]* shot.'

Poole became a Port of Staple in 1433 and was allowed to levy duties on 'every stranger or foreigner' who unloaded goods. The present Staplecross, otherwise known as the Town Beam, is a replica of the medieval man-sized scales, dating from 1947. Beside it, the Wool House or King's Hall – subsequently known as Town Cellars – dates from about 1433. It seems to have been built by John, Duke of Bedford, who held the manor of Canford. The King's Hall, as it became after the manor reverted to the Crown in the Tudor period, faced the central quay.

It was originally 120ft long and remained that size until Thames Street was extended through it, early in the nineteenth century. The western end of the original building survives behind the Harbour Office. The eastern part remains almost intact, complete with buttressing, arched doorways, two-light windows with cusped heads and almost all its original collar-beams and tie-braces.

Because of its general appearance 'the fine stone house by the quay' has at times been assumed to have been an ecclesiastical building. No such mistake would have been made in the Middle Ages; well-heeled secular and religious builders shared the same masons. It just happens that although many of their churches survive, most of the other buildings have since been demolished. Town Cellars, a remarkable exception, is now Poole Maritime Museum. In the process of conversion the floor was lowered, through 4ft of accumulated archaeology, to its original fifteenth-century level.

As with the Strand, in London, now running inland from the River Thames though parallel to it, Strand Street in Poole marks the original shoreline at Poole. Bell Lane, taking its name from a former tavern, preserves, as a narrow but disjointed highway, an echo of the route from the High Street south to Strand Street – where it is now blocked by modern buildings – and onwards to the present waterfront, beside the Poole Arms.

John Beaufort, 1st Duke of Somerset (1403–44) became lord of the manor of Canford shortly before his death. He had commanded Henry V's forces in France with his younger brother, Edmund, who was created Earl of Dorset in 1442 and succeeded John at Canford. Edmund Beaufort was killed at the first Battle of St Albans in May 1455. The building known as John of Gaunt's Kitchen at Canford School is the lasting link with this period. John of Gaunt, Duke of Lancaster, of Beaufort Castle, Anjou, founded the illegitimate but noble English Beaufort family through his liaison with Catherine Swynford, widow of Sir Hugh Swynford. Parliament granted them legitimacy in 1397, but denied them any claim to the royal succession.

Canford passed to Edmund's son, Henry Beaufort, 3rd Duke of Somerset (1436–64). Defeated at Newnham Bridge but successful at Wakefield, he shared the attainder of Henry VI. He was taken prisoner and summarily executed after the Battle of Hexham, which ended the male line of the Beauforts. Canford Manor reverted to the Crown and was granted to the King's brother, George Plantagenet, Duke of Clarence (1449–78), whose main mark on

The Watergate in the sole surviving section of Poole's Town Wall, with a medieval corbel-table (top right), *seen from St Clement's Lane.*

Medieval Tudor walls of Scaplen's Court (left and right), *the lighter coloured stonework and bay windows dating from restoration as a museum after its rediscovery in 1923.*

history was the manner of his going after being sentenced to death on conspiracy charges. The act was carried out secretly in the Tower of London, the popular account having it that he was drowned in a butt of vintage malmsey wine.

Edward Plantagenet, 1st Earl of Warwick (1475–99) inherited his father's possessions but was regarded as a threat to the Yorkist cause. As a result he spent most of his short life in dungeons until conviction and execution on a charge of trying to escape from the Tower of London. The Crown seized his possessions. One of the manorial products was alum, mainly from exposed beds at Durley Chine, near Alum Chine, which preserves by its name the memory of industrial activity. The chines between 'Bourne Mouth' (then only a farm) and Canford Cliffs were then regarded as part of Dorset, and early map-makers generally show the Bourne Stream as the county boundary with Hampshire.

The reign of Edward IV (1442–83), from 1461 to 1483 with a break in 1470 when Lancastrian exiles tried to replace him with the helpless Henry VI, saw trading privileges being granted to Poole. These were in thanks for the town having given sanctuary and a base to dispossessed Channel Islanders. They mounted a successful assault on Mont Orgueil Castle (Gouray Castle, as it was) and recaptured it from the French. It was the reign in which printing and silk manufacture were introduced to England, as the autocratic King did his best to encourage cosmopolitan culture in troubled times.

Edward IV was succeeded in April 1483 by his eldest son, the Prince of Wales, Edward V (1470–83). The boy was seized by his paternal uncle, Richard, Duke of Gloucester, who had him thrown into the Tower of London with his younger brother, the Duke of York. In June 1483, both were deposed by Parliament on the ground of their father's betrothal to Lady Eleanor Butler before he married Elizabeth Woodville. It is widely believed that their uncle not only assumed the Crown as Richard III but had the boys smothered to death. One of the most despicable and widely debated actions in English history, the story has resonated through the ages, and returns to these pages with Victorian developments on Brownsea Island.

The Earl of Richmond sailed from St Malo on 12 October 1483 with 5,000 men in 40 ships, but had his fleet scattered by a storm. Most of the ships turned back for France but Richmond persevered and arrived alone in Poole Bay. The cliffs were lined with an inquisitive and potentially hostile reception committee. Richard III was in the West Country at the time and Richmond was a swipe away from a polished blade on a misty morning at Tower Hill. It was during this time, John Leland tells us, that Poole's wall was built: 'King Richard III began a piece of a town wall at one end of the quay, and promised large things to the town of Poole.'

These precautions against the threat from 'Richmond in Dorsetshire' – to quote Shakespeare – were overtaken by events. Firstly, he was swept back to sea by the tail of the same gale that brought him, which delivered him from Dorset and thereby English perils to the security of Normandy.

Secondly, it was Henry Tudor, Earl of Richmond, who became King Henry VII (1457–1509) on defeating and killing Richard III at the Battle of Bosworth on 22 August 1485.

Poole was included on the royal 'progress' into Dorset of Henry VII on 26 July 1496. He had been in Christchurch the previous day and went on to Corfe Castle on 27 July. Henry was buying Purbeck marble for Richmond Palace, which was his major domestic diversion at a difficult diplomatic time, with Perkin Warbeck proclaiming himself King Richard IV and being encouraged by King James IV of Scotland.

Scaplen's Court, facing Sarum Street from the south-western end of the High Street, dates from between 1475 and 1525. Built of Purbeck and Bath stone, with cobbles that probably came to Poole Quay as ballast, it was most likely the home of a rich merchant. The original building was in an L-shape with a central parlour, but later wings have since surrounded the courtyard on the eastern and northern sides.

Local historian and schoolmaster Harry Smith identified it as a Tudor building when it was derelict in 1923 and a collapsed chimney revealed the roof structure. He was convinced that gale-damaged Scaplen's Court was Poole's 'Old Town House' – its first Guildhall – but based this on not much more than wishful thinking. Poole's town shield of arms, with the initials 'WP' and the date 1554, appear over a courtyard doorway but are not firm evidence of public use.

Later history is also somewhat vague. It may have been the George Inn in the seventeenth century, before being bought by John Scaplen early in the following century. His name is the building's one certainty. Scaplen is also known to have had the cellar excavated beneath what he described as his 'best parlour'. Changes and additions, in the mid-eighteenth century turned Scaplen's Court into tenements. Most of the extraneous architecture was removed in 1927, following Harry Smith's Tudor discoveries. Inspired by Smith's commendable enthusiasm, and also believing it to have been the town's Guildhall, the Society of Poole Men bought the freehold for £16,000. Scaplen's Court was presented to the borough for use as a museum.

Poole (centre right) *and Parkstone* (central foreground) *from Constitution Hill in a view that remained like this for centuries, until being drawn by J.M.W. Turner and engraved by George Cooke in 1849.*

Poole Quay in about 1900, westwards from the Harbour Office (right) *to Burden's coal yard* (centre right) *and a meeting of masts towards Poole Bridge* (left).

Poole Quay (centre) *in 1905, still with a full line of sailing ships, the newest and smallest craft being the yacht* White Kitten *on the Hamworthy side of the water* (lower right).

Poole Quay in about 1908, with timber being unloaded (foreground), *coal hauled on horseback, and a grain warehouse* (left) *in a timeless view eastwards from Poole Bridge.*

✥ CHAPTER 5 ✥

Newfoundland Tudors

Display of Newfoundland-related exhibits in the Maritime Museum, including a model of a merchant ketch and a statuette of Captain Wills from Poole.

The earliest carvings of dried cod fish that adorn Poole's architecture date from the sixteenth century. The cod symbolised the mainstay of the town's prosperity and arose as the local fishing fleet extended its range far into the Atlantic Ocean. Their course, once at sea, was west-south-west, by the lodestone, towards what the magnetic compass gives as 247.5 degrees.

There, 3,000 miles west of the Bay of Biscay, the cold shallows under frequent fogs supported an unimaginable abundance of easily caught fish. Dozens of hand-lines with hundreds of hooks, each baited with a decaying morsel of fellow fish, did the business. The Poole carvings depict the cod dried, the traditional method of curing. The world's premier fishery was open for business, yielding cod oil that was worth £25 a ton in England, brought back several tons at a time, the oil 'pressed off' from the livers, which were left to decay in barrels. Each ship caught an estimated 50,000 cod per summer season.

The long voyages to the Grand Banks took on another dimension after John Cabot sailed from Bristol in 1497 and sighted what would become the first British colony. There, to the north, lay 'New Found Land' which was settled by a few West Country people from 1500, unofficially at first but with legal authority from London after 1583. A century later, institutionalised as Newfoundland, which also incorporated the coast of Labrador, the permanent settler community still numbered only 120. Onshore, the principal economic resource was a product known as train oil – 'trane' being a Dutch word for a 'tear' or drop of lamp-oil – which was extracted from slaughtered seals. Boom times followed and the population grew a hundredfold during the next century.

Richard Blomfield, in *Poole Town and Harbour*, credits Henry VII with commissioning the accidental discovery of Newfoundland, which cost the King the grand sum of £10, according to a long-standing joke. Cabot did receive a pension of only £20 per annum but, Blomfield points out, he was allowed 'a trading monopoly' of the lands he discovered provided that the King received 20 per cent of the profits.

The King regretted having missed the opportunity of sponsoring Columbus in 1492 and encouraged Cabot to explore 'all parts, regions and coasts of the eastern, western and northern sea' in search of an alternative route to the East that avoided Venetian competition and harassment. The flat-earthers were beginning to concede that we inhabit a globe but the old Norse knowledge of North America had failed to leave its mark on the European mind.

Poole's burst of building in Tudor times has left a few survivals, inside a single section of the Town Wall, at the western Watergate which now stands at the inland end of St Clement's Lane. It still incorporates a sixteenth-century doorway and an imposing corbel-table (see page 22). Excavation has shown that beach shingle came up to this Water-Gate with the waterline deposit also having been traced southwestwards to the King Charles Inn. No other length of the town's medieval wall has been preserved.

The Bull's Head Inn in the High Street, delicensed in 1965 and turned into newspaper offices, appears in the borough archives as the oldest public house in the town. The earliest dated reference is from 1552. In the seventeenth and eighteenth centuries civic meetings were held at the Bull's Head; for reasons of comfort and facilities, the official excuse being that the old Guildhall in Castle Street was too draughty. Internal fittings include a Tudor fireplace that was later hidden behind tiles. Upstairs the Tudor treasure is a perfectly preserved plaster ceiling in a first-floor room.

Tudor Poole was a merry place. The annual accounts show payments for the daily services of a minstrel 'that went about the town in the mornings and evenings' and a piper. Strolling players, including 'Robin Hood and his Company', made regular visits, for civic dignitaries at mayoral dinners, and the wider population in the Parish Church. Feudal lords staying at Canford House often brought troops of actors. They were among their regular retainers and carried noble such names as Lord Arundel's players, Lord Lyle's players, and the players of the Marquis of Dorset.

Henry VIII granted Poole a charter in 1526 to exempt it from control by the High Court of Admiralty. This confirmed the power of its mayor to act as Admiral of Poole and hold a local court 'as of time out of mind'. These were the basic regulations and rights of a harbourmaster, though the officer of the court was a water-bailiff. Rules restricted the gathering of immature shellfish, provided for actions to salvage shipwrecks, and enabled the apprehension of felons and pirates. To emphasise the independence of the Admiral from his duties as mayor of Poole, a location for the occasional court was chosen across the water at Broomhill, which appears to be the 75ft high plateau of Ham Hill on Ham Common, in the centre of Hamworthy peninsula. Options for quayside punishment included the whipping post, pillory and the stocks – mostly used for humiliating males – plus a 'clonking stool' for ducking offending females into the harbour. The instruments of deterrence were renewed and replaced in 1524.

The first effective defensive work to protect Poole Harbour dates from 1547 and remained unchanged for nearly 400 years, when the Royal Artillery fortified the same location, positioning guns to fire directly into the narrow entrance to Poole Harbour. Henry VIII's square single-storey blockhouse, with walls 40ft long and 9ft thick, stands on the eastern end of Brownsea Island, surviving largely intact in the basement of eighteenth-century Branksea Castle. An hexagonal gun platform faced seawards towards North Haven Point.

No vessel coming into either the Main Channel or South Deep could avoid passing within half a mile of the guns. Outside the harbour, on the south side of Poole Bay, a similar fortification, Studland Castle, beside Old Harry Rocks, acted as a further deterrent, though its main purpose was to provide watch-guard. A cannon was kept ready to fire, as a signal to alert Brownsea, plus Hurst Castle and Yarmouth Castle – placed on either side of the entrance to the Solent – if a suspicious vessel was sighted.

Dating from the mid-sixteenth century, the King's Head in the High Street is another of the oldest hostelries in the town. The King Charles Inn, with its first floor overhanging the pavement at the quayside end of Thames Street, dates from the same time but was a private house until 1770. It then became the New Inn and kept this name until the early-twentieth century. The renaming has been claimed for King Charles II of England (who came to the quay in 1665) but is more likely to be for King Charles X of France (who arrived as an exile in 1830), in celebration of Edwardian diplomacy having achieved the *entente cordiale* between Europe's ancient adversaries.

In 1563 the fortifications on Brownsea Island were brought back into operation, the costs being itemised in the town's accounts. There were '2 pairs of wheels for the ordnance' (£1.15s.0d), described as 'the great brazen piece'. We know that it was manned by 'George the gunner' from his 'one quarter's wages' (£2.5s.6d.). His eyes were the watchers, four men being required to maintain a shift system, and coverage for a fortnight is listed (£1.17s.4d.). George requisitioned 'half a hundred of lead to make shot' (£0.6s.8d.). There was also a food bill, for cheese and bread, plus a barrel of beer when the gun barrel was set on its rebuilt carriage (£0.7s.6d.).

The paymaster was the mayor, Thomas Bingley, who signed off the accounts for the year with a budgetary deficit which these days would be regarded as of Californian proportions. Total expenditure of £70.14s.6d. had to be met from quay charges and other income that came to just £18.16s.4d. 'So the

Byngley House, named for Thomas Bingley, and its courtyard towards Cinnamon Lane.

Tudor timbering at the rear of Nos 12 and 14 High Street, built as a single house for mayor and merchant Thomas Bingley in 1567.

Newfoundland-generated opulence represented by West End House, on the corner of Thames Street (foreground) *and St James's Close* (right), *built for the Slade family in 1740.*

whole that the town oweth me is £51.18s.2d.,' Bingley writes. Costs included two shillings for the rent of Poole Quay, still in its original location at Baiter, that was paid to the reeve of Canford Manor.

Byngley House, at Nos 12 and 14 High Street, is named for Mayor Thomas Bingley, who had it built in 1567. In the Civil War it was the local headquarters for Parliamentary officers. It retains Tudor timber-framing behind the surviving part of its contemporary stone frontage but was split into two dwellings in the eighteenth century. The original porch was removed and it now has a shop front and pair of front doors. Above, there are ten original roof-trusses, some having being described by the Royal Commission for Historical Monuments, for their contemporary cambered collars and tie beams.

Thomas Bingley personified the pride of Poole. He was the architect and dynamo who turned Baiter into a national port. In 1568 the peninsula community of just 1,400 inhabitants won its legal independence from Dorset and Dorchester jurisdiction, being designated 'the Town and County of Poole'. Queen Elizabeth, through her Privy Council, granted Poole's 'great charter' at a cost to the town of £500. Poole was joining an exclusive club.

There were only 16 such incorporated independent towns, run by their own county corporations, in the country. Poole was now the equal of Bristol and Southampton. Each appointed its own sheriff and its ships were exempted from paying docking dues when they visited other English ports. To exercise these enhanced powers, Poole needed a courthouse and prison – from which to exercise full judicial powers through to executions – and a new Town House was built in 1572. This stood in Fish Street (renamed Castle Street in the twentieth century), on which Nos 20 and 22, plus the Rising Sun, incorporated these buildings on the west side. The County Court Offices opposite remained in use, beneath an intact sixteenth-century roof of six bays, almost until this most historic of streets suffered mass demolitions and complete redevelopment.

Christopher Saxton's county map of 1575 shows 'The Mynes' – mines worked for alum and copperas – on Poole Heath. This area was still known as Mines Heath in 1707. Alum, as a double sulphate of aluminium and potassium, was a salt much used in the arts and medicine. Copperas, a sulphate of iron, was also known as green vitriol.

In 1577 piracy, provoking the Spanish and French, was upsetting European diplomacy and causing concern to Queen Elizabeth. She required its 'Reformation' and appointed commissioners in 1578 who were tasked with apprehending pirates in their waters. They were required to name suspect vessels and those who had fitted them out 'in warlike manner and not in trade or merchandise without her Majesty's special licence' – the distinction between a privateer and a pirate – over the past five years. The first Poole Harbour Commissioners were:

> *Our trusty and well-beloved Mayor of the Town and County of Poole for the time being, Giles Escorte*

St George's Almshouses, in Church Street, probably incorporate stonework dating from 1429 or earlier.

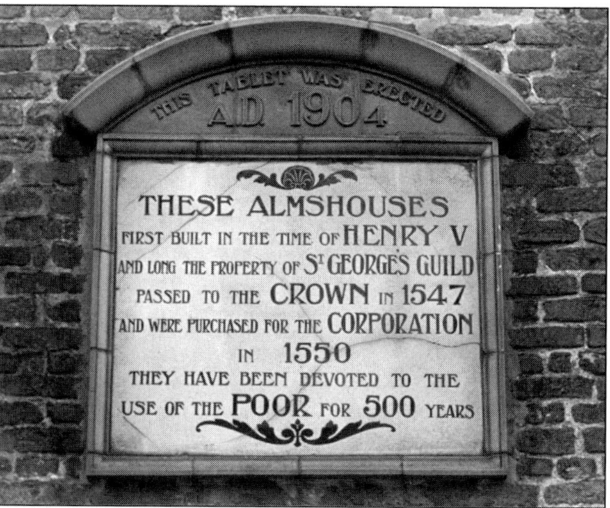

Rebuilding in 1904 removed a projecting timber storey from St George's Almshouses but provided the building with a plaque to record its long history.

> *Esquire, Recorder of the same town, William Newman, William Greene, John Rogers, and William Dyker.*

Queen Elizabeth I made a life gift of Brownsea Island to her favourite, Sir Christopher Hatton, who was described as 'a mere vegetable of the court, that sprang up in the night'. He took up residence in Branksea Castle long enough to fall out with his neighbours in Poole and Purbeck. His confiscation of traditional ferrying rights between Sandbanks and the South Haven peninsula was challenged in the Court of Admiralty. The verdict, which went against him in 1581, shows the importance of such passage rights in medieval times.

Ownership of Newfoundland as a British colony was proclaimed in the name of Queen Elizabeth by Sir Humphrey Gilbert in a ceremony at St John's Harbour witnessed by the crews of 20 British ships who were warned that, 'if any person shall utter words sounding to the dishonour of her Majesty, he shall lose his ears and have his ship and goods confiscated'. Acquisition of the northern Americas, he announced in equally unambiguous terms, would not only 'annoy the King of Spain', but pare Spanish nails by shaving them 'to the stumps'.

Back at home, Francis Rogers of Poole was among those implicated in piracy but was protected by his brother, Sir Richard Rogers, High Sheriff of Dorset during these troubled times, whose country residence was Bryanston House. Several pirates were hanged on Studland beach in 1581 and 43 pirate vessels were seized by a pair of Royal Navy warships in a sweep of the Dorset coast in 1583. Sir Richard Rogers was implicated and received what amounted to a gentlemanly warning in the shape of a £100 fine. Pirates by the name of Courte at Lulworth Cove and Vaughan at Swanage were both said to dine regularly at their respective parsonages. Richard Blomfield, in *Poole Town and Harbour*, writes of the extent to which pirates lived up to their *Treasure Island* stereotype. Not only was scarlet their colour, in satin and silk, but some did carry parrots on their shoulders. Exotic pets were *de rigueur* in Dorset society. Lord Howard of Bindon's cook had both a monkey and a parrot. There were also parrots in residence at Corfe Castle.

La Lune, a captured French vessel, was burnt on Studland beach after Nicholas Curry from Poole 'salvaged' its cargo of salt in 1585. Several masters of English and Scottish vessels also complained that they had fallen victim to pirates while at anchor off Swanage and Purbeck. They were robbed of fish, cargo, tackle and personal possessions. Poole, to them, was synonymous with piracy.

Relations between Poole and the offshore island deteriorated in February 1586 over the behaviour of James Mounsey, a Londoner, 'who farmeth the mines of Brownsea, at my Lord of Huntingdon's hands'. The accusation, made to Sir Francis Ashley, was that Mounsey and his brother ('a very bad fellow, and of an odious religion') forced their workers 'to labour the Sabbath day' but rest on Saturday, which they celebrated instead.

These mines appear to have been along the island's central southern shore, in the area of South Shore Lodge and Barnes's Bottom, according to the description by Philip Brannon in his *Guide to Poole and Bournemouth* in 1857:

> *Below, on a piece of level land between the bank and the water were some kilns, which are now destroyed. Not far from this were discovered, in carrying on the works, some of the old cisterns formed on solid oak staves, which had been used in the former alum and copperas works we have mentioned in the historical remarks. It is most probable, too, that on this low land were some of the salterns supposed to have been in the island. On the rolling land between the ridge and the water are placed some detached cottages for the forester and gamekeepers*

of the estate, and it is intended near them to erect a laundry, fowl-house, and kennel.

The *Primrose*, a 120-ton vessel from Poole engaged in the fish trade with Newfoundland, defied an official embargo on 31 March 1588 and slipped from port. The royal proclamation required all English craft to stay in port on account of the threat by Philip of Spain to capture any of Queen Elizabeth's vessels found at sea. The mayor and burgesses of Poole ordered that Peter Cox, master and owner of the *Primrose*, should be imprisoned on his return.

Poole reluctantly contributed one ship, joining two from Weymouth, in the English fleet which gathered to meet the threat from Philip of Spain. His Armada set sail on 30 May 1588, heading across the Bay of Biscay and up the English Channel with the intention of picking up Spanish soldiers from the Netherlands and then returning to invade England. Quite apart from fire-fights and other military measures, the complicated plans almost totally ignored the vagaries of the weather, and that alone played its part in causing complete chaos.

Beacons were operational and Brownsea Castle was placed under the command of Sir Richard Rogers. Gunpowder was released from the magazine in Poole and taken into the English Channel to rearm the *Anne Royal*. Action off Portland, including a daring dash around Portland Bill to counter enemy progress, was followed by a running battle towards the Isle of Wight. Sir Francis Drake's *Revenge* duelled with the *Gran Grifon*. English vessels, light and manoeuvrable, could run rings around their heavier foes. More than 100 of them harried and harassed the 'Invincible Armada'.

Then, in sight of Purbeck with St Catherine's Point marking the next objective, the climate played a crucial card. The wind dropped and allowed the Spanish to drift up-Channel, south of the Isle of Wight, with the English following. Later, the fast-changing summer weather nearly drove the Armada to its doom on the Zeeland Banks in the North Sea. Once again the wind changed direction but the matter was already decided. The grand plan to call at Calais for barges and soldiers to invade England had been rendered impossible. The only option for the battered Spanish fleet was to attempt an escape. This had to be the long route home, via a hazardous circuit of Scotland and Ireland.

The threat had passed, leaving in Dorset only the wreck of the carrack *San Salvador*, an armed three-masted trading vessel. She was Miguel de Oquendo's vice-flagship, and had carried the Spanish Paymaster-General along with his gold. After the vessel had blown apart off Plymouth, in an accidental explosion which tore off the stern and killed 200 crewmen, the Spanish realised the *San Salvador* had to be abandoned. The Duke of Medina Sidonia brought his own vessel alongside to fight fires and remove most of the treasure. An attempt at scuttling failed and the *San Salvador*, with her injured still aboard, was left to the English.

Thomas Flemyng, captain of the *Golden Hind*, towed her into Weymouth. An inventory of fittings and contents totalled £846.5s.8d, the 'meticulous valuation' including 5,460 gallons of wine. In November 1588 the Privy Council ordered that the wreck – which had been partially repaired – should sail to Portsmouth. Having rounded Durlston Head, by which time she was badly taking on water, the crew seem to have attempted to beach her on Studland sands. Instead she went down off Old Harry Rocks, where Wimborne diver Roy Parker found Spanish timbers in 30ft of water in 1984. Of the crew of 57, the *Lyon*, from Studland, took off 34, but the remainder drowned.

After the rout of the Armada, Poole vessels were free again to venture onto the high seas, though local bureaucracy remained an irritant if not an obstacle. Sir Francis Hawley, as Governor of Corfe Castle, and Sir Christopher Hatton as Vice-Admiral of Purbeck, reminded the mayor and Corporation of Poole that they should not 'suffer any barque, ship or vessel to pass out of your port other than in small vessels from port to port within this realm'. If offenders were identified, 'I require you to take away the sails of all such ships'.

This order led to a shooting incident, in February 1589, when the commander of Branksea Castle, Walter Partridge, rejected the pass presented by the *Bountiful Gift*. The barque, with a cargo of copperas, was outward bound from Poole. The vessel refused to stay and two shots were fired from the castle battery. The master, Walter Merritt, and one of his men, William Drake, were killed.

As a result, a coroner's inquest at Corfe Castle passed a verdict of wilful murder against Partridge. Standing trial at a special court, he was found guilty of manslaughter and sentenced to death 'without the benefit of clergy', because the felony had been committed at sea. The sentence was never carried out. Partridge, not unreasonably in the circumstances, was pardoned on the ground that the shots had been intended merely 'to stay the sail ship'.

Judge Julius Caesar, on his appointment to the Admiralty division of the High Court in 1590, visited Poole to see the defensive situation for himself. He was lavishly entertained. Among those he met were Sir Christopher Hatton and Christopher Anketill, Governor of Branksea Castle, both of whom profited from dubious activities. Two French vessels were intercepted in the Channel and taken into Mupe Bay on its sheltered western side, from where one of them was brought around the coast to Poole by George Fox, who was employed by Hatton. Anketill also traded in goods removed from such vessels, landed on remote spots around the inlets of Poole Harbour and spirited inland. Robert Gregory, a Poole freeman

Scaplen's Court, drawn by Sheila Sturdy in 1949, showing the fifteenth-century walls as revealed by the collapse of a chimney in 1923.

Boat building at Poole in the 1920s, still using traditional methods, in the yards of West Quay and Hamworthy.

Conversion of Scaplen's Court into the Maritime Museum, in the early 1970s, also saw the pedestrianisation of Providence Street (right).

Ropes and rigging of the British tall-ship Royalist, *manned by the Sea Cadet Corps, on one of the nostalgic visits that bring the age of sail back to Poole Quay.*

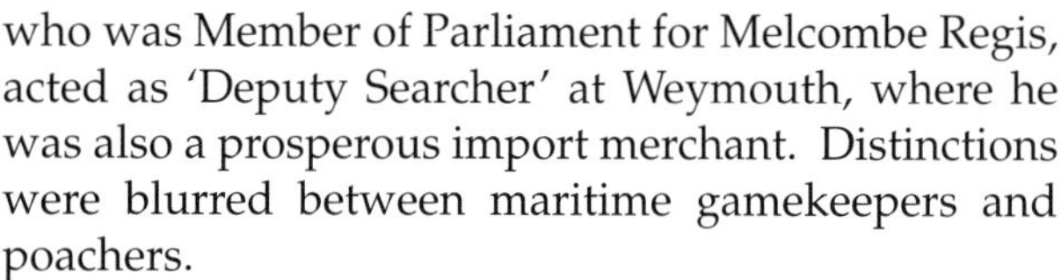

who was Member of Parliament for Melcombe Regis, acted as 'Deputy Searcher' at Weymouth, where he was also a prosperous import merchant. Distinctions were blurred between maritime gamekeepers and poachers.

There were 46 ships from Poole on the Newfoundland run in 1591 but the subsequent attrition rate was considerable, largely due to French warships and pirates from 'the Barbary coast' of North Africa, reducing their 'spread of sail'. The number of ocean-going operators at Poole dropped to just 16 masters and their vessels in 1627. They had real fears the moment they left the harbour. Two Turkish pirate ships not only sailed up the English Channel but audaciously entered the Thames estuary before being captured by Sir John Mainwaring.

The murder of Richard Mead by 'three wicked men' took place at Haven House, Sandbanks, in 1598.

Rogers' Almshouses on the east side of West Street, south of the junction with King Street, were founded by Robert Rogers in 1604. A wealthy London leather merchant, he left over £3,000, including 500 marks for this 'almshouse to house six poor couple'. The northernmost of the original six dwellings, facing the Old Inn, was cut in half early in the nineteenth century to widen King Street. A further six cottages were then added to the south in 1852. They were all altered and modernised in 1927.

As a result of the Poor Law Act of 1601 – the 43rd year of Queen Elizabeth's reign – the common-law edict 'that none should die for default of sustenance' was given a statutory mechanism under which overseers were appointed in each parish. As a result, two-and-a-half per cent of grain (by value six pence in the pound sterling) that passed through Poole Quay was retained for purposes of humanitarian relief. A total of between 40 and 50 needy people were supplied with bread.

✦ CHAPTER 6 ✦

Puritan Politics

The Old Rectory at Hamworthy dates from between 1600 and 1610. In 1943, when it was the home of Revd Edward Hounslow and his wife Kate, who came to the parish in 1913, its future was in doubt. That remained the situation for many years. Its most articulate defender was the architect Miss Elisabeth Scott, who described it as 'the finest bit of early Jacobean architecture in the south of England'. Originally named Hamworthy Manor, it was built by the Carew family, and is said to have billeted Sir Thomas Fairfax as head of the Parliamentary Army in 1645, and the Duke of Wellington when he came to review his troops during the Napoleonic Wars. In 1826, on passing out of the hands of the Carews, the property became absorbed into the immense Canford estate, but was then provided as a rectory for the parson of newly-rebuilt St Michael's Church.

The quay at Baiter was extended westwards, towards the town and away from the windmill on the exposed spit, with a new quay and fish market being built in 1612. This seems to have been the 'Little Quay', which collapsed into Little Channel in 1754.

The three major islands of Poole Harbour, named 'Brunksey' (Brownsea), Fursey (Furzey) and 'little Helen' (Saint Helen, now Green Island), feature in *Poly-Olbion*. This celebrated topographical description of the English counties, in twelve-syllabled verse, was published in 1613 by Michael Drayton (1563–1631). He personifies these islands as the children of 'Great Albyon' – beget of Poole – which appears as a 'lustie sea-borne lass' in the epic fairyland poem 'Nymphidia'. This is accompanied by one of the rarest of Dorset and Hampshire maps, which features nymphs arising from Poole Harbour and the surrounding rivers and forests.

Poole's harbour rights, dating back to the Winchelsea Certificate of 1364, were being asserted on the ground and in the water by beating the bounds ceremonies. Traditionally they were linked with Rogation week in the spring (ecclesiastical Rogation days are the three days before Ascension day, which falls on the sixth Thursday after Easter).

They were a ceremonial entertainment, with boys being swished to imprint a lasting memory of the precise location of key points, and being bent over boundary stones such as Shag Rock. This stood at what is now known as Russel Quay – these days sandy and unpopulated – on the Arne shore opposite Holton Mere. Men played football along access tracks, with their hats if nothing better was available, to maintain the free use of rights of way leading from the sea to the nearest highway. Barrels and boats bobbed about offshore to mark the outer limits in Poole Bay. The standard format for the day's perambulation, such as that in 1631, was for it to end with the Lord's Prayer. Unless stopped by war or weather the colourful event continued at regular intervals until being suspended in 1834.

In 1638 the *Concord* from Poole brought back a Turkish prisoner and three released Christian hostages.

The post-medieval transition of feudal England into a free-market economy, which had been evolving since the Peasants' Revolt of 1381, received a major jolt in 1634. The ramifications of a decision by Charles I to re-invent ship money – a tax first levied in 1007 to raise a navy to resist the Vikings – would reverberate for the rest of the first half of the seventeenth century. The issue has been cited as a reason for the revolution of 1641 and the Civil War that followed, and the final resolution cost King Charles his head at the Banqueting House in Whitehall on 30 January 1649.

Ship money cost London dear. It was required to fund seven ships, of 4,000 tons in all, manned by 1,560 men. Bristol had to pay for one ship of 100 tons. Some towns and officials refused to pay the tax, but the Exchequer division of the High Court declared it legal on 12 June 1637. As a result, the county of Dorset had to find £5,000, of which Poole's contribution was £60. In common with other trading towns, Poole declared for Cromwell and Commonwealth on the Puritan side of the great divide, between Parliament and commerce and King and countryside.

Mayor Henry Harbin refused to allow the Royalist Marquis of Hertford to advance around the harbour from Wareham to Poole in 1643. Parliament provided two ships and arms. One vessel was kept in the Brownsea Road anchorage to prevent any attack from the sea. Poole men took part in the early ineffectual sieges of the virtually impregnable fortress of Corfe Castle. By this time the Parliamentary commander, Sir Walter Erle, from Charborough, controlled Wareham, until he moved westwards to block a Royalist threat to Dorchester.

There was a close call in 1643 when John Bingham from Bingham Melcombe was Governor of Poole. It came about through treachery, but Captain Francis Sydenham (1617–45), from Parliamentary Poole, had in fact double-crossed the Royalist Earl of Crawford. Sydenham was known to be debt-ridden. It was therefore convincing that he should make an

Seventeenth-century trade tokens from Poole, produced during coin shortages, ranging in date from that issued by William Minty (1657) to 'His half-penny' carrying the name of Michael Tree, at the Oak (1668).

Town token issued 'For the Mayor of ye Town and County of Poole' during the currency shortage of 1667.

arrangement through Captain Phillips, a 'malignant' intermediary, to leave the Towngate open at the neck of the peninsula when he was the officer of the watch. Royalist horsemen duly approached at night, on cue, but instead of an unbarred gate they faced barriers of chains overlooked by primed guns mounted on piles of stones. Ten were killed as they turned and fled – the Royalists conceded – but the Parliamentarians claimed several cartloads of dead. Both sides had to admit 'the narrow escape of Lord Crawford'.

Poole assumed special significance in 1643 as this was the year the King was winning the war. Waller's Parliamentary Army was destroyed on Roundway Down, Devizes, on 13 July, and Prince Rupert stormed Bristol – then the second biggest city port in the land – on the 26th. Of the Dorset garrisons, only Lyme Regis and Poole remained in Parliamentary hands, and in the region as a whole Gloucester, Exeter and Plymouth were crucial in preventing the King's men from turning their back on the West and marching on London. On 19 August 1643 Gloucester successfully defied the King in person, and the high-water point of Royalist supremacy began to recede. General Sir Ashley Cooper eventually recovered Wareham for Parliament and in 1645 was ordered:

> *You are desired forthwith to repair to the Isle of Purbeck and draw together as speedily as may be out of the garrisons of Poole, Wareham, Lulworth and Weymouth such members of foot and horse as are sufficient to block up Corfe Castle.*

In the event it fell by an act of treason rather than force of arms and was reduced to a ruin on orders from the House of Commons in 1646. Branksea Castle, with a 20-strong garrison, was provided with four large guns and several chests of muskets. By this time the conflict had moved, via Marston Moor and Naseby, to the King's base in Oxford.

Even the beheading of King Charles did not draw the intended definitive line under the English Civil War. There was succession waiting in the wings. The King's son, Prince Charles, landed in Scotland, where he was proclaimed King Charles II and crowned by the Marquess of Argyll on the historic stone of the Scottish Kings, at Scone, in July 1650. Parliament, regarding it as inevitable that the Scots would invade England, sent its New Model Army northwards in a pre-emptive strike which almost served its purpose at the Battle of Dunbar on 4 September 1650. The remnants of the Scottish forces retreated to Stirling but Oliver Cromwell lacked the strength to storm the town.

The outcome was that Cromwell had to withdraw and a revived Royalist force, under David Leslie with Charles at his side, crossed into England in August 1651. This time the clash of arms was decisive, in the meadows between Worcester Cathedral and Powick Church, where the tower is still pockmarked from the impact of musket balls on 3 September 1651. King Charles fled for his life via Trent Manor on the Somerset–Dorset border and, after an abortive attempt at sailing from Charmouth, rode in disguise (alias Mr William Jackson) inland of the South Coast towns before finding the *Surprise* at Shoreham.

His supporters in Dorset had commissioned Captain Nathaniel Tattershall to slip out of Poole and pick up the royal party in Sussex. They sailed towards the Isle of Wight and then turned south as, in Shakespeare's phrase, the elements 'set fair the wind for France'. A favourable northerly took them to Fécamp in Normandy. There the King stepped into exile, and the *Surprise* returned to Poole, on what then became an equally helpful southerly wind. Both Charles and Tattershall lived to savour the sequel. At the Restoration, the *Surprise* was commissioned into the Royal Navy and renamed *Royal Escape*, her former master being rewarded with a pension of £100 a year.

Poole was preoccupied by postwar outbreaks of bubonic plague. The town's isolation hospital, the Pest House, as it was called, was supplied with mutton, broth, bread and prunes, together with pills, pots and shrouds, and a fumigating jar which was also used for 'smoking of houses'. Famine was another concern as a consequence of the disruption caused across great tracts of countryside. Oliver Cromwell, now the Protector of the Commonwealth, found more difficulties with the politics of peace than the winning of war.

In 1651 martial law, in the person of Colonel John Rede as Governor of Poole, was resented and resisted by Mayor William Williams. The town petitioned the Council of State for his removal, complaining that 'our civil rights' had been 'devoured by the power of his arbitrary sword'.

Religious turmoil followed. Revd John Haddesley was ousted as Presbyterian rector of St James's and faced imprisonment. His official replacement, Pastor Gardiner, was resented as a radical 'leveller, ranter and dipper'. George Fox (1624–91), who founded the Society of Friends, repeatedly came to Poole and converted William Bayly in the town. As 'ranters reversed' he and his followers preached extreme austerity. 'Tremble at the word of the Lord,' was Fox's phrase that led to the epithet of Quaker. Bayly also became an ardent pamphleteer, his final outburst *Against Drunkenness and Swearing* contributing to his sentence of transportation to the West Indies. He never arrived, as he died on the outward journey in 1675.

From a deep black cloud 'it rained warm blood' on the port of Poole on 20 June 1653. It was supposed that the water had come from the sea where the British and Dutch fleets had clashed in the English Channel, and that the blood of sailors had somehow been sucked into the sky. Similar red rain fell on the Isle of Wight in 1176; the colour, and the fact that the rain of 1653 was warm, suggest that the phenomenon was caused by Saharan dust being blown high into the sky, rather than the fallout of ash from a volcanic eruption.

Colonel Thomas Pride and a section of his regiment from the Commonwealth Army was stationed on Brownsea Island in 1654. Pride was both famous and notorious – depending which side one favoured in the Civil War – for having carried out the most audacious act in Parliamentary history. 'Pride's Purge' was the original colonels' revolt, on 3 December 1648, when, on orders from Sir Thomas Fairfax, he barred the door of the House of Commons and prevented 80 Presbyterian members from taking their seats.

In 1655 a 'shallop man-of-war' – a light boat without decks – approached the boats of George Skutt, the Governor of Branksea Castle. The defenders were taken by surprise but managed to capture the intruder, which turned out to be sailing under a Royalist commission from James Stuart, second son of executed monarch Charles I, who later became King James II. The restoration of the monarchy by Charles II in 1660 saw the end of Brownsea as a functioning fortress until re-fortification by the Royal Artillery in the Second World War.

Charles II and his court, including the 16-year-old Duke of Monmouth (his illegitimate son) and Lord Ashley (afterwards the Earl of Shaftesbury), escaped to Dorset from plague-ridden London during the Great Plague. They were rowed across Poole Harbour on 15 September 1665, on a day-trip to Brownsea Island, with Colonel William Skutt steering at the rudder and six ships' masters as oarsmen. The visitors did not land, however, most likely because the island's owner was Sir William Clayton, one of the wealthiest men in the City of London, from whom Charles had borrowed large sums. Though Clayton rarely visited Brownsea, he may have fled from London that disease-ridden summer.

The royal party was accompanied by the Earls of Lauderdale, Oxford and Suffolk and Lords Arlington, Crofts and Gerrard. Colonel Skutt, the son of Poole's Republican commander in the Civil War, had the honour of hosting one of two banquets in 'the sacred royal presence', as the *Corporation Record Book* puts it. All were self-proclaimed Royalists now. Charles nominated Skutt as the next mayor of Poole (though the burgesses reasserted their independence by electing Stephen Street instead). 'Favour for favour' was another matter. The moment was grasped for securing for the town charter concessions and other bureaucratic benevolence.

Revd Samuel Hardy (1636–91), from Frampton, was appointed rector of St James's in 1667. He raised £500 by public collection 'for the purpose of redeeming captives from slavery'. Religious reforms, however, had gone into reverse since the Restoration

Plaque to King Charles II and the Duke of Monmouth, set in a wall on the east side of the central High Street, commemorating their visit to Poole to escape the Great Plague in 1665.

'Town and County of Poole' boundary stone at Towngate – focal point of Civil War activity – re-set in the bridge built across the spot in 1970.

of 1660. Hardy was accused of shunning the *Book of Common Prayer*. Conformity Commissioners arrived in Poole in 1681 and disqualified the mayor and Samuel Hardy for refusing to take an oath of submission. Another 20 burgesses were also dismissed from public office. Revd John Wesley, an independent pastor in Poole, was imprisoned for six months in the Fish Street gaol for preaching in contravention of the Five Mile Act. He is also significant, in retrospect, as the grandfather of the founder of Methodism, John Wesley.

One of the first mentions of the press-gang, impressing civilian sailors into military service, comes from 1672, when a total of 150 Poole men were forced to enlist in the Royal Navy. Some, it was claimed, had been pulled from their beds as the town was subjected to a nocturnal raid.

Dorset lawyer Anthony Ettricke (1622–1703), 'a little man' who was the recorder at Poole, lived at Holt Lodge Farm, near Wimborne. One of the closest friends of the antiquary John Aubrey, they travelled together to Ireland in 1660, 'and returning were like to be shipwrecked at Holyhead, but no harm done'.

In 1685, following the Battle of Sedgemoor, the defeated Duke of Monmouth was captured less than a mile from Ettricke's home and brought to him for committal proceedings. Aubrey's *Life of Monmouth*, a commentary on these events, is lost. Ettricke is best remembered for his eccentric coffin, set in the wall of Wimborne Minster – he requested a position neither inside nor outside the building – which originally carried the date 1691. He was sure he would die then, at the age of 69, because these 'magic' numbers read the same either way up. In the event Ettricke stayed alive for another 12 years and an amended date appears on the wooden coffin.

The 'turbulent and aspiring politician' Sir John Trenchard (1640–95) was born at Lytchett Matravers and is buried just inside the entrance to the north chapel of Bloxworth Parish Church. In June 1685 he was with his brother-in-law, Charles Speke, in Ilminster, when news came that the Duke of Monmouth had landed at Lyme Regis. Implicated as a potential conspirator against James II, Trenchard realised the danger of being regarded as a Monmouth supporter and rode home to Lytchett to pack his bags. He sailed from Weymouth into exile on the continent. It was a prudent move, as Speke was strung up and hanged outside his house.

Later, in 1687, Trenchard's friends obtained him a pardon from King James and he was elected Member of Parliament for Dorchester. He then weathered the Glorious Revolution with flying colours and was knighted by King William III in 1690. By now he was sitting in Parliament for Poole and capped his career by being appointed His Majesty's Principal Secretary of State in 1692. He reformed the network of British spies in French ports and devised a complex system of numerical ciphers. Poole did its bit for the transfer of power from King James to Prince William of Orange by impounding one of the King's fire-ships, the *Speedwell*, after having taken its captain hostage in the Antelope Hotel.

The French were more of a problem for Poole than the ousted monarch, who had headed for Ireland. Comte de Tourville defeated an Anglo-Dutch fleet between the Isle of Wight and Beachy Head in 1690, and gathered invasion barges at Cherbourg, creating a climate of fear along the South Coast. The mayor of Poole, Henry Jubber, reactivated the battery on Brownsea Island and mounted 'four great guns' at Towngate. Veterans recalled the Civil War sieges and skirmishes as a public appeal was issued for muskets and pistols. These were serviced by gunsmiths and put into an armoury at the Town Hall. The peril was greater at sea, where Poole merchants suffered a series of seizures by French privateers, and the threat continued until Tourville was defeated towards Barfleur and Cap de la Hague on 29 May 1692. The French admiral had his revenge, off Cape St Vincent on 26–27 May 1693.

In 1694 King William III presented Captain Peter Joliffe from Poole with a gold medal and chain for his boldness in attacking with his hoy a French privateer that was three times his strength. He had seen it capturing a Weymouth boat that was fishing the

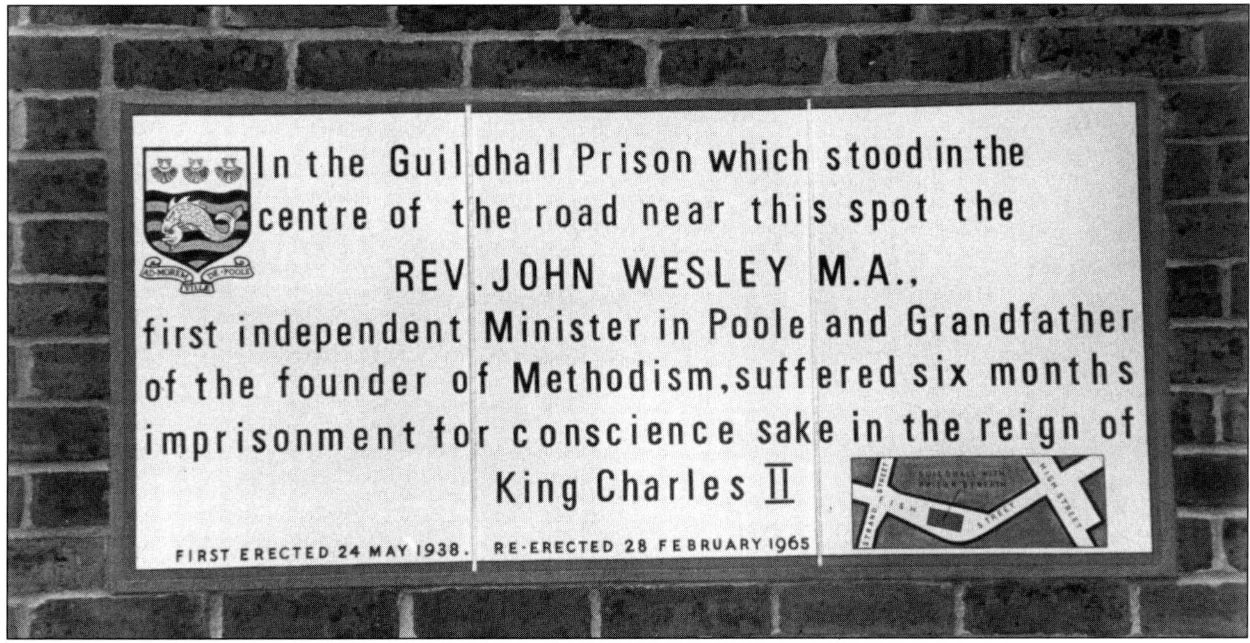

Guildhall Prison, which stood in Fish Street (now Castle Street), where Revd John Wesley (grandfather of the founder of Methodism) spent six months behind bars in the 1660s.

Lulworth Grounds. Joliffe not only forced the enemy to release his prize but forced him to beach near Lulworth, where local people took the crew prisoner. The medal was inscribed:

> *His Majesty's gift as a reward to Peter Joliffe of Poole, for his good service against the enemy in retaking a ketch of Weymouth from a French privateer, and chasing the said privateer on shore near Lulworth in the Isle of Purbeck where he was broken in pieces.*

Poole's Peter Thomson also received a medal for having turned the tables on a French vessel that was in the process of seizing an English ship. The Royal Navy, Poole sailors complained, could be as much of a threat as the French. They cited the example of a merchant ship which was fired upon by soldiers and a press-gang from an English vessel in Studland Bay. Five were killed on board the *Maria* as she escaped into the Channel.

Interruptions in long-distance Newfoundland and European commerce focused attention on possibilities and profits from local waters. The mainstay of this home trade at Poole lay in the oysters of Poole Harbour. This natural resource was fished in huge quantities and has left an underground layer of shells up to 4ft deep beside the eastern part of Poole Quay. Thousands of barrels of pickled oysters left Poole each year.

Sir Robert Clayton revived the copperas works on Brownsea Island. This was visited by the chemist Celia Fiennes on her *Great Journey through Britain* in 1698–99. She sailed from Poole and found the manufactory operated by the collection of quantities of 'copperice' stones from the shore which were then allowed to decay and drain naturally in the rain, the resultant liquid being accumulated in deep iron pans and boiled 'to a candy', which was hanging from branches 'like a vast bunch of grapes'. The 'great furnaces under' kept 'all the pans boiling'.

Left: *Hogarth-like caricature of Mayor Benjamin Skutt set in the rebuilt Harbour Office in 1727.*

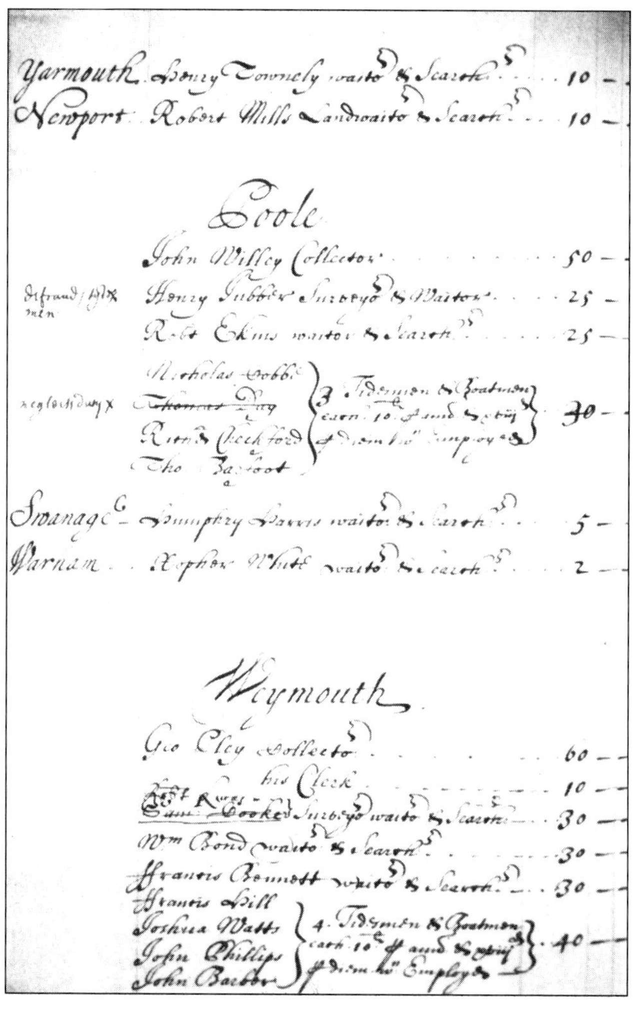

Yarmouth Henry Townely waiter & Searcher . . . 10 –
Newport Robert Mills Landwaiter & Searcher . . . 10 –

Poole

John Willey Collector . . . 50 –
[illegible] Henry Gubbins Surveyor & Waiter . . . 25 –
Robt Ekins waiter & Searcher . . . 25 –
[illegible] Nicholas Hobbs, ~~Thomas Day~~, Richard Checkford, Tho Barfoot } 3 Tidesmen & Boatmen each 10 [illegible] employed . . . 30 –

Swanage Humphry Harris waiter & Searcher . . . 5 –
Warham Xpher White waiter & Searcher . . . 2 –

Weymouth

Geo Cley Collector . . . 60 –
his Clerk . . . 10 –
[illegible] ~~Saml Cooke~~ Surveyor waiter & Searcher . . . 30 –
Wm Bond waiter & Searcher . . . 30 –
Francis Bennett waiter & Searcher . . . 30 –
Francis Hill, Joshua Watts, John Phillips, John Barber } 4 Tidesmen & Boatmen each 10 [illegible] employed . . . 40 –

Right: *Excise staff at Poole and Weymouth in 1671, when John Willey was the Poole Collector, as listed by contemporary accountants.*

Left: *Armed smugglers from Sussex breaking into the Custom House at Poole, to recover a confiscated cargo of tea, in October 1747.*

Right: *The New Inn (now the King Charles Inn), Thames Street, is the oldest surviving tavern behind the quay.*

✦ CHAPTER 7 ✦

Crusoe and Smugglers

London merchant Henry Harbin was elected a free burgess of Poole in 1701. He reciprocated by leaving the town £200 in his will towards buying land, so that the rent could provide an income for a schoolmaster to teach poor children. Appropriately, to this day, one of the town's largest schools still carries his name.

The Meeting House in Hill Street was built in 1704. Though known as the Presbyterian Meeting House it was in fact run by Congregationalists and Hill Street was a renaming of Hell Street. Its first pastor, Revd William Madgwick, was ordained on 11 October 1704. William Minty was the senior member of a congregation numbering 55 which soon grew. In 1721 the building was doubled in size.

The equivalent of an anti-social behaviour order was placed on Elizabeth Serrell, who was denounced in Poole in 1708 as 'a common scold and abuser of her neighbours'. She was threatened with a ducking from the quay.

There is a line in a Tennyson poem about sailing wherever a ship could sail. Poole-born, apparently, Captain Woodes Rogers (1679–1732) was among the first to do just that and came back with a tale of discovery and human isolation that holds a permanent place in the national psyche. Little is known about Rogers in earlier life, though he was still living in Poole at the age of 11. His father, also named Woodes Rogers, had definitely been born in Poole and lived there with his wife, Frances, prior to moving to Bristol. 'Woodes Rogers, Francis his wife, Woodes their child,' is how they appear in a poll-tax document of 1690.

Their son did well for himself by marrying Sarah Whetstone, the daughter of Sir William Whetstone, and as a sea captain aged around 30 was also based in Bristol. There, in 1708, Woodes Rogers was appointed captain of the *Duke* and given overall command of a privateering mission in which she and the *Duchess*, fitted out by West Country merchants, were sent off to harass the Spaniards in the South Seas. It was at latitude 79 degrees south, longitude 33 degrees west, on 31 January 1709 that Woodes Rogers found a bearded white man wearing a goat-skin on one of the otherwise uninhabited South Pacific islands of Juan Fernandez to the west of Valparaiso.

Speaking only broken England – as do most true Scots – the strange figure turned out to be Alexander Selkirk (1676–1721), from Largo, in Fife. He had been marooned there for four years after having been cast off in a rowing-boat following a violent row with Thomas Stradling, the master of the *Cinque Ports*. On the island his feet and clothes had been gnawed by rats until Selkirk befriended cats which 'became so tame that they would lie about him in hundreds and soon delivered him from the rats.' Richard Steele, the hack who first recorded the story for *The Englishman* journal, is now all but forgotten. So too is Woodes Rogers, who wrote his own memoir, as *A Cruising Voyage round the World*. The story, however, was too big for Woodes Rogers, Richard Steele or even Alexander Selkirk himself.

It was author and traveller Daniel Defoe who captured world attention by turning the tale into *Robinson Crusoe*. The story grew in one dimension, the period of exile and isolation being stretched to 28 years, but in another it literally lost most of its mileage. Rather oddly, Defoe moved the island towards home waters, around Cape Horn and across the Equator into the North Atlantic. As for the Islas Juan Fernandez, which belong to Chile, there the fiction has become fact. The larger eastern one is now known as Isla Robinson Crusoe and the 1,650m high western rock has become Isla Alejandro Selkirk.

Alexander Selkirk died as master's mate of the *Weymouth* on 12 December 1721. Woodes Rogers went on to become the first governor of the Bahamas, where he hanged ten of its notorious 'nest of pirates'. He died at Nassau on 16 July 1732.

Some time after the death of Sir Robert Clayton in 1707, probably in 1710, his heirs sold Brownsea Island to William Benson (1682–1754) for £300. He pretended he had also bought Branksea Castle and occupied it as if it were his own, although it was still Crown property, as he well knew. He added a 'Great Hall' to the building. Nationally, as a pamphleteer, he published *A Letter to Sir Jacob Bankes* which sold 100,000 copies and argued that kings were accountable only to God. He also sponsored literature by printing Samuel Johnson's *Psalms*, and erected a memorial to John Milton in Westminster Abbey. The poet Alexander Pope lampooned Benson for both: 'On two unequal crutches propell'd he came. Milton on this, on that one Johnson's name. On poets' tombs see Benson's title writ.'

The Harbour Office on the quay was built as the Town House in 1727, and has a bas-relief caricaturing the mayor of the time, Benjamin Skutt. It is not an unkindly likeness, but something of an unlikeness for all that. The sundial, dated 1814, was provided for the benefit of voyagers. The imposing classical colonnade was added during the reconstruction of the building into the Harbour Office in 1822.

Before 1729, when the post of consul or *chargé d'affaires* in Newfoundland was taken over by a naval commander, the first 'fishing admiral' to arrive from England at the start of the season was rewarded with the post. Much prestige attached to winning the race, which traditionally began on Poole Quay on the first day of March, and fogs and icebergs were defied in the annual contest.

Thomas Missing, who was returned as one of Poole's two Members of Parliament in 1745, endowed the town's first workhouse which stood in West Street. It carried the following inscription:

How commendable are the works of charity. This public edifice erected for the reception of the poor, was finished in the year 1739; the necessary charges of £500, were voluntarily defrayed by the sole generosity of Thomas Missing Esq.

Built for a Newfoundland trader in about 1740, West End House is the most impressive home in the Old Town. Dominating the setting with an impressive balustrade, it stands on the corner of Thames Street and St James's Close. Many of the Poole traders had businesses on both sides of the Atlantic. Shipbuilding yards in Newfoundland were operated by families with names familiar in Poole, such as Fryer, Garland, Gosse, Green, Kemp, Lester, Pack, Pike, Slade and Spurrier.

Frederick, Prince of Wales, was among the visitors to William Benson on Brownsea Island. By 1741, however, Benson was suffering a mental breakdown in Branksea Castle, as a result of which his former love of books turned to iconoclastic rejection of all that he used to cherish. Strange things were said to happen and Brownsea was henceforth synonymous with magic and mystery, as fishermen came back to Poole with tales of witchcraft and worse.

Sir Peter Thompson's House, in what was then the northern part of Market Street, towards Hungry Hill, was built between 1746 and 1749. Its provincial Georgian style is attributed to Blandford architects John and William Bastard. The house dates from the height of Thompson's fame and fortune, with a knighthood to celebrate for his services in the '45 rebellion. Above the door is his coat of arms with its modest motto 'Nil conscire sibi' (Conscious of no fault). Inside, the building is equally assertive. A magnificent oak staircase has Spanish mahogany banisters. The mantelpieces are finely carved and the moulded ceilings are a marvel of pargetting, with Thompson armorials.

Sir Peter Thompson (1698–1770) lived in Bermondsey and made most of his money as a Hamburg merchant, retiring to his home town of Poole in 1763. The house frontage looked out across the shrubbery, which hid from public view an ornamental lake in the shape of a very long swimming-pool, described as 'an ornamental canal', which was set on the same axis as the three-storey house so that it was overlooked from the bedroom windows. Beyond the shrubbery was Love Lane and the nineteenth-century buildings of Grove Place, Strickland's Yard and Providence Row. All except Sir Peter Thompson's House have been redeveloped. A large staircase window incorporating national coats of arms, which had been collected by Sir Peter, was removed to the new municipal buildings at Park Gates East in 1931.

Poole's Custom House featured in 'one of the most daring and brutal episodes in smuggling history'. The notorious incident took place on the night of 7 October 1747, when it was broken into by the 'Hawkhurst gang', from Sussex, who recovered 1 ton 17cwt of imported tea (4,144 lbs, worth £500) which had been recently taken from them. Captain William Jackson, in a Customs cutter, had seized the contraband in *Three Brothers* in Poole Bay, after an evening chase during which shots were fired, on 22 September 1747. The *Sherborne Mercury* recorded the details of the sequel:

We have the following extraordinary account from Poole in Dorsetshire. Viz., that on Wednesday morning, about two o'clock, a numerous company of persons unknown, armed with blunderbusses, pistols, swords, etc., came into that town, broke open his Majesty's Custom House there, and forcibly carried off a large quantity of tea, which had been lately brought in by the Swift *privateer, who took a smuggling vessel. They told the watchman, that they came for their own, and would have it; but would do no other damage. And accordingly did not.*

In taking back what was theirs, the men of Sussex ignored the guns of a naval sloop moored beside the building on Poole Quay, and no one was hurt either in the raid or the consequent cavalcade of carts northwards through Ringwood and Fordingbridge. Up to this point it was heroic defiance.

There followed, however, a despicable sequel. The passage of the smugglers across the ancient humped bridge had been witnessed by a shoemaker, Daniel Chater. He exchanged greetings with one of the smugglers and, as a result, was tossed a bag of tea. This, inevitably, drew attention to Chater's relationship with the men and caused him to face questioning in February 1748. Both Chater and another who recognised some of them, retired tidewaiter William Galley, from Southampton, agreed to give a statement to the authorities in Chichester.

News of this spread ahead of the two informants. Their initial undoing was to call for directions at the New Inn in Leigh, near Havant, where they met George Austin and two members of his family who agreed to show them the way to the village home in East Murden of Major William Battine.

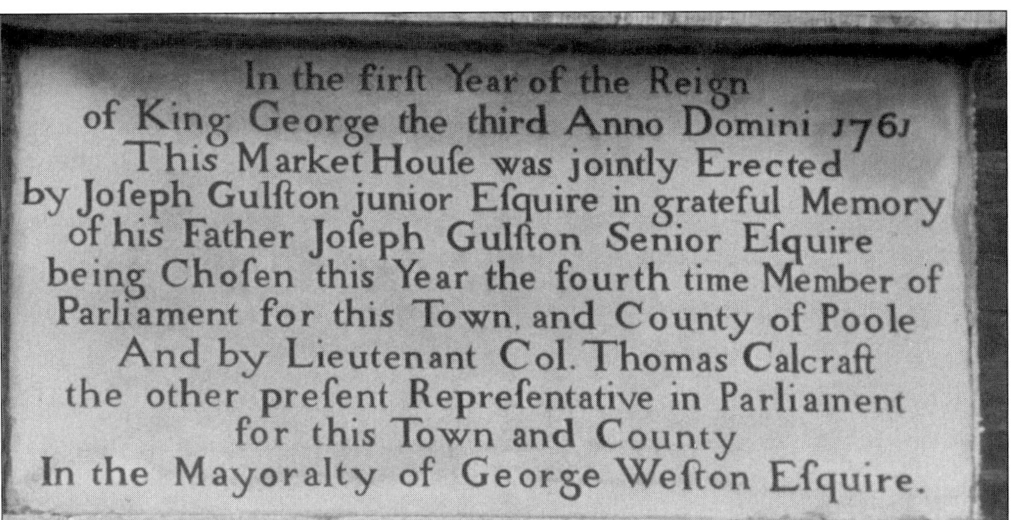

Plaque on the Market House in Thames Street recording its erection at the personal expense of the town's Parliamentarians, Joseph Gulston and Lieutenant-Colonel Thomas Calcraft, in 1761.

The following day, for a swig of rum, they stopped off at the White Hart Inn, Rowlands Castle, on the Hampshire–Sussex border. This stop proved to be a fatal mistake.

The landlady, widow Elizabeth Payne, had two smuggler sons. Having established that the men from Fordingbridge were heading for the home of Major Battine she sent word to William Jackson and his friends from the Hawkhurst gang. They came and seized Chater and Galley, subjecting them to prolonged beatings and other mutilations before throwing their half-dead victims to their deaths, near the Red Lion at Rake, where landlord William Scardefield was told that the men had been in a skirmish with excise officers. Galley was left to expire in a pit and Chater was thrown into a well, where stones were piled down on to him.

It took the remainder of the year for the law to catch up with the Hawkhurst gang. More than six months later, it seems to have been Scardefield at Rake who passed on details of the whereabouts of Galley's body, and then identified William Steel (alias Hardware) as one of those involved. Steel and his friend, John Race, both turned King's evidence and fingered their associates in return for immunity from prosecution.

The barbarity of the crimes was regarded as exceptional even to a nation accustomed to high thresholds of cruelty. The London judges arrived in Chichester to preside over a special Assize on 16 January 1749. Seven were in the dock, accused of one or both of the murders – William Carter, John Cobby, John Hammond, William Jackson, Richard Mills senr and Richard Mills junr, and Benjamin Tapner. They denied the offences but were found guilty. Each was to hang, with five of them suffering the further humiliation of having their bodies strung in chains from gibbets. The Mills, father and son, were excused that and Jackson managed to cheat the hangman by dying of shock as he was being measured for his chains.

The law caught up later with accomplice Henry Sheerman (alias Little Harry), who was condemned at East Grinstead Assizes in March 1749. Roger Guttridge, who details the multiple twists and turns of the story in his standard work *Dorset Smugglers*, quotes Sheerman's confession to *The Gentleman* newspaper in Chichester. 'Hot', the smugglers' favourite tipple – a mix of gin and beer – was the excuse for things going too far:

> *He said the smugglers, both masters and riders, drink drams to great excess, and generally keep them themselves half-drunk, which was the only thing that occasioned them to commit such outrages as they did some times.*

Sheerman's body was hanged in chains at Rake, where he had taken part in burying Galley alive. John Mills (alias Smoaker), the younger son of Richard Mills senr, was also convicted and hanged at East Grinstead but for another offence, namely the whipping to death of Richard Hawkins for a supposed indiscretion of which he was innocent.

The three leaders of the Hawkhurst gang – William Fairall, Thomas Kingsmill and Richard Perrin – were taken to London and convicted at the Old Bailey. They were hanged at Tyburn – now London's Marble Arch – on 26 April 1749. Two other smugglers were pardoned. In all, Roger Guttridge records, a total of 35 'East Country' smugglers went to the gallows as a result of a two-year campaign led by the Duke of Richmond. Ten more died in prison while awaiting trial. There was just one loose end, Guttridge adds, to round off Poole's principal contribution to *Dorset Smugglers*:

> *But what of Dorset's John Diamond (alias Dymar), the*

former shepherd whose generous act in throwing tea to an old friend led to the deaths of two innocent people and eleven of his smuggling colleagues? Like Race and Steel, Diamond turned King's evidence and like them, saved his neck by so doing.

Smuggling recurs in Poole's story, particularly after the Napoleonic Wars, though generally without the savagery of the Hawkhurst gang. The 3rd Earl of Malmesbury, as a young boy in 1800, met his Poole Bay smugglers while bird-nesting near his Hurn Court home. They merely asked for and received his silence. Likewise, at Ansford in south Somerset, parson James Woodforde, after just momentary apprehension, had his spirits lifted by the appearance of a free-trader at the inland end of one of the great smuggling trails from Purbeck and Poole Harbour across the Blackmore Vale and Cranborne Chase:

Andrews the smuggler brought me... a bag of Hyson tea 6 pound in weight. He frightened us a little by whistling under the parlour window just as we were going to bed. I gave him some Geneva [gin] *and paid him for the tea at 10s.6d per pound.*

The psalmist William Knapp (1698–1768) is remembered for his long-metre hymn tune 'Wareham', named for his home town, though by then he had moved to Poole. A glove maker by trade, living in Castle Street, he was the parish clerk for 39 years. While at St James's Church he composed *A Set of New Psalm Tunes and Anthems* in 1738, and followed this in 1753 with *New Church Melody*. 'Wareham' generally accompanies the words 'Rejoice, O land, in God thy might'.

One of Knapp's contemporaries, a tall man named Day, had a much-quoted memorial in St James's Church:

As long as long can be,
So long as long was he;
How long, how long, dos't say?
As long as the longest Day.

A wealthy new name arrived at Poole in 1751. Ralph Willett (1715–95) purchased the Merley estate from William Ash. Its manor-house, Merley Hall Farm, is now cut off by the A31 dual carriageway from a virtual riverside position looking out across the meadows towards Wimborne. It had been in the hands of the Constantine family until the death of Harry Constantine in 1712, and remains to this day as an intriguing warren of old buildings. Ralph Willett had the means to transform it but decided instead to build an entirely new mansion.

The cash came from slavery and sugar. An earlier Ralph Willett (1652–94), the eldest son of Henry Willett, sailed from London in the 1670s and found his way to the English colony of St Christopher (also known as St Kitts) in the Leeward Islands of the West Indies. By 1678 his brothers, William and Henry, had joined him there. The island was divided between the English and the French until the matter was settled by the Treaty of Utrecht, under which France ceded its colony to England in 1713.

The Ralph Willett who came to Merley in 1751 was Henry Willett's son. Slavery, upon which their sugar-cane plantations depended, could not legally exist in England – as Lord Mansfield confirmed in 1772 – but there was nothing to prevent the practice in British overseas territories until 1 August 1834.

Ralph Willett set about creating Merley House as a three-storey rectangular building. The classical work, in brick with Portland stone facings, dates from 1752 to 1759 and was undertaken either by provincial builder Francis Cartwright or the Bastard brothers from Blandford. The finest flourish, at the centre of the north façade, has steps rising from each side between temple-like Ionic columns to enter the building beneath a massive pediment. Willett lived in opulent elegance. Cultured and learned, being a Fellow of the Royal Society from 1754, he acquired books and paintings. Two separate two-storey wings, on either side, were added in 1772. Reached by curving corridors, they housed Willett's art gallery and library.

The Meeting House in Hill Street was taken over in 1753 by Revd Samuel Phillips. An evangelical preacher, he balked at the past practice of including members of the Arian sect, who rejected the doctrine of the Trinity. He demanded of them 'an application in your name of Father, Son and Holy Ghost.' This split the congregation. After a decade of divisions, Phillips 'was locked out of the pulpit' in October 1759, and 'withdrew'. George Kemp, George Olive and the Coward, Durrell, Gillingham, Ledgard, Linthorn and Miller families 'were amongst the seceders' who established another Congregational Church in Lagland Street. Meanwhile, members of the Bird and Young families 'continued with the old cause' and the Meeting House was later rebuilt as a Unitarian Chapel.

The Guildhall is imposing in plan and position. Its grand curving double staircase and 1761-dated symmetry look down on Market Street from the heart of the Old Town. It was given to the town by Poole's two Members of Parliament, Joseph Gulston and Thomas Calcraft. A typical Georgian Town Hall, costing £1,500, it shows the fusion between bureaucracy and commerce, the ground floor originally having arched openings for market-place commerce and stalls which were sealed in the mid-nineteenth century. Upstairs, entered from the imposing outer steps, an elegant main room hosted the Town Council beneath a moulded ceiling, and doubled as a court.

The red-brick façade is embellished with stone string-courses and quoins but its major flourishes are concentrated above the entrance, where the two flights of steps meet beneath a portico and pediment. It continued to host the Town Council until completion of the Municipal Offices in 1932. It is now one of the town's museums, with displays that explain the origins and development of the surrounding Old Town streets.

The Blandford and Poole Trust completed a turnpike road in 1765, in a straight course across Canford Bottom and Corfe Hills, north-westwards from Darby's Corner to Corfe Mullen. From there the main road system headed up the Stour Valley via Sturminster Marshall, Spetisbury and Charlton Marshall.

The smuggler Robert Trotman was shot dead in the spring of 1765 when a landing party from the Excise cutter *Folkestone* intercepted 'a desperate gang of smugglers'. Trotman, from Rowd (the place is misspelled on his gravestone) in Wiltshire, was said to be their leader. The skirmish took place at Canford Cliffs, and the fatal bullet could have come from either side, but his gravestone in St Andrew's churchyard at Kinson says he was 'barbarously Murder'd'. An official account of the incident which survives was shown in 1969 to a reporter from the *Evening Echo*, Bournemouth, who transcribed it as follows:

> *The smugglers, about 20, were loading tea on to their horses when they were surprised by Lieutenant Down and 14 hands from the cutter* Folkestone *which was lying in Brownsea Road. A midshipman was the first on the scene but the smugglers beat him in a most cruel manner with the great ends of their horse whips. Mr Down's clerk suffered a similar fate and was wounded by a pistol shot. The smugglers dragged him into the sea and left him, presumably to drown, but he crawled out and concealed himself in one of the chines while the affray lasted.*
>
> *Mr Down ordered his men to cut the bags of tea from the smugglers' horses but even while they were doing that, they were being whipped and one of them received a shot wound in the leg. They then made use of the means of their power to defend themselves and rescue the goods and one, Robert Trotman of Rowd, near Devizes, the head of a desperate gang of smugglers, was killed, but as it was dark, Mr Down, nor any of his men, can be certain who shot him, whether them or the smugglers; and some of their horses died on or near the shore of their wounds.*

Other smugglers went to Ringwood to inform the coroner, who held an inquest the following afternoon at North Haven House, Sandbanks. Several smugglers attended and gave evidence but, in the words of the report, the jury failed to give 'the least notice' to Lieutenant Down and his men, as they brought in a verdict of 'wilful murder by person unknown'.

Those committed to Poole's Salisbury Gaol in Sarum Street – named for the Earls of Salisbury who used to own Canford Manor – were also suffering in 1765, petitions claiming it to be 'unfit to retain prisoners'. The mayor of Poole was also blamed for failing to maintain the stocks on the quay.

Brownsea Island was purchased in 1765 by Humphry Sturt (1725–86) of Crichel House, near Wimborne, who set about enlarging Branksea Castle into a four-storey tower with wings branching off all sides. The grounds were also transformed into ornamental gardens with thousands of trees planted beyond as the island was turned into offshore parkland. The enhancement schemes cost £50,000.

James Oliver's mansion, on the eastern side of the High Street, was built in about 1765 and faced the wide junction with Hill Street and Towngate. The house became the home of the Garland family and was later extended at the back for the Freemason's Hall of Poole's Lodge of Amity. That name was preserved when it was converted into the twentieth-century Amity Cinema, but this remarkable building was demolished during the town's postwar decade of clearances.

Among the public nuisances for which townspeople were 'presented' to Quarter Sessions in 1767 was Mrs Elizabeth Christian's kitchen chimney, which was reported to be 'so low that the sparks' were 'in most eminent danger of setting fire to the straw and litter on the dung mixen of the Lion and Lamb Inn.' Hygiene was also a problem beside the old Town Hall in Fish Street, where the scholars of Mr Willis's private school 'do their necessary occasions' against the walls. Richard Blomfield's list of contemporary cases also features the failure of the ferrymen to maintain regular services across 'ye passage' between Poole and Hamworthy.

The national demand for clay began to increase after 1764, when potter Josiah Wedgwood married his wealthy cousin, Sally, and had the means to unite art and craft and establish himself as Britain's leading Neoclassicist. The Staffordshire Potteries became the biggest in Europe as a result of what Dr Johnson called an age 'running mad after innovation'. As a result, by 1797, a Swiss traveller noted that:

> *From Paris to St Petersburg, from Amsterdam to the farthest point of Sweden, from Dunkirk to the southern extremity of France, one is served in every inn from English earthenware.*

Thomas Hyde, born in 1731, was the notable member of a powerful Poole family, and the man who dominated the Corporation for 20 years. The doors and windows of his town house were 'all smashed' in an election riot in 1769. He was also working on an inspired revival of commercial clay-digging on a scale unknown in Dorset since Roman times. The family had been involved for a century in mining and merchandising pipe-clay from the shores of Poole Harbour.

After 1770, with the opening of the Trent and Mersey Canal, Josiah Wedgwood was able to expand

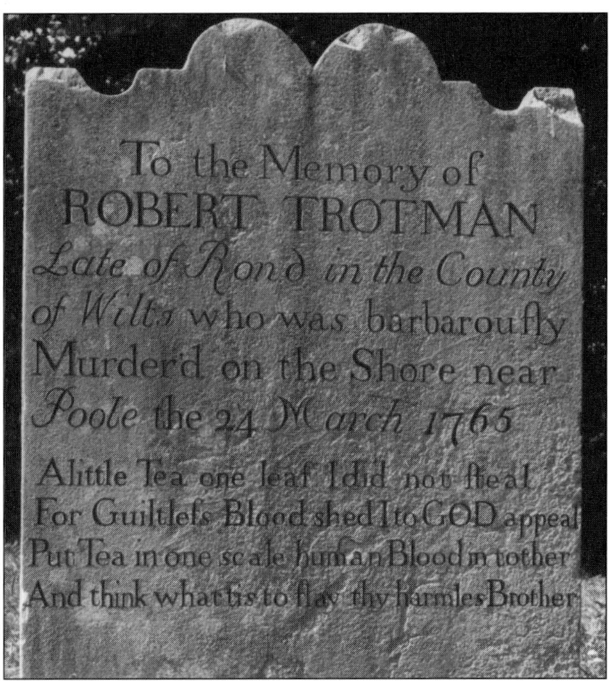

Sympathetic gravestone at Kinson for smuggler Robert Trotman, 'barbarously Murder'd' by excisemen 'on the Shore near Poole', 24 March 1765.

his operation on an industrial scale. That year Thomas Hyde began clay-digging at Arne, where he paid £30 for mining rights and began his workings on what is still known as Hyde's Heath, facing Gigger's Island, on the Purbeck side of the Wareham Channel off Swineham Point. His contracts included an agreement to supply Wedgwood with 1,400 tons of clay from the Rempstone estate, which was brought across the heath by donkey-cart to Russel Quay, between Hyde's Quay and Gold Point Heath. Other major business customers were at Queenborough, Kent, and in London. Sailing barges with ball clay from Poole Harbour and china clay from Cornwall, became a regular feature of Channel and North Sea shipping. The economics of its forward transfer to Staffordshire, and the even more important outward movement of products, were both revolutionised by the canal network.

Hyde also dug beside the shore to the west of Gold Point, directly opposite Rockley Sands, where the legacy was a lake beside Froxen Copse. This area was extensively re-dug for modern, deeper workings in the late-twentieth century. Arne's eighteenth-century business ceased, however, in 1792, when failing health caused Hyde to retire.

William Morton Pitt wrote from Encombe to Josiah Wedgwood to offer clay from his lands in Purbeck – which included the Arne peninsula – and appointed shipping agents both in Poole and the Potteries. They suggested that ship-coal could be brought back from the Midlands to Poole as a return cargo by the empty clay boats. Such plans were soon rendered impossible as a result of the disruption to coastal shipping by deteriorating relations with France.

The abortive Dorset and Somerset Canal, as envisaged in 1793, would have circumvented this problem by connecting Poole Harbour with the Bristol Channel. It had as its two main prospective sources of income the Somerset collieries and Purbeck potters' clay. Part of the canal was constructed in the colliery district, linking with the Kennet and Avon Canal, but the project ran out of money in 1803. Its backers had already abandoned the aim of reaching Poole Harbour and were intending to link with the turnpike road system at Shillingstone in the Blackmore Vale.

The Powder House on former Hospital Island, nearly a mile east of the Parish Church, was a rectangular building 22ft 4ins long by 18ft wide, with stone cladding on the outside and an inner shell of brickwork. Poole Corporation appointed a committee of burgesses on 14 June 1775:

> *... to order the building of a Store-house or Magazine for depositing and keeping gunpowder landed and brought into the said town at any place on the Point* [Baiter] *beyond the Windmill.*

In the town, the prison incorporated in the Town Hall was little better than a doss-house or, in the phrase of the day, 'a common bawdy house' which its keeper, John Galton, was summoned to bring up to an acceptable standard in 1777.

Splitting his life between Oxford and a Somerset parish near Castle Cary, Revd James Woodforde captured numerous insights into eighteenth-century living in *The Diary of a Country Parson,* which covers the period 1758–81. It includes what Richard Blomfield points out, in *Poole Town and Harbour*, is among the earliest evidence that 'use of cod liver oil was widespread before its official recognition' at Manchester Infirmary in 1782. He quotes an extract which I also selected, for reading at a dinner in the clergyman's honour a couple of centuries later. 'Keep taking the vitamins', was my take on the entry: 'Mr Thorne sent Nancy over today some Cod's Liver Oil to make use of about her still arm and lame knee. Pray God! Send thy blessing upon it for her good.'

Poole in 1784 had nine shipbuilders and seven sail-makers, as well as two iron-founders who produced anchors, grapnels and pintles, the latter being the pin which attached the rudder to the gudgeon. The port also had 11 surgeons whose principal sources of business arrived via the quay.

The rectory, built to impress in 1786, faces St James's Church from the crescent of Georgian buildings known as The Close. Beside it is St James's House.

A new Fish Shambles – the word means meat market – was erected towards the eastern end of the quay and replaced the historic building behind the Custom House.

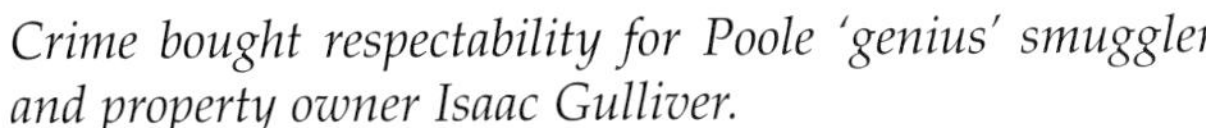

Crime bought respectability for Poole 'genius' smuggler and property owner Isaac Gulliver.

Betty Gulliver, wife of Isaac, after he had turned his talents to banking.

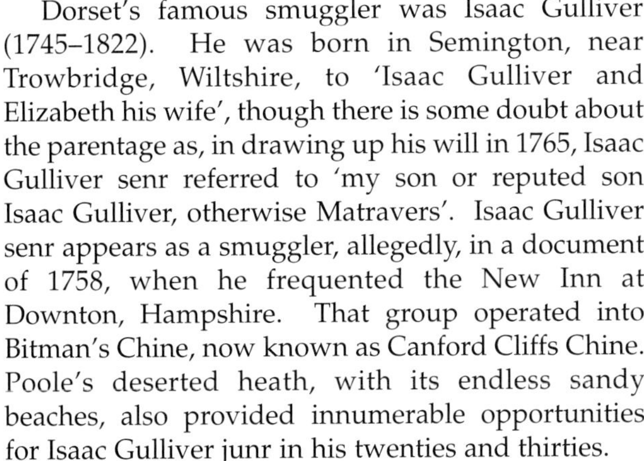

Dorset's famous smuggler was Isaac Gulliver (1745–1822). He was born in Semington, near Trowbridge, Wiltshire, to 'Isaac Gulliver and Elizabeth his wife', though there is some doubt about the parentage as, in drawing up his will in 1765, Isaac Gulliver senr referred to 'my son or reputed son Isaac Gulliver, otherwise Matravers'. Isaac Gulliver senr appears as a smuggler, allegedly, in a document of 1758, when he frequented the New Inn at Downton, Hampshire. That group operated into Bitman's Chine, now known as Canford Cliffs Chine. Poole's deserted heath, with its endless sandy beaches, also provided innumerable opportunities for Isaac Gulliver junr in his twenties and thirties.

He married innkeeper's daughter Betty Beale at Sixpenny Handley on 5 October 1768. His father-in-law's hostelry, the Blacksmith's Arms at Thorney Down, was on the main road from Blandford to Salisbury. Horse-shoeing was William Beale's other trade. He is said to have disapproved of his daughter's liaison but quickly adapted to reality. Gulliver took over tenancy of the inn. His first daughter, Elizabeth, was born there in 1770 and his second, Ann, in 1773.

Gulliver's 'great speculating genius' is the subject of a report from the Custom House, Poole, to His Majesty's Commissioners of Customs in London, on 10 December 1788, which goes on to say:

> *Gulliver was considered one of the greatest and most notorious smugglers in the west of England and particularly in the spirits and tea trades but in the year 1782 he took the benefit of His Majesty's proclamation for pardoning such offences and we are informed dropped that branch of smuggling and afterwards confined himself chiefly to the wine trade which he carried on to a considerable extent having vaults at various places along the coast to the westwards of this port some of which it is said were situated in remote places and we are well informed that he constantly sold wines considerably under the fair dealers' price from which circumstances there is no doubt that he illicitly imported that article but which trade we are informed he dropped some time since. He is a person of great speculating genius and besides the smuggling he has carried on a variety of other business, but we find he is not known at present to be concerned in any sort of merchandise and lives retired at a farm in this neighbourhood having acquired it is reported a very considerable property.*

Gulliver's far-flung estates included Howe Lodge at Kinson, near his eastern beach-heads, which was demolished in 1958. He rented out nearby Pelham's House and Manor Farm. Towards the harbour, at the end of Luscombe Valley, Parkstone, he is said to have owned both Ledgard House and Flag Farm, where lowering the flag was a warning signal of trouble ahead as his men hid kegs in the sand-dunes. Gulliver is the name that links nearby Lilliput with the giant of Jonathan Swift's scathing satire.

The Dean of St Patrick's in Dublin, Jonathan Swift (1667–1745) wrote *Gulliver's Travels* between 1720 and 1726, handing it to his friend, Alexander Pope, who obtained £200 for the copyright and had it published anonymously. It was instantly successful, 'at once a favourite book of children and a summary of bitter

The Georgian Custom House on the quay, the replacement for an earlier building been destroyed by fire in 1813.

scorn for mankind,' to quote the *Dictionary of National Biography*. He went on to publish *A Modest Proposal*, advocating the eating of babies to alleviate hunger and at the same time prevent another generation becoming a burden on society. Swift died as Isaac Gulliver was born. The two names were already inextricably linked and our Gulliver was no pygmy.

On the Parkstone coast, 'Lillypute' first appears as a name in 1783, and assumes standard spelling with the first Ordnance Survey map in 1811. Lilliput was the land of the pygmies and in its midst Isaac Gulliver owned Ledgard House and its pier. A further association is that a member of the Gulliver family, almost certainly a relation, was baptised at East Orchard, near Shaftesbury, with the same name, Lemuel Gulliver, as Swift's hero. The names Lemuel, Gulliver and Lilliput had become inseparable.

At Corfe Mullen, beside a triangle of roadside grass, 'Gullivers' carried his name on the gate to a thatched cottage until new owners renamed it Apple Tree Cottage. Gulliver's Farm, West Moors, was also close to one of the principal cart-routes inland and is known to have been owned by Isaac Gulliver. On the foothills of Cranborne Chase, as well as Thorney Down, he owned Thickthorn Farm, Long Crichel and nearby North-East Farm. At the other end of his operations, inland from the western end of the Chesil beach, he bought North Eggardon Farm, Askerswell. His associate at Poole, John Fryer, named a boat *Eggardon Castle* for its hill-fort, upon which Gulliver planted a clump of pines as a seamark.

Isaac and Elizabeth's only son, the third Isaac Gulliver (1774–98), died unmarried, but their daughters married into the Fryer family, whose interests ranged from the Newfoundland fisheries to English banking. Gulliver retired to the brick-built Gulliver's House in West Borough, at Wimborne. He died there on Friday 13 September 1822, leaving an estate of £60,000 – multi-millions in modern values – with properties in Dorset, Hampshire, Somerset and Wiltshire. His gravestone is in the floor of Wimborne Minster.

In February 1791 *Neptune*, a Swanage stone-boat, was beached and abandoned in Poole Harbour. She had 'bulged', to use the nautical term for a vessel with split sides.

Among the merchants who split their lives between Poole, Dorset, and Trinity, Newfoundland, with homes on both sides of the ocean, were Benjamin Lester, George C. Pulling and Thomas Stone. From Lester's diaries and a manuscript in Pulling's hand we know of the persecution of the native Beothuk. These so-called Red Indians – named for their use of red ochre – were discovered by the French sailor Jacques Cartier (1491–1557), who explored the Gulf of St Lawrence in 1534.

By the late-eighteenth century their descendants were suffering disease, harassment, starvation and worse – including massacres amounting to genocide – as white settlers encroached on their hunting and fishing grounds. During one such excursion, Pulling wrote, a father was surprised in his wigwam and shot dead as he tried to escape while his son, in his arms, was wounded and left to bleed to death. Then, after the remaining Indians had fled, a little girl was found in bed and abducted by the settlers.

Thomas Stone took her into his home at Trinity and named her Oubee. She went with him when he returned to Poole in January 1792. Unfortunately, she contracted tuberculosis and died in England in about 1795. Stone lived at Howe Lodge, Kinson, but a search of local parish records by Professor John Hewson of the Memorial University of Newfoundland, in 1971, failed to reveal a burial entry. John Hewson told me of Oubee's significance:

The writer would appreciate any information that might help in this quest, since this little girl has a place in the history, archaeology and ethnography of the whole of north-east North America. She was the informant for the document that we know as the Clinch Vocabulary *of the Beothuk language, one of three surviving fragments, containing scanty and garbled detail. From 400 surviving glosses of this now extinct language, present research is attempting to spell out the relationship of the Newfoundland Indians with the Indians of the North American mainland, and thereby shed some light upon the prehistoric movements of peoples in the north-eastern part of the continent.*

✣ CHAPTER 8 ✣

Napoleon's Wars

Poole Quay in the 1830s, in a view north-westwards from the Ballast Quay on the Hamworthy side of the Quay Channel to the wooden Poole Bridge (top left) *and St James's Church* (top right).

England declared war against France in 1793. George III spent his summers at Gloucester Lodge on the Esplanade in Weymouth, from where 'he bathed, yachted, rode and made excursions'. His son Frederick – 'the grand old Duke of York' in popular memory – marched his men up and down the slopes at Bincombe before taking them to the Low Countries. The King reviewed Lord Howe's fleet at Spithead on 30 January 1794 and expressed 'infinite pleasure' that peace talks had failed. Made paranoid by the threat of French invasion and the possibility of a Bastile-style revolution in London, he urged the defence of the South Coast by a counter-attack of barges, in what a Gillray cartoon satirised as an explosion of 'bum boats' emanating from Dorset.

Sugar magnate Ralph Willett, of Merley House, died in 1795. Though twice married, he had left no children and bequeathed five cane plantations on St Christopher's and the Merley estate to John Willett Adye (1744–1815), the son of a cousin, who was required to change his name to John Willett Willett. John's son and heir was Henry Ralph Willett (1786–1857), a barrister, who received £15,370 under a Parliamentary grant, when slavery was abolished in the British Empire, as compensation for the emancipation of the 351 slaves he owned in the West Indies.

The *General Wolfe* from Poole was intercepted by a French privateer in 1797 while en route to Newfoundland, but lived up to her name by outwitting the attacker and escaping. Seven English vessels, including one or two from Poole, were captured by a French warship off Newfoundland in 1702.

The poet and travel writer Robert Southey (1774–1843) ventured into what he described as an enchanted wilderness, on Poole Heath, in 1797. He delighted at the experience of 'walking in desolation' and contrasted it with London life. His conclusion was that 'much as I love society, rather than purchase it by residing in that great denaturalised city, I would prefer dwelling on Poole Heath'. The Southeys then did so, almost, by moving to a similar spot on the other side of St Catherine's Hill, on the edge of the New Forest near Christchurch.

Beech Hurst, facing Hill Street, was built in 1787. Ivy House in the High Street, which became the Westminster Bank, was built in 1800. Out of town, as fears of French invasion reached a peak before the Battle of Trafalgar, Lytchett Beacon was the communication link for Poole Harbour. It signalled to the national network at Badbury Rings, inland to the north, from where the next links in the chain were Woodbury Hill to the west and St Catherine's Hill to the east. The closest muster point for cavalry was in Wareham. Poole was also placed on a war footing, the following expectations being set out for the town

The first Poole Bridge, in wood, drawn by Philip Brannon in 1860, in a view westwards from the quay to the pottery chimneys (centre) *and church in Hamworthy and Lytchett Beacon beyond* (top right).

The New Inn (centre) *and west side of Thames Street, as sketched in 1880.*

Poole from the Hamworthy shore beside Poole Bridge, north-eastwards to the quay warehouses and tower of St James's Church (centre).

in the event of a French landing:

III Dorset Division. 287 Voluntary Infantry to be assembled from population of 729 men aged 15 to 60 who are capable of service. Livestock 226 oxen, cows and sheep. 54 riding horses. 59 draught horses. 33 wagons and carts. 16 ovens. Availability of loaves of 3 pounds in 24 hours – 2,030 for a constancy, 3,030 for an emergency.

Coastal signal points along the English Channel were operated by the Royal Navy: Round Down, St Alban's Head and White Nothe covered the coast westwards from Swanage to Portland North Point and Portland Bill, while Ballard Down and Hengistbury Head overlooked Poole Bay.

Between five and six o'clock on the evening of 2 October 1806 the Wareham and Poole *Passage Boat* left Poole Quay. It was a Thursday and the vessel was deeply laden with shopping and supplies. On board were 12 passengers (two men and ten women), William Gillingham of Wareham (the owner) and William Turner and Charles White junr (boatmen). A contemporary account records what happened next:

The wind was right ahead. Between six and seven o'clock it blew hard. Darkness hastened on, with a thick fog and rain, just as they entered the Wareham River at a place called the First and Last Boom. The boat ran aground and remained athwart the channel, the wind blowing so strong on her larboard side, and the sea inundated the vessel several times. They perceived their danger and all crowded towards the mast and rigging. The men got aloft. In a few moments she sank! The current running against the sails drove all under water, so that those who had got to the top of the mast for safety were obliged to commit themselves to the mercy of the waves.

Edward Everett from Wareham, the only man to survive, attempted swimming to the shore of the Purbeck parish of Arne, only 100 yards away. It was even more of a struggle because he had to contend with the presence 'of a poor woman of the name of White', who refused to drown:

Being encumbered with a great-coat and the woman having hold of him prevented his swimming so much that (self preservation getting the better of humanity) he had formed the dreadful (though necessary) resolution of shaking her off and leaving her to her fate, but at that moment one of the oars floated just before him which he eagerly caught at, and placed the woman upon it. After struggling with the waves for one hour and a half he found himself on the shore with the woman who was much exhausted to proceed a step. He hastened immediately to a house and requested their assistance, but they were deaf to his entreaties, [so] *he then went to the next house where he obtained it and went on to Wareham, about two an a half miles from where he landed.*

Captain Bartlett recovered the distressed Mrs White and brought her in a post chaise to his own house. There she was revived, by the fireside, with the added warmth and slobbering of a large dog, before being restored the following day to a grateful husband and family in Church Knowle. Otherwise, however, that village and Isle of Purbeck generally was in mourning for 13 lost souls:

Jane Barnes of Church Knowle (aged 33).
Betty Brown of Wareham (aged 39).
Sophia Dorey of East Stoke (aged 19).
Elizabeth Forster of Wareham (age not given).
William Gillingham of Wareham (aged 52).
Elizabeth Mintern of Wareham (aged 38).
Mary New of Church Knowle (aged 33).
William Oxford of Wareham (aged 37).
Elizabeth Pindar of Wareham (aged 27).
Amelia Randall of Stoborough (aged 19).
Edith Randall of Wareham (aged 24).
William Turner of Wareham (aged 52).
Charles White junior of Wareham (aged 33).

Even during the Napoleonic Wars, which caused an economic boom for that section of the community at the top of the pyramid, the supposed trickle-down effect through society as a whole left base-level poverty on a massive scale. When the bullocks and sheep were slaughtered for a series of quayside barbecues to celebrate 'with great rejoicing' the jubilee of King George III, on 25 October 1809, no less than 647 Poole families were regarded as impoverished and therefore qualified for free meat and a total of 2,000 loaves. Allowing for their children and aged relatives, the total treated in the name of the King must have exceeded 4,000 people, half the population, who were regarded as disadvantaged. The problem with calculating the scale of communal poverty by an average measurement is that half the sample inevitably falls below the line that is regarded as normal. In terms of wealth, rather than lack of it, the other 2,500 inhabitants of the town held an estimated 90 per cent of Poole's assets and possessions.

The Town Pump on the seaward side of Town Cellars is inscribed 'John Strong, Mayor 1810'. Cynics pointed out that all other water on Poole Quay that was safe to drink had first passed through a brewery. The pump was restored by the Society of Poole Men in 1929.

The masters of Poole fishing smacks were issued with exemption certificates in 1810 to prevent them 'from being impressed into His Majesty's Service'. This was granted under the terms of:

An Act for the better supplying the Cities of London and Westminster with Fish, and to reduce the present exorbitant Price thereof, and to protect and encourage Fishermen.

The historic open look of Poole Quay, looking eastwards to the Fish Shambles (left centre) *and Poole Pottery, though by 1890 it was dissected by rails, with wagons carrying the initials of the London & South Western Railway.*

The central section of Poole Quay, from a cluster of old buildings beside the Portsmouth Hoy Inn (left), *looking eastwards to the Coal Wharf and its overhead gantry* (centre left) *in an early Edwardian view, after the introduction of gas lighting.*

The Eagle *from Yarmouth, in a photograph from 1900, looking westwards from the Harbour Office* (far right) *to H. & A. Burden's coal yard and the Ship Supply Stores* (right centre), *and the boatyards and potteries of Lower Hamworthy* (left).

The document issued 'By the Commissioners for Exercising the Office of Lord High Admiral of the United Kingdom of Great Britain and Ireland, &c' was addressed 'To all Commanders and Officers of His Majesty's Ships, Press-masters, and all others whom it doth or may concern.'

The Custom House, midway along Poole Quay, which had been modified around the former Red Lion Coffee House, was destroyed by fire on 22 April 1813. Its rebuilding, more or less as a replica, includes an outer double staircase similar to that of the Guildhall.

A dog biscuit preserved in a glass case by Poole's Lodge of Amity, in Freemason's Hall in Market Street, is proof that the brotherhood can transcend national enmities. It is a memento of an incident during the Napoleonic Wars in which a French freemason ended his seizure of an English freemason's vessel with a masonic handshake. He released into the custody of the fortunate Poole master and his crewmen a little dog which had come into their hands from another Dorset mason, Captain Storey, who had been similarly apprehended and set free a few days earlier. The treasured exhibit is accompanied by an inscription which tells the story:

> *This biscuit is preserved by the Lodge of Amity, as a memorial of their gratitude and brotherly affection for Jacques de Bon, captain of the* Junon, *French privateer of St Malo, who captured at sea, on the 13th of December 1813, at 11 am, in latitude 49 degrees 50 minutes north, longitude 7 degrees west, the brig* Oak of Poole, *brother Stephen Pack, master, belonging to brothers G.W. Ledgard and John Gosse, on her passage from Bilbao to Poole, who after treating him with every mark of kindness, returned him to his vessel, and sent on board a dog (which had been taken from a brother) with this biscuit suspended by a string round his neck, signifying that he would not see a brother's dog in bondage, or see him want bread.*

The premature end of the French Wars, later extended by Napoleon's departure from exile on the Mediterranean island of Elba, was celebrated across the country after the triumphant arrival of the allies in Paris on 31 March 1814. Poole hosted the biggest party in its history. Two breweries, both owned by the Corporation provided 1,280 gallons of 'strong beer' at a cost of £96. A further £367.2s.6d. was spent on municipal festivities.

The Sturt family sold Brownsea Island to Sir Charles Chad, who held it until 1840 and built cottages called Seymer's House, now in ruins, overlooking the northern shore.

Between 1816 and 1819 a cabin boy named William Pardy (1802–72) left Poole and jumped ship at Twillingate on Change Island, beside Notre Dame Bay on Newfoundland's deeply indented northern shores. By 1825 he had married into the Young family, who gave him land at Little Harbour which their descendants own to this day.

The Napoleonic Wars had brought unparalleled prosperity to Poole. By the time of the Battle of Waterloo, on 18 June 1815, there were 317 fishing vessels operating from Poole Quay. Then the bubble burst and the number dropped to 19 in 1828.

Meanwhile, smuggling enterprises experienced a revival, as the town archives show. On 11 April 1816, at the Guildhall, Kent, victualler Joseph Brooks appeared before magistrates Samuel Weston and Peter Jolliff. He was prosecuted by David Lander, Collector of Customs, for 'harbouring and concealing' two silk shawls, one silk half-handkerchief and 19 yards of lace 'well knowing them to have been clandestinely run and imported'. Brooks, who was fined £10.6s.0d., appears again in the records later in the year, standing bail for alleged smugglers.

Co-defendant Martha Hurdle was accused of possessing contraband on 26 February 1816 and being 'employed in carrying the same'. Her illicit goods comprised 1 silk shawl, 5 silk half-handkerchiefs, 13 silk handkerchiefs, 24 pairs of leather gloves, 1 *[further]* silk shawl, 2 lace silk half-shawls and 21 yards of lace. She was fined £20, including costs.

On 15 June 1815, three officers from Poole Custom House deposed evidence on oath relating to the master and crew of the *Elizabeth and Mary*, from Rochester, who were 'charged with having contraband abroad.' The informants were John Scaplen Stansmore, Charles Sandy and James Botley Street.

Bail terms, set in a recognisance of 7 August 1816, identify the crew as Robert Loft (mate) and Thomas Fielding, James Woolvill, and William Cooper (mariners). Their recognisance was £100 and the same was received on their behalf from sail maker William Atkinson Erratt and victualler Joseph Brooks from Strood on the Medway.

The Customs officers affirmed that, when apprehended near Poole, the vessel was carrying contraband comprising 15 gallons of Geneva (Holland's grain spirit, which we know as gin), seven pounds of tea, two pounds of chocolate, ten pounds of salt, and a half-pound of tobacco. On being questioned, the officers claimed, 'the mate and master confessed that they had been on shore at Jersey and had taken some spirits on board there'.

John Foot, town clerk of Poole, received a letter in July 1816 from Knight, Jones & Knight – London solicitors in the Temple – relating to John Galton and Timothy Ellis. They had been impressed for service in the Royal Navy:

> *... on the 17th of last month two lads named John Galton and Timothy Ellis were detected in some sort of smuggling by Joseph Carter, a sitter of the Preventive Customs belonging to Swanage, and have been consequently sent into the Navy under the* [Act] *47 George III, chapter 66, section 15, the cases having been*

Sea Cadet Corps' training ship Royalist, *berthed to a capstan on Poole Quay, in a timeless view from the 1970s.*

> *referred by the Admiralty Board to their solicitor, we have be obliged to you to send for and take Mr Carter's deposition... acquainting us with their respective ages.*

This evidence was duly taken down, on 14 August 1816, on the back of a Longfleet property sail handbill from three years earlier. Carter, who was on duty at midnight at North Haven House, Sandbanks, with the 'Preventive Boat' from Swanage, hid in seaweed on the shore after seeing a suspicious light. Galton and Ellis were observed putting 'a tub of liquor' into a boat at North Haven Quay. They were challenged and seized as a third person ran off. Galton and Ellis were taken to the Custom House at Poole and held in the watch-house before being conveyed to Swanage, where they were impressed and transferred to the sloop HMS *Algerine*.

Further information from Joseph Carter was written on the back of an old political handbill, dated 26 August 1811, which carried the election address of one John Dent.

From May 1818 we have a mittimus (warrant for committal to prison) against Edward Hopper. It was granted at the Guildhall by Mayor James Seager and fellow magistrate Peter Jolliff on evidence from Robert Aldrich, chief officer, and Preventive boatmen John Mercer and John Rigler. They had seized 'a large quantity of foreign spirituous liquors' which were being smuggled:

> *And whereas the said Edward Hopper not having proved to the satisfaction of the said Justices that he was a passenger on board such a boat, we therefore hereby command you the said keeper to receive the said Edward Hopper into your custody in the said Gaol, and there safely keep* [the accused] *to abide such judgement as may be given against him.*

On 24 September 1818, information sworn by Thomas Mundy, officer of the Revenue Cutter *Hawk* was put before Mayor Joseph White Orchard and magistrate James Seager in the Guildhall. The boat from the *Hawk* had come across a vessel suspected of smuggling near Beer Head, Devon, and chased her for some time. At the end of the pursuit they found 20 tubs 'of foreign spirits' in her, and about as many alongside, all of which were seized. Then four men aboard were also taken, according to Thomas Mundy:

> *Who saith that in the night of the 22nd instant he captured a boat taken with 11 casks of spirits on the sea near Portland on board of which were four persons which he took into custody, and who are now present before the magistrates.*

Thomas Flann, a seaman from the *Hawk*, attended at the Guildhall on 26 October 1818 to say that 'at four o'clock the previous morning' he had seized James Davis – who appeared as 'the prisoner' – along with 'a boat lade with spirits subject to forfeiture on the north shore to the westward of Cliff House'.

In 1819 the Terrace was built in the High Street. It later became Rose's Dairy. The great change in the town's skyline in 1819 was the demolition of the medieval church of St James and its replacement in Georgian Gothic style.

The lock-up in Sarum Street, rebuilt with an 1820 datestone, was known as the Salisbury. This may have arisen as a result of the street name, ecclesiastic Sarum being synonymous with secular Salisbury, but it also preserved the memory of the medieval Earls of Salisbury from Cranborne, who held the manor of Canford and were therefore responsible for providing such facilities. Regular clientele included the inevitable drunks, possibly either celebrating their return to this sceptred isle or preparing to depart from it.

Between 1820 and 1860 the export of clay from Poole Harbour rose from 20,000 to 60,000 tons a year. Purbeck and Poole were being credited with producing the raw material for 35 per cent of all the pottery made in England. Since Thomas Hyde's time, before the French Wars, the Staffordshire kilns were the main buyers of greyish-white ball clay from the Dorset heaths. It was also known as pipe clay, being the stuff of the archetypal prop for the common man. Back home tobacco pipes were soon to be surpassed by drainage pipes as the construction industry flourished.

The Town House was rebuilt and expanded, with a colonnaded frontage, in 1822. It became the offices of the Poole Harbour Commissioners and has since been known as the Harbour Office, though in the 1980s it was transferred to Coastguard and Fisheries personnel.

The Poole Inclosure Award of 1822 records the last gasp of a medieval landscape. Even the present wilderness, such as at Delph Wood, was nothing of the kind, but laid out as a series of allotments, the land being owned by John Willett Willett and Martha Snooke. Their name, the Moorlands, captured the spirit of the past and was to become the future look of the land as nature eventually ousted the cultivators. The poor had been handed rights to a wild expanse of heathland which would beat them in the end.

Smuggling, already the town's fastest growing industry, gained further momentum as increasing rates of taxation put an end to any concept of free trade, and austerity at home put luxury items beyond the means of ordinary people. The crime wave became endemic at all levels of society. In 1822 a confidential report to the Board of Customs in London commented cryptically: 'Much must be doing on the Dorset coast. Brandy is offered in Yeovil at eight shillings a gallon.'

Among those who indulged in an older illegal trade was Maria Williams, sent to the House of Correction by Poole magistrates in 1822 for idle or disorderly behaviour in the public streets as she carried out her trade as 'common prostitute or night-walker'. Samuel Hart was a regular raider of the harbour oyster-beds, dredging them at night, for which he was arraigned in 1821 and again in 1824.

Poole labourer John Harding (born 1805), of Longfleet, whose height was recorded as 5ft 4.75ins, was convicted of 'stealing bank notes and wearing apparel' and sentenced to death at Dorchester Assizes in June 1824. He was reprieved, however and, his sentence commuted to transportation for life, was taken to the *York* prison hulk at Portsmouth on 6 October 1824.

Another contemporary convict was Thomas Barnes. The offences of this 'seafaring man' were documented by town clerk James Foot on 29 July 1824. He was seized on a vessel at Southampton 'not proceeding on her voyage although the wind and weather permitted the same'. Customs officer Samuel Charles Umpreville then found on board 650 lbs of tobacco and Barnes and the boat were brought to Poole. On appearing before George Welch Ledgard and James Seager, the mayor, the accused was convicted and 'adjudged to serve in His Majesty's Naval Service'.

Thomas Barnes was saved from naval service by two officers on HMS *Victory* in Portsmouth Harbour. On his own request, on 28 August 1824, he was returned to prison to be dealt with 'according to law' because of his unfitness for duty due to 'old ulcers on his leg'.

The Commander-in-Chief North Sea, Admiral Thomas Macnamara Russell (1740–1824) 'died suddenly, in his carriage, in the neighbourhood of Poole' and was buried in Canford Magna Church, where his elegant and fulsome memorial tells of his 36 engagements in 'the wars of America and France' and enigmatically states that he 'was offered a knighthood' in 1784.

Russell blockaded Texel, at the mouth of the Zuyder Zee, Holland, in gales 'and was the first to anchor a fleet on enemy's lee shore'. Newly appointed as Commander of the North Sea Squadron, he heard that Denmark had declared war on Britain, and on his own initiative took the fleet to the offshore island of Heligoland, receiving its surrender on 5 September 1807.

One of the results of the collapse of the Dorset and Somerset Canal Company, plus the new opportunities for railways as a more viable alternative, was a meeting at the Red Lion Inn, Wareham, on 26 November 1825. It was chaired by John Calcraft MP of Rempstone Hall and agreed to support moves to build a railway, costing up to £300,000, that would run from Poole Harbour to the Somerset coalfield. As with the canal, nothing came of the plan, and the arrival of the first train in Dorset was postponed for two decades.

Market Street in 1874, northwards to the barrel of a cannon beside the Guildhall (centre), *this Crimean War trophy having been captured from the Russians at the siege of Sebastopol.*

Pre-1870 photograph of the upper High Street, before the building of the railway through the centre of the town, north-eastwards from Beech Hurst (right) *to Towngate* (top left).

✥ CHAPTER 9 ✥

Lifeboats and Railways

Given its location inside a usually well-protected harbour, Poole held little priority for the Royal National Institution for the Preservation of Lives from Shipwreck when it was founded in 1824. Rowing-boats in Poole were effectively landlocked in that they could fight their way out of the Swash Channel, into Poole Bay, in adverse conditions. Therefore the first local lifeboat, un-named but built at Plenty's Boatyard, in Newbury, was based at Studland in 1826. The second in Dorset – Portland had the first – she was 20ft in length and had a crew of eight or nine. Studland Bay saw a daring rescue that year, of two sailors from Christchurch boat *Lark*, but it was carried out by Lieutenant Joseph Elwin with two other members of His Majesty's Coast Guard. The Studland lifeboat stayed on station for a quarter of a century but seems to have been little used.

The Lifeboat service – pictured here as 'The Red Cross of the Sea' – has become synonymous with Poole as a result of the RNLI basing itself in the town.

The 'Poole canoe', as the flat-bottomed harbour punts was known, was described in 1830 by Colonel Peter Hawker in his manual on *Guns and Shooting* in such detail, he says, as 'a carpenter ought not to mistake in building one.' For wild-fowling, beside the marshes, a heavy punt-gun was fired from one end as, at the other, the boatman held the craft in position with a pole:

> *The Poole canoe is built sharp at both ends, on the plan of the Greenland whale-boat, except being so flat at the bottom as to draw about two inches of water, and so light as to weigh only from 60 to 100 pounds. Dimensions – from stern to stern, 12 feet; length of bottom, 10 feet; bottom, at centre, 3 feet 2 inches; width at ditto, from gunwale to gunwale, 3 feet 7 inches; height 11 inches at centre, rising to 13 ditto fore and aft; weight about 100 pounds. Timbers yew or oak. Bottom to be three pieces of elm or pine an inch thick. Caulk the seams with oakum, then pour in rosin* [turpentine resin], *softened with a little oil to prevent it from cracking, and paint the bottom (outside) with red lead.*

Eminent biologist Philip Henry Gosse (1810–88) began his career by collecting sea anemones in Poole Harbour. The family had moved to Gosse House, Skinner Street, Poole, in 1812. As a 15-year-old Gosse began work as junior clerk to George Garland, whose comfortable counting house in Poole contrasted with the austere end of the trade, from which the profits came, over the water in Newfoundland. Gosse sailed there to work in a whaling office from 1827 to 1835, where 'Dirty brawling vulgar fellows' cussed, swore and abused others, amid the filth and grease. Gosse's task was to count rancid seal hides in snowy gales. He longed to see the arrival of the last schooner before the ice closed the sea lanes for another long winter.

Then Gosse went off to enjoy other discomforts, endured without complaint, in order to collect the colony's insect life, which he was the first to put under the microscope. From there he moved on to Canada and completed his unpublished *Entomology of Newfoundland* in 1836. Further travels did get into print, with the *Canadian Naturalist* in 1840 followed by his *Introduction to Zoology* in 1843, *Birds of Jamaica* in 1847 and *A Naturalist's Sojourn in Jamaica* in 1851.

Back in the Old World, Gosse described *The Antiquities of Assyria* in 1852 and *A Naturalist's Rambles on the Devonshire Coast* in 1853. This, and his early Poole discoveries, led to *The Manual of Marine*

Zoology in 1855–56, for which he produced 700 woodcuts. Then he jumped into the evolutionary debate with *Life*, in 1857 (two years before Darwin's *On the Origin of Species*), and *Omphalos*, in 1857, before tidying his boyhood sea-anemone studies into *Actinologia Britannicus* between 1858 and 1860, the first standard work on the subject. *Letter from Alabama*, in 1859, also recalled his younger days. In *The Romance of Natural History*, in 1860, he put forward the notion that the sea-serpent of mariners' tales was a surviving plesiosaurus.

A Year at the Shore, in 1864, and *Land at Sea*, in 1865, rounded off his literary efforts and in retirement in Devon he grew orchids and drew microscopic plates of rotifers, the minute wheel-shaped animalcules. Philip Henry Gosse was the father of Sir Edmund Gosse (1849–1928), his only child, born in London, who found fame as a literary critic and was author of *Father and Son* and friend of novelist Thomas Hardy.

Looking back to 1820, when Poole was a town of 6,000 souls, people and place were imprinted with the smells of tar, turpentine, train oil, and 'fresh fish in the act of becoming stale fish.' A big windmill still stood on the isthmus at Baiter, which was reached from Mount Street and Green Lane. Edmund Gosse captured this vignette of quayside life as 'my father's impression of the Poole of his early childhood':

The Quay with its shipping and sailors: their songs and cries of 'Heave with a will yo-ho'; the busy merchants bustling to and fro; fishermen and boatmen and hoymen in their sou' westers, Guernsey frocks and loose trousers; countrymen, young bumpkins in smocks seeking to be shipped as youngsters for Newfoundland; rows of casks redolent of train oil; Dobell the ganger moving among them, rod in hand; Customs officers and tide-waiters taking notes; piles of salt fish loading; packages of dry goods being shipped; coal cargoes discharging; dogs in scores; idle boys larking about or mounting the rigging.

All this makes a lively picture in my memory, while the church bells, a full peal of eight, are ringing merrily. The Poole men glory somewhat in the peal, and one of the low inns frequented by sailors in one of the lanes opening on the Quay had for its sign the Eight Bells duly depicted in full.

Owing to the narrow, winding channels of Poole Harbour, skilled pilots were indispensable for every vessel arriving or sailing. From our upper windows in Skinner Street we could see the vessels pursuing their course along the Main Channel, now approaching Lilliput, then turning and apparently coasting under the Sandbanks at North Haven Point. Pilots, fishermen, boatmen – a loosely-trousered Guernsey-frocked sou' westered race – were always lounging about the Quay.

The Newfoundland trade was still in recession. The Spurrier family from Upton House went bankrupt in 1830, despite owning the 340-ton *Upton* and wider shipping interests.

The Fish Shambles, on the eastern part of the

Ironwork of the second Poole Bridge, newly built in 1885, with remains of its timber predecessor alongside, looking north-eastwards from Hamworthy to the grain warehouses on Poole Quay.

quay, was replaced in 1830. That was a year long remembered in the town for the unexpected arrival of exiled French monarch Charles X (1757–1836), who packed his treasures, assembled his entourage and departed from Cherbourg. The 73-year-old arrived in Poole on Monday 23 August 1830 aboard the English steamboat *Comet*. He was politely received at the Ballast Quay, an occasion commemorated on a plaque near the King Charles Inn.

The Prime Minister, the Duke of Wellington, ordered the Custom House authorities not to inspect any of the royal baggage. Ten days after his arrival, £500,000 was invested in consolidated annuities, as a coffer of the French state was emptied into British Government stock. Charles arrived with 120 servants, and he and his court were taken to Lulworth Castle, where the Catholic Weld family were sympathetic hosts.

For the Government there was a diplomatic crisis, for allowing the ex-King to set up home on the South Coast was deemed a provocation against the French, and there were fears also that an attempt might be made to land and carry off the young Duke of Bordeaux. It having been decided that Holyrood, at Edinburgh, would be a more suitable location, the Admiralty steam-packet *Lightning* arrived at Poole for the purpose on 14 October, and the King sailed for Scotland on 20 October 1830.

Poole Corporation at this time comprised a mayor, four aldermen and 28 burgesses. The town's worthies – who totalled 126 men out of a total population of 6,390 adult persons – exercised the historic right to return two Members to Parliament. In 1830 they were the Hon. William Ponsonby, who inherited Canford House after the Webbe family departed, and Benjamin Lester, a major operator of the Newfoundland fisheries. Both backed the Reform Bill, which led to resistance and riots even though, in the first instance, it would only extend the town's plebiscite to 540 voters. There was also a review of the town's boundaries, extended to include the new suburbs of Hamworthy, Longfleet and Parkstone, increasing the population to 'about 8,000 inhabitants'. Passions were aroused by this supposed diminution of the town's 'independence' being open to 'corruption and nomination', though cynics pointed out that patronage was endemic in the previous system.

Ponsonby's father was Frederick Ponsonby, 3rd Earl of Bessborough, and his only sister Lady Caroline Ponsonby, well known to history as Lady Caroline Lamb (1785–1828), one of the most colourful characters of the age. In 1805 she had married the Hon. William Lamb, later 2nd Viscount Melbourne (1779–1848), who was appointed Home Secretary by Lord Grey on 19 November 1830. It was Melbourne's sister, Emily, who remarked of Ponsonby that he was 'reckoned an ass and a jackanapes by everybody'. The Lambs had had one of the best recorded broken marriages of the time, as Lady Lamb had become infatuated with Lord Byron, confiding to her diary that he was 'mad, bad and dangerous to know', an epithet she went on to prove when she finally went mad after accidentally coming upon the poet's funeral cortège en route to Newstead in 1824.

Back in Poole, at the time of Caroline's death in 1828, her brother William Ponsonby was preparing to make rather lower-key contributions to the cause of literary appreciation. Together with fellow MP Benjamin Lester, he endowed the town's first public library and saw the completed building open for use at the bottom end of the High Street in 1830. In 1827 Ponsonby also founded the charitable Bethel Company as a ships' lending library for mariners both ashore and on the high seas.

Defeated by Lord Ashley at a by-election in 1831, William Ponsonby slipped back unopposed when a third county seat was created for Dorset in 1832. Ponsonby owned the immense Canford estate, which covered almost all the land from the sea at Poole Bay to the River Stour in the shadow of Wimborne Minster. He was created 1st Baron de Mauley in 1838.

Poole Gas & Coke Co. was founded in 1833, with a capital of £4,000, with a standard tariff for regulated lighting – by agreeing to 'lights out' at a curfew time – or metering if unrestricted use was required. Farmer & Co., traditionally bell-hangers and furnishers, now advertised themselves as gas-fitters.

Parkstone, a tithing in what was known as Great Canford, was formed as a civil parish in 1833 and retained its separate identify for the rest of the century. It was not absorbed into the municipal borough and civil parish of Poole until the Poole (Extension) Order came into operation on 9 November 1905. The ecclesiastical parish of Parkstone dates from 1834, when it too was taken from Canford Magna and provided with St Peter's Church, which was rebuilt and extended in 1876, 1892 and 1901.

When St Mary's Church was erected at Longfleet in 1833, this was also a tithing of Great Canford. Built in Early English style, its tower was topped by a 108ft spire which became a seamark for harbour shipping. The ecclesiastical parish was formed in 1837 and Lord Wimborne gave an acre of land for a churchyard in 1886.

The National School at Longfleet dates from 1839 and was enlarged in three stages – in 1874, 1883 and 1886 – to accommodate 260 children. The population of Longfleet was 2,406 in 1881, though this figure included 138 officers and inmates of Poole Union Workhouse, an institution which resulted from the Poor Law Act of 1834, replacing a much smaller building in West Street.

The need for regulated fishing to safeguard diminishing stocks can be traced back to 1835 in Poole Harbour, when management of the oyster-beds was annulled by the Admiralty and a free

The westernmost and first of the two viaducts built across Surrey Road, Bourne Valley, during construction in 1884.

market came into play. Until then, traditionally, an average of 50 licences had been issued, and it was not until 1885 that measures for their re-establishment were put in place, renewed by Poole Oyster Co. in 1858. In 1973 the faster-growing Pacific oyster was introduced and proved a beneficiary of global temperature rises, as it would not have survived traditional northern European winters.

The National School in Perry Gardens, on the corner of Lagland Street and South Road, was opened in 1835, the master in 1851 being William Drew. This became the boys' school, with an average attendance of 159 in 1889, when Thomas Laws was the master. The girls and infants had their school in Church Street, where Miss Alice Price was the mistress for 121 girls and Miss Laura Cross Goff looked after 126 infants. National Schools comprised the educational wing of the Anglican Church, functioning under the auspices of the National Society for Promoting the Education of the Poor in the Principles of the Established Church. Because Poole Corporation donated £100 towards the building, the mayor and aldermen retained a right of veto over staff appointments. Initially this was a master for 22 boys, his wages being met by the 'free school' bequest of philanthropist Henry Harbin from more than a century earlier.

The role of the National Schools, and their British School equivalents for Nonconformist offspring, was gradually eroded by state education. Poole's National School was demolished in 1959. The town's British Schools were in Skinner Street and Chapel Lane. The former premises, on the corner with Lagland Street, started with the section that became the girls' school, in 1777. In 1851 the master was Henry Whicher and by 1889 it had 124 female pupils in the care of Miss Edith Lowe. The building in Chapel Lane dated from 1793 and was enlarged in 1843. It remained a Sunday school until 1884, when it opened as a day school for 140 infants with Miss Isabel Rattray as mistress.

In 251 pages of evidence, plus a scathing six pages of findings, a select committee of the House of Commons investigated and denounced the election of two Poole councillors in a ward election on 26 December 1835. On 25 March 1836, the committee found that George Lidgard and George Major had been 'illegally and fraudulently returned' (in place of George Conway and Samuel Salter). The mayor at the time, Robert Slade, and his deputy, Richard Lidgard, had connived in accepting false votes by at least one person not on the roll, invalid second votes by people who voted twice, and substitution of a false paper for that signed by William Lilly. To compound the offence, they had then failed to announce or publish the 'count' of votes against the name of each candidate, thus contravening election legislation, which required 'that the councillors who have the fewest votes shall be the first to go out of office.'

Although the result was queried at the time by bookseller John Lankester and a Mr Scott, they were prevented by Slade and his deputy from seeing the voting papers. Robert Henning Parr, the town clerk, joined the conspiracy as 'vexatious difficulties were thrown in their way, under the most frivolous pretences.' Only winning councillors from the opposite party had been allowed to inspect them. The scandal led to Parr, a solicitor, being discharged from office, but even this raised the committee's suspicions as it appeared to be 'with a view to the compensation to be claimed.' This, 'whatever may be its amount, must be an injury to the property of the Corporation and a heavy burthen upon its limited finances.'

Queen Victoria's accession in 1837 was marked in Poole by the opening of a facility that had been an aspiration for centuries – the first Poole Bridge, between the Old Town and Hamworthy. Its eventual construction involved a local Act of Parliament piloted through Westminster by William Ponsonby.

This rickety timber structure changed the life of the town for ever. Before, all Poole people had been at least occasional mariners, crossing 80 at a time in the *Passage Boat*, which plied to and fro throughout the day, hauled from the shore by a rope which stretched across the narrows. Hamworthy residents and those from Poole who worked in its ship and timber yards held virtual season tickets. Payment of four pence gave a family passage for a year, while strangers and travellers paid a half-penny to cross.

Indecision and intrigues had accompanied the bridge project for years. In accepting a timber bridge (estimated price £9,612), the town elders had turned their backs on the modern cast-iron option (£28,471, including stone piers). William Ponsonby, as lord of the manor of Canford, gave a graceful nod to the prospect of having to pay the price of progress but in the process was accused of financial betterment by turning his land at Hamworthy into potential building plots. Though influential supporters could be counted on the fingers of one hand, they wielded considerable power, comprising as they did the senior town Member of Parliament, Sir John Bying; Captain Parrott and his employer, Quaker businessman George Penney; shipbuilder Richard Pinney; and Customs collector David Landor.

Ranged against them was a multitude comprising every business and professional person in the Old Town. Everyone, from old salt Tiptow Jolliffe to his namesake the rector of St James's parish, Revd Peter Joliffe of Sterte House, seemed to find cause for concern. Although paying lip-service to worries about obstructions to navigation (unwarranted) and tide-flows (also unwarranted), they were mainly disturbed by the migration of cash to new businesses and churches across the water (correct) and the consequent adverse effects on property prices on the Poole side of the water (also correct).

Church and Chapel made common cause with the 68-year-old rector in supporting 78-year-old aristocratic Congregationalist deacon George Kemp, a dapper dresser, in a petition to Parliament. Both men had to abandon the principles of a lifetime in order to play at politics for the day. Appearing before a House of Commons committee, in Westminster, required a ride out of Poole on the Sabbath-breaking coach-and-four. Their most ingenious objection to the bridge was based on a claim that beggars and tramps did not pass through Poole because it was a cul-de-sac and they would have to return across the same ground, whereas with a bridge 'it would bring them this way'.

Their efforts were in vain and the nod of royal assent was granted by King William IV on 16 June 1834. Who was to pay the lawyers? Having failed to block the scheme the town clerk, Robert Parr, claimed to be out of pocket to the tune of £1,250. The money was found by raiding the accounts for harbour dues. William Ponsonby bailed out the town, effectively paying for the opposition he had overcome, and then found himself having to subsidise the entire construction costs of Poole Bridge.

Only usable in one direction at a time, the bridge had just 1ft 8ins of footway and 6ft 8ins of carriageway. Despite these constraints, and being denounced as an 'alien abortion' by Richard Sydenham's conservative *Poole Pilot* newspaper, the engineering was of high quality. Big flat-topped nails, forged by local firm Furnell & Joyes in West Quay Road, were driven into well-chosen timbers. Those nails, and the piles which attached it to the harbour, outlasted the structure they supported.

The opening ceremony was typical of civic and national pageantry, as it has remained ever since. James Harvey, from South Haven Point, headed the celebrations with the Union Flag while brass bands played. The municipal good and great assembled to hear the praises of a scheme they had fought so long to thwart. Their revenge on those in Hamworthy, which lasted until 1904, was to charge them tolls for the privilege of returning to the Old Town to register their votes at elections. This was literally a poll-tax.

On his retirement in 1840, diplomat Sir Augustus John Foster (1780–1848) bought Brownsea Island. He boasts a place in history that remains unchallenged to this day, as the last man to put Britain into a state of war with the United States of America. The crisis began in 1811 when, as Minister Plenipotentiary to Washington, he failed to defuse a simmering row over orders to impress American sailors into the Royal Navy, a matter which should have been settled in 1807.

Although London backed down on 16 June 1812, cancelling the contentious orders, no one knew that

Broadstone Hotel and Broadstone Station (left), *which opened as New Poole Junction in 1876 is seen here after closure in 1966, looking southwards along platform 3* (centre) *and platform 4* (right), *which carried London & South Western Railway trains using the 'Old Road' of Castleman's Corkscrew.*

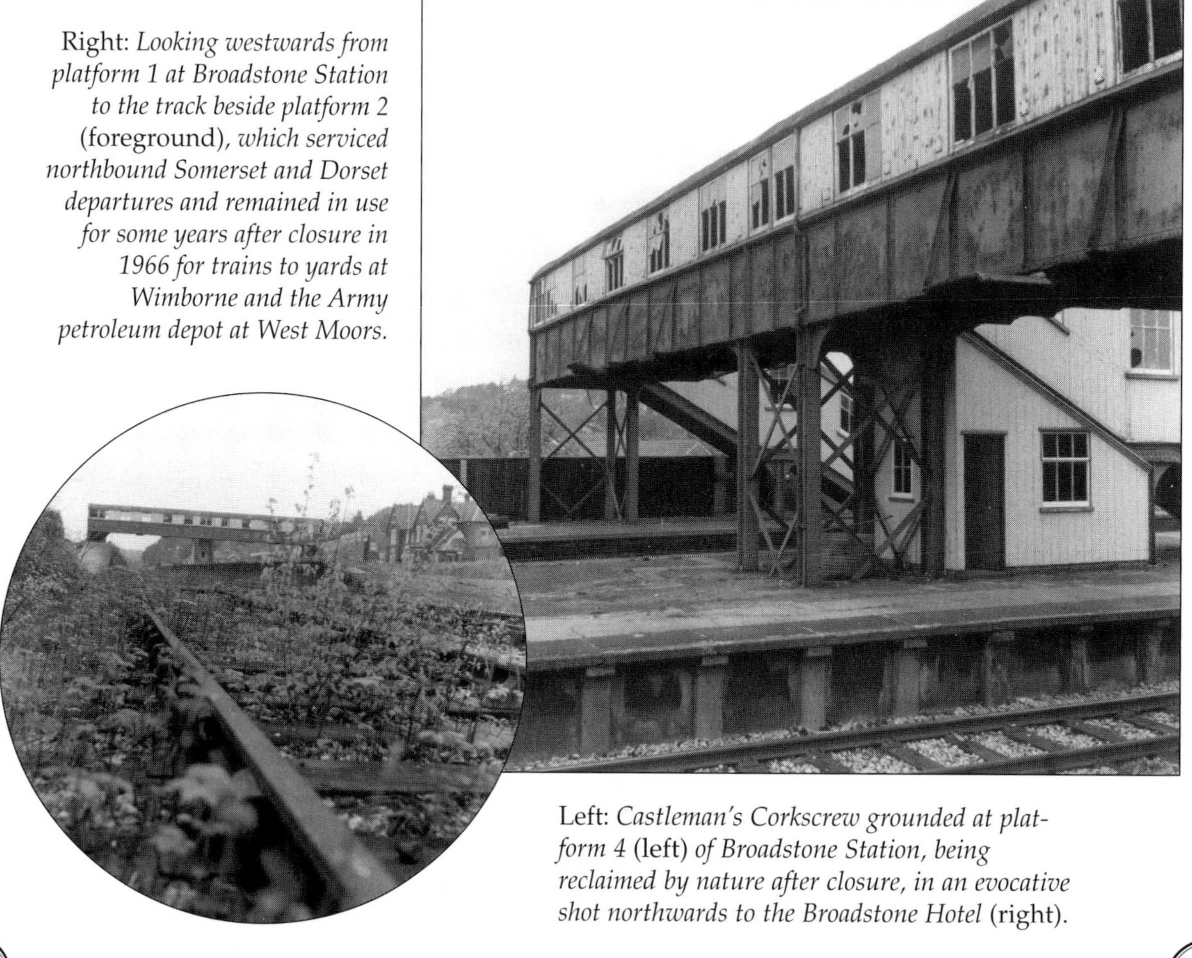

Right: *Looking westwards from platform 1 at Broadstone Station to the track beside platform 2* (foreground), *which serviced northbound Somerset and Dorset departures and remained in use for some years after closure in 1966 for trains to yards at Wimborne and the Army petroleum depot at West Moors.*

Left: *Castleman's Corkscrew grounded at platform 4* (left) *of Broadstone Station, being reclaimed by nature after closure, in an evocative shot northwards to the Broadstone Hotel* (right).

on the other side of the Atlantic. As a result, the Americans declared war on 18 June 1812 and prepared to invade Canada. Their offensive was outmanoeuvred as British troops marched south to burn the Capitol in 1813 and destroy most of the Library of Congress. The great American victory, at New Orleans, did not take place until 1815.

Foster's career suffered, to say the least, and his subsequent postings, to such places as Copenhagen and Turin, were of little consequence. Sir Augustus Foster found Brownsea far from an island paradise. He experienced bouts of deep depression and took his own life, slitting his throat in Branksea Castle, on 1 August 1848.

The local colony of natterjack toads, established between Poole and Wareham, was discovered by W. Thompson, who wrote in 1843 to the *Zoologist* of a new species, 'which I believe to be distinct and not yet described.' With a distinctive yellow line down the back, the natterjack, which habitually digs into soft ground, had done so to hibernate in a sandpit. In March they emerged in quantity and set off on a 2-mile journey to a heathland pond, where they spawned, their migration accompanied by their mass slaughter as birds and rats found them easy prey. The return journey took place in the autumn. This activity, which Thompson had observed from 1830, came to an end when he cut a dyke across their path, letting in sea water. Although a few survived for a time around other ponds, the colony became extinct.

Radical writer William Taylor Haly (1818–74) was born in Poole and is buried in its cemetery. His work on *The Opinions of Sir Robert Peel* was praised by *The Times* on its appearance in 1843 as 'a perfect encyclopaedia of political knowledge'. The author, however, failed to apply this knowledge personally, with four unsuccessful attempts at entering Parliament, two of them in Poole. As an 'advanced Liberal' he came south from Paisley and tried to oust the established sitting Liberal, Henry Danby Seymour, in 1857. In a three-way fight for the town's two seats, Seymour was returned to Westminster with 211 votes, as was Tory George Franklyn, with 189 votes. Haly had only 98 votes.

On the death of his previous opponent, Haly returned to Paisley only to find he had lost all credibility by turning his back on Scotland and, with his former support just about wiped out, he returned to Poole for the 1859 election. Once again, with the same slate of candidates, it was to no avail. The figures were: Franklyn 208, Seymour 193 and Haly 143. Although Haly had gathered a few more votes, his political career was over before it had started.

Railway mania was at last catching up with Dorset. Amongst other schemes, in 1836, the Bath & Weymouth Great Western Union Railway received its Act of Parliament and was set to steam to the coast via Cerne Abbas. In 1844 the scales were tilting further east, with promises from the Bristol, Bath & Poole Harbour Railway, for 'a trifling outlay', to turn Poole into 'the most sheltered, safest, and most commodious port in the Southern Kingdom'. With the offer of 50,000 shares at £10 each, Castleman and Kingdon were the secretaries on behalf of the promoters.

Their principal competition came from the same wealthy Wimborne solicitor, Charles Castleman (1807–76), second son of attorney William Castleman, whose family seat was Chettle House on Cranborne Chase. He made his move from the east, where Southampton was already flourishing from its adoption of the 'Iron Road' provided by the London & South Western Railway. The inaugural public meeting in the Royal Hotel, set to run out of space, was hastily transferred to the Town Hall. A committee then appointed as project engineer Captain William Scarth Moorsom, his first report being heard at the Crown Hotel, Wimborne, on 18 July 1844.

While Charles Castleman wanted a 52-mile semi-direct route from Southampton to Dorchester, crossing from the New Forest into Dorset via Wimborne, Bere Regis and Puddletown, Moorsom made a strong case for a more circuitous 60-mile route. He argued that this was necessary in order to connect a scattering of small towns – of which Poole was by far the largest, with a population of 6,093 at the 1841 census – while at the same time avoiding costly geographical obstacles. Though there were few high hills, a deeply indented coastline, on clay and soft sands, presented formidable difficulties.

Moorsom's alternative route linked Southampton, Brockenhurst, Ringwood, Wimborne, Poole, Wareham and Dorchester. There would be single-line track with passing loops at stations. The costs totalled £450,000, while estimates of income from traffic, calculated by William Pare, were for receipts of £48,750, yielding a profit of £29,250. Going further, across or through the great chalk barrier of Ridgeway Hill would require a further £104,000 if the line was to extend the last 8 miles to Weymouth. Moorsom's suggestions were backed by a public meeting in Dorchester on 19 July 1844.

On 3 October 1844, realisation of the adverse strategic implications of the Dorchester line – effectively an extension of the London & South Western Railway – led the rival Great Western Railway to host a conference at Paddington. The greatest of all railway builders, Isambard Kingdom Brunel, turned his attention from the *Great Britain* steamship, under construction in Bristol, to offer a draft agreement. It required Castleman to build his railway to GWR broad gauge (7ft) specifications rather than standard gauge (4ft 8.5ins). Brunel would link it, at Dorchester, with the broad-gauge metals of his proposed Wiltshire, Somerset & Weymouth Railway.

Hamworthy Station, on a branch line from Hamworthy Junction which opened on 1 May 1847. This was Poole's first station.

The line into derelict Hamworthy Station, looking north-eastwards, in 1972.

Sidings eastwards from Hamworthy Station, to Corralls' oil-tanks (top left) *and the wharves and yards at the end of the line, in 1972.*

Pillbox for machine-guns (left) *and the closed Hamworthy Station* (centre), *in a view north-westwards from the sea wall in 1972.*

The Railway Tavern in New Quay Road, Lower Hamworthy, looking south-eastwards from Bridge Approach in 1972.

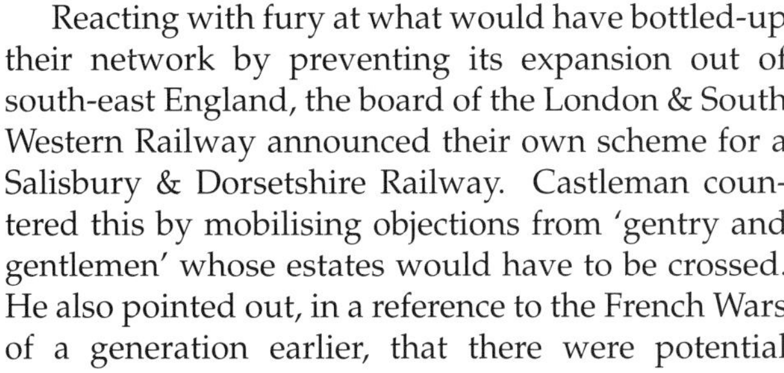

Reacting with fury at what would have bottled-up their network by preventing its expansion out of south-east England, the board of the London & South Western Railway announced their own scheme for a Salisbury & Dorsetshire Railway. Castleman countered this by mobilising objections from 'gentry and gentlemen' whose estates would have to be crossed. He also pointed out, in a reference to the French Wars of a generation earlier, that there were potential military advantages in having a linear railway close to the Channel coast.

Moorsom finalised the details of the route for the Southampton & Dorchester Railway while on a fact-finding trip to Poole. This and another of its few coastal sections were causing concern. Those to the east were settled by the agreement to build a 480ft tunnel under the Lammas Lands at Southampton. Poole caused another lengthy debate, which ended

Western Pride *pushed and pulled wagons along the waterside tramway at Hamworthy, until being withdrawn for scrap in 1964.*

With the opening of the Holes Bay Curve across Poole Harbour, over a mile and a half of mud and water in 1893, the main line from Waterloo to Weymouth became the route that we know today.

Fojo *working the light railway at Creekmoor, operating pits and potteries in the mid-twentieth century, for Sykes & Sons who manufactured 'sanitary stoneware'.*

with Moorsom deleting the Old Town from the plans. Instead, due to the 'insurmountable complications' of inlets and reed-beds, there would be a separate branch from Turland Farm, in the chapelry of Hamworthy, to the Ballast Quay near the far end of the peninsula.

Railway mania was about to reach its peak. Trains had been brought to within striking distance of the Dorset coast in 1840, when Joseph Locke and Thomas Brassey completed the 'massively engineered' line through and under the Hampshire Downs from Basingstoke to Southampton, inevitably drawing attention to the next significant towns to the west. The Southampton & Dorchester Railway Bill was just one of 248 Parliamentary measures proposed for Britain as a whole in 1845. The result was bureaucratic chaos that threatened both to gridlock Whitehall and to then criss-cross the country with a network of competing lines that would mostly run into bankruptcy. There had to be a filtering mechanism. William Ewart Gladstone, President of the Board of Trade, and Sir Robert Peel established a Railway Board chaired by Lord Dalhouse, vice-president of the Board of Trade.

The committee chose the Southampton & Dorchester Railway as one of its approved projects but then transferred the running of the line from the broad-gauge Great Western to the standard-gauge London & South Western. The three companies signed up to the compromise arrangements on 16 January 1845. Henry Compton, MP for South Hampshire – a New Forest verderer – was the sole objector when the Southampton & Dorchester Railway Bill passed through the House of Commons in April 1845. Other past opponents, such as George Bankes MP of Kingston Lacy House, took the pragmatic view that any local line was better than none at all. Lord Palmerston persuaded Compton to withdraw his motion so that the Bill would receive an unopposed second reading on 21 April 1845.

So that both companies could operate around Dorchester and Weymouth, the House of Lords required 8 miles of broad gauge on the line east of Dorchester in return for 8 miles of standard gauge on that of the Wiltshire, Somerset & Weymouth Railway. Queen Victoria consented to works on Crown lands in the New Forest and Duchy of Cornwall properties in Dorset, giving royal assent to

Somerset & Dorset 7F-class 2-8-0 locomotive 53808 pulling the 07.43 Saturday service from Birmingham New Street to Bournemouth West, in a view northwards as the train crosses the points at Broadstone Junction, on 7 August 1954.

George Jennings (centre), *named for the founder of the South Western Pottery* (background) *at Parkstone, operated its tramway from 1902 until being removed and scrapped in 1964.*

Diesel locomotive 6520 at Oakley Gates, beside the gatekeeper's cottage at Cruxton Farm, with a weekly train heading south to Poole from the Army petroleum depot in West Moors in 1972.

The network of closed railway lines curving around Broadstone became leisure trails in the 1970s before being engulfed in the advance of suburbia.

what was an Act of Parliament on 21 July 1845.

The company's capital was £500,000. Directors of the London & South Western Railway held large numbers of shares. John Mills (1789–1871), of Bisterne Park, the largest Hampshire and Dorset shareholder, had a £25,000 stake, and William, 1st Baron de Mauley (1787–1855), of Canford House, and Charles Castleman both invested £5,000. The £420,000 contract was awarded to Grissell & Peto, headed by the dynamic entrepreneur Samuel Morton Peto (1809–89), who personally invested £25,000 in the project. Though single-line working was specified throughout, apart from a 4-mile length of twin lines from Southampton to Redbridge, bridges and viaducts were to be built in anticipation of the later laying of double track. Architect Sancton Wood designed the engine sheds and stations with lofty flourishes for gables and chimneys.

Even before the Bill had received the royal assent, Peto had started preliminary work by shipping quantities of rails into Hamworthy. In the following month, by 31 August 1845, his navvies had built a mile of cul-de-sac embankment westwards across Hamworthy Common. Pile-driving was necessary for the foundations of a viaduct between Rockley Sands and the inlet channel of Lytchett Bay.

✦ CHAPTER 10 ✦

Canford's Guests

Lady Charlotte Guest of Canford House, one of the greatest Welsh scholars of all time, who translated and published the medieval manuscripts of the Mabinogion *between 1838 and 1849.*

Coinciding with the arrival of the railway, one of Britain's leading industrialists, Sir Josiah John Guest MP (1785–1852) ploughed a spare £350,000 into buying Canford Manor and its 83,600 acres from Baron de Mauley in 1846. The inventor of the blast-furnace, he owned Dowlais Ironworks, Merthyr Tydfil, which produced the rails for the nation's expanding railway network, and had been created a baronet in 1838. The Poole purchase was 'a reluctant indulgence' for the benefit of his health. Breathing difficulties were exacerbated by the dirt and fumes that emanated from his Welsh enterprises. Though he conceded that Dorset brought some relief, Sir Josiah resented every moment 'wasted' at Canford, and continually returned to Wales. He refused to relinquish control of his great firm, on which the livelihoods of 12,000 families depended, and he took an active interest in civil engineering and was chairman of the Taff Valley Railway.

The immense tracts of Canford lands had their own private road – rebuilt by navvies to railway engineering standards with causeways, cuttings and bridges – which led from Canford Bridge at Wimborne, via Canford House, then skirting Canford Heath, all the way to the sea at Canford Cliffs. Known as Lady Wimborne's Drive, great lengths remained walkable until the concrete bridges over the A341 and A3049 were demolished in the 1980s.

On his arrival in Dorset in 1846, Sir Josiah Guest's first priority was to set about enlarging Canford House, for which purpose he commissioned architect Sir Charles Barry, who was then rebuilding the Houses of Parliament.

In 1833 Josiah Guest married the Hon. Charlotte Elizabeth Bertie (1812–95), daughter of the 9th Earl of Lindsey, who, over the next 13 years, provided him with ten children. She also found time to become one of the great Welsh scholars of all time by translating the medieval manuscripts that formed the *Mabinogion*, published between 1838 and 1849. These gave her friend, Alfred Tennyson, the Arthurian legends that formed the basis for his *Idylls of the King* in 1859.

Animal feed importer Christopher Hill also came to Poole in 1846. The company was initially based on the quay, where Poole Aquarium has taken its place, and moved to Castle Street and West Street before being taken over by Rank, Hovis, McDougall in 1980. The firm was still turning out 60 tonnes of animal feed a day when it passed to Dalgety Agriculture Ltd, who still trade from PO Box 274 in Poole.

The race to bring rails into Dorset had been won by the Southampton & Dorchester Railway, though its approach from the north-east missed Poole by 3 miles when the first through train – belonging to and named for contractor Samuel Morton Peto – ran on 1 May 1847, ahead of the public opening of the line on 1 June 1847. Even this closest point to the town missed out on having a station for nearly three decades, and Poole Junction Station was established at Hamworthy, from where a cul-de-sac line led to the boatyards opposite Poole Quay. Poole Junction,

Lady Cornelia Henrietta Maria Spencer-Churchill, daughter of the 7th Duke of Marlborough, who, as Lady Wimborne, headed a political dynasty based at Canford House.

renamed Hamworthy Junction on 2 December 1872, was the town's closest main-line connection for London, via Wimborne, Ringwood and Brockenhurst. The peninsula branch-line station at Hamworthy – then named Poole – shared with Dorchester the distinction of employing 12 staff, giving it equal-top status on the new network.

John Mills, speaking as the principal investor, defended the line's first snaking layout from its detractors' epithet of 'Castleman's Corkscrew' – for its agent Charles Castleman – at a celebratory dinner in the Crown Inn, Ringwood, on 8 June 1847. Among those who had been less than impressed was Captain Coddington – the government inspector who checked the track for public use – who calculated that curves comprised half the length of the line. Coddington did, however, compliment Peto on general construction standards and Moorsom, the engineer, added his personal thanks to Peto's navvies for having 'continued to work through so many nights'. Indeed, seven men had contributed their lives, the local fatality being 17-year-old George Cherret, who fell to his death while tipping gravel at Canford Bottom.

The railway narrowly escaped what could have been a calamitous collision when two locomotives heading towards each other were derailed at Worgret, near Wareham, on 20 September 1847. Only two men were injured. There were also a number of accidents at work as newly appointed staff familiarised themselves with railway equipment and procedures. Vandalism, another threat, was the cause of two derailments near Poole, when boys placed stones on the rails.

The single-track line transformed travel at a stroke. The weekday journeys of the Age stagecoach, a coach-and-four which left the Antelope Hotel for the capital at 6.30 each morning, ceased operation within weeks. The same applied to the Wellington (three times a week) and then the Emerald, from the London Hotel on the coastal route from Weymouth to Southampton (twice a week). The western terminus of Castleman's Corkscrew was at Dorchester.

Buoyant with success, the directors of the Southampton & Dorchester Railway planned and negotiated with investors, landowners and politicians to build a series of branch lines. These ranged from Eling, on Southampton Water, to Lymington

Cricket at Canford House which was bought by iron-maker Sir Josiah John Guest from Dowlais, Glamorgan, in 1846.

and the Solent, to Blandford in central Dorset, and to Weymouth, to take the line south from Dorchester to the sea. All would be built, eventually, but most by other operators, some time after the railway boom had ended.

The London & South Western Railway, operating out of Nine Elms before the building of Waterloo, took the chance to consolidate its supremacy. The Dorchester & Southampton Railway was amalgamated into the capital-based company by a private Act of Parliament which received the Queen's nod on 22 July 1848. Each Dorchester share was replaced by a £50 share in the LSWR. John Mills became a director and Charles Castleman joined him on the board in 1855. The latter was vice-chairman from 1859 to 1873, when he finally achieved his ambition of becoming chairman, until failing health forced his resignation in 1875. He died on 17 July 1876 and is buried at Melcombe Regis, Weymouth.

The first British record of the purple-and-white-flowering Liliaceae *Simethis bicolor* lily was made in Branksome Chine by Miss Charlotte Wilson in 1847. The species still grew there in 1911, and specimens are preserved in the Bournemouth Natural Science Society's herbarium. By then the plant had been appropriated by the Victorian new town and was known as the Bournemouth Lily. Poole patriots sigh when incomers do the same with their 'Bournemouth' addresses.

The area of general distribution of the lily is in the western Mediterranean, with an outlying colony on the coastal heath near Derrynane, in Kerry. As for the plant's survival around Poole and Bournemouth, it is said to be 'very rare among the pines' and it is thought that it was introduced possibly between 1800 and 1810, reaching maturity to become the lasting symbol of the town that sprang up amidst the trees.

Nonconformists were first to realise and respond to the spiritual needs of the new community that was beginning to turn Canford Bottom into Broadstone. To provide for them, and the original heath-cropping natives, a Congregational chapel was built in 1848. The Congregationalists had the 'undulating heather country' to themselves. The Horwood family claimed credit for coining the Broadstone name after placing a flat boulder across the muddy Backwater stream in the vicinity of Brookdale Farm.

By 1851, industrial Poole had two foundries operated by separate branches of the Furnell family in West Quay Road, while George and William Burt made anchors and other marine fittings in Thames Street and on Hamside. The Waterloo Foundry beat competition from all over Britain and won first prize in the 'Iron' category at the Great Exhibition in Crystal Palace. This was for a cast-iron bas-relief depicting Leonardo da Vinci's famous painting of the Last Supper. The casting returned to the town and is exhibited in Scaplen's Court.

Rope and twine for fishing lines, nets and sailcloth was being manufactured across the town. Rope-walks, being several hundred yards in length, extended along many streets and yards, including the Ladies' Walking Field beside the railway line at Towngate. Manufacturers included Balston & Co. in the High Street, Robert Major & Son in Longfleet, George Penney on the quay and Charles Weeks & Son in East Quay Road. West Shore Twine Works was established beside West Quay Road.

There were five breweries in the town. These are listed in the Hunt & Co. *Dorsetshire Directory* as being Thomas Ballard in High Street, John Buttress in East Street, John Gardner in Taylor's Buildings, Joseph and James King in Towngate Street and Tom Rickman in Market Street. The list of the borough's public houses and hotels is an interesting mix of medieval survivals and the new Victorian age:

Angel Inn, Market Place (Henry Best)
Baker's Arms, Strand (John Lacy)
Bell, Fish Street (also John Lacy)
Bell and Crown, High Street (John Harden)
Blue Anchor, Market Street (William Cobb)
Brewer's Arms, Towngate Street (John Marder)
Britannia, Parkstone (G. Barrett)
Coach and Horses, Strand (John Shave)
Crown, Market Street (Michael Carroll)
Eight Bells, Quay (John Cook)
George, Longfleet (Charlotte Stickland)
Globe, High Street (Samuel Simmons)
Greyhound, Market Street (William White)
Harbour View, East Quay Road (Frederick William Lacy)
Jolly Sailor, Quay (James Wheeler)
King's Arms, High Street (Henry Green)
King and Queen, East Quay Road (Robert Ellis)
Lion and Lamb, Salisbury Street (George Wickham)
London Tavern Hotel, High Street (William Furmage)
Lord Nelson, Quay (Reuben Brett)
New Antelope, New Street (Elizabeth Gilbert)
New Inn, Thames Street (John Starks)
New London Tavern, Lagland Street (Elizabeth Frampton)
Old Antelope Hotel, High Street (George Knight)
Old Inn, West Street (Charles Foster)
Poole Arms, Quay (Samuel Fricker)
Port Mahon Castle, Longfleet (George Purton)
Portsmouth Hoy, Quay (George Dunford)
Rising Sun, Fish Street (Edward White)
Royal Oak, Baiter (Job Short)
St Clement's, Thames Street (Eli Allen)
Ship, Salisbury Street (Elias Webb)
Sloop, Parkstone (Joseph James)
Star, West Street (James Dunford)
Swan, Lagland Street (James Weeks)

One of the conquerors of Lagos, Lieutenant-Commander Russell Patey (1818–52), who is buried on Ascension Island in the South Atlantic, has his

The chapel ceiling in St Mary's Church, Brownsea Island, brought from Crosby Place, Bishopsgate, in the 1850s.

memorial in Canford Magna Church. In the action fought to suppress the slave trade, he commanded HMS *Bloodhound* as part of the squadron led by Commodore Bruce, which sailed up the Bight of Benin on 26–27 December 1851. Patey, the son of George Edward Patey, died a few weeks later.

Thomas Bell (1792–1880), the son of a Poole surgeon, became a dentist and produced a study on tooth decay in 1829. His main interest, however, was zoology, and in the early Victorian period he published three standard works which were something between textbooks and popular guides to the country's animal life. These were the *History of British Quadrupeds*, in 1837, the *History of British Reptiles*, in 1839, and the *History of British Stalk-eyed Crustacea*, in 1853. In 1869 he retired from Poole to the Wakes at Selborne, Hampshire, which had been the home of the naturalist Gilbert White. Bell immersed himself in his predecessor's memorabilia, preparing a biography of White, and reissued his *Natural History of Selborne* in what, in 1877, was acclaimed as its classic edition.

Albinia Jane Hobart, widow of Sir Augustus Foster of Branksea Castle, sold Brownsea Island to Colonel William Petrie Waugh for £13,000 in 1852. His commission had been with the XXth (East Devonshire) Regiment of Foot, which served in India. As director of the London & Eastern Banking Corp. he had no difficulty in raising £237,000 after a geologist identified 'a most valuable bed of the finest clay' worth 'at least £100,000 an acre'.

From 1853 the money was used to excavate claypits and build Branksea Pottery. Waugh also restored and embellished Branksea Castle, built St Mary's Church (named for his wife) at a cost of £10,000 and embanked and drained St Andrew's Bay.

The foundation-stone of St Mary's Church on Brownsea Island was laid on 2 July 1853 by Major-General Sir Harry Smith. The consecration service, on 18 October 1854, was conducted by Bishop Hamilton. Among the guests were Sir Percy Florence Shelley (1819–89), the poet's only surviving son, and Lady Shelley, of Boscombe Manor, Bournemouth.

Among the most remarkable of the treasures brought to Brownsea Island, where it was set in the roof of Colonel Waugh's private chapel on the north-east side of St Mary's Church, was a ceiling of 12 panels from Crosby Place, Bishopsgate, which in 1853 was being converted into a restaurant. The project failed and it was demolished.

The panels, from the main roof of the hall, had been witness to one of the greatest conspiracies in English history. Richard III (1452–85), while Duke of Gloucester and Protector acting for his 13-year-old nephew, Edward V, had lived in Crosby Place. This arrangement ended with the treasonous murder of the princes – Edward and his brother – in the Tower of London, which, in 1483, had put Richard on the throne.

The Victorian Gothic east window in ancient Canford Magna Church was inserted in 1855 as a memorial to Sir Josiah John Guest. Sir Josiah, who had retreated to Canford to relieve his failing health, was determined not to die in Dorset and his final return to Wales, in 1852, enabled him to breath his last amidst his beloved industries. His main monument is at Dowlais Parish Church, Glamorgan, where he is buried.

Lady Charlotte Guest, his widow, entered into her second marriage, to Charles Schreiber MP, which lasted until his death in 1884. Mrs Charlotte Schreiber made a major impact on British culture through one of her 'good works'– providing a shelter for London cabmen. The shelter, which was kept supplied with newspapers, helped create one of the most articulate and opinionated groups of people in the land. After Charles's death, Charlotte presented her porcelain collection to the Victoria & Albert Museum, in his memory. She then published illustrations of her collection of painted fans in two lavish volumes, given to the British Museum in 1891.

Sir Ivor Bertie Guest (1835–1914), who inherited the Canford estate, came of age in August 1856. The occasion was celebrated at Canford House by a series of parties that lasted 18 hours. Events began with tea for 800 children and progressed to a ball for 800 members of county and national society. This, punctuated by a huge fireworks display, continued through the night and concluded with the playing of 'God Save the Queen' at six o'clock in the morning.

Although he launched the heyday of Canford House – and fathered its political dynasty – Sir Ivor himself had a disappointing career at Westminster. Having failed in four attempts to enter the House of Commons, he arrived in Parliament through the back door on being created Baron Wimborne in 1880.

CHAPTER 11

Fortunes and Follies

Branksea Pottery on Brownsea Island – perhaps the least likely location for such an enterprise – which underpinned Colonel William Waugh's plans for its Victorian heyday.

The 14-year-old Prince Bertie, Queen Victoria's son and heir – the future King Edward VII – included Poole on his walking tour of the West Country. Having slept almost incognito at the Bath Hotel, Bournemouth, on 24 September 1856 the Prince of Wales and two aides followed the beach to Sandbanks. They took the ferry from the landing stage near the Haven Hotel to Brownsea Island and later walked through Parkstone to Poole, where they spent the night at the Antelope Hotel. Next day they moved on to Wimborne to see Wimborne Minster, staying at the Crown Hotel on the night of 25 September. The tour eventually had to be abandoned, at Honiton on 1 October 1856, because the secret was out and stirring an embarrassing wave of public interest.

On the death in 1857 of Henry Ralph Willett, who was unmarried, the Merley estate passed to Willett Lawrence Adye. That year the Architectural Pottery Co. was established in Hamworthy and soon became one of the half dozen large players in the town. It specialised in glazed ceramic tiles, which were in increasing demand as Romanesque mosaics became highly fashionable.

The expensive transformation of Brownsea Island at the hands of Colonel William Petrie Waugh ended in failure. By 1857 Branksea Pottery was not only running at a loss, but Waugh's unwise spending and other debts had brought the London & Eastern Banking Corp. to the brink of insolvency. The story goes that Mrs Mary Waugh was on the island's quayside when a group of civic dignitaries arrived from Poole to ask if her husband would consider becoming the town's Member of Parliament. Mrs Waugh, who had hearing difficulties, responded by asking for time to pay. The couple then fled to Spain.

Logsbooks from the 1860s give a snapshot of life on the ocean wave. Poole's prolific fleet of little ships ranged widely across the North Atlantic and around the Mediterranean. A basic rule was that no alcoholic spirits were allowed on board, and swearing was also banned. Basic sailing rations were 1.5lbs of salted pork or beef on alternate days (unless replaced by fresh fish) plus 1lb of bread (or pease) daily. There

Grandiose developments on Brownsea Island, including a quay (left), *rebuilt Branksea Castle, battlemented cottages and St Mary's Church* (right) *engraved by Philip Brannon in 1857.*

'High Street, Poole', engraved by Newman & Co. in 1870, with the Post Office on the corner with Hill Street (right).

was also 1oz of tea, ½oz of coffee or chocolate, and 2oz of sugar or molasses a day. Port rations promised fresh meat except in Newfoundland and Labrador, where supplies could not be guaranteed.

This free bed and board, along with the inherent discomfort and danger, came at the lowest of wages – £1.10s.0d. per month. For some, such a trip was a way of working a passage that would otherwise be unaffordable.

The temptation to jump ship was often irresistible. The *Alarm* (98 registered tons) sailed for Newfoundland in 1861 with a crew of seven, three of whom deserted on arrival in St John's. The *Heart of Oak* (124 tons) also made for Labrador, with a master, five seamen and a cook. On the return voyage she gave passage home to John Patterson from the *Hermione,* who was languishing on the virtually uninhabited Labrador coast with a seriously infected leg. Disease and accidents were likely to be lethal when the nearest doctor was on the other side of the Atlantic Ocean.

In 1863, in Plymouth, Massachusetts, Henry Thomas left the *Rosina* (634 tons) during the night and, although he returned, there were three further desertions when she reached Quebec. Among them was William Poole, who had also stayed ashore at Plymouth where, although he claimed to have hurt himself in a fall, the doctor could find nothing wrong with him. George Lucas had second thoughts about deserting and did come back from Quebec, but then fell asleep in the forecastle, refusing to work. He was replaced by a temporary labourer from the mainland, paid 8s. a day, which was deducted from Lucas's wages. John Chown appeared in court in Quebec after a public-house brawl in which he was 'in a very queer way through the effect of liquor.'

Abraham Trisse was one of those who stayed in Canada. He had already accumulated such criticisms in the ship's log as tossing a canvas bucket overboard, and doing the same with a quantity of bread that was 'good and fit for food', and was judged 'not competent to steer the ship'. His replacement, Thomas Davis, more than matched this record by 'breaking a jar of molasses valued at 12s.0d.', failing to steer the ship, and then showing he was completely useless, 'not knowing one rope from another'. Deck-hand Fred Munich, who knew his ropes but was found in a drunken stupor, lost 6s.8d. from his wages to pay a replacement for the day.

Outward bound, the crew of the *Aurora* (629 tons) came close to mutiny in the South-Western Approaches. Battered for three days by gales, the crew told the master they would not 'proceed any further as the ship was making much water.' The wind drove them towards Milford Haven, where they put in for repairs before proceeding to Quebec. The captain suffered a debilitating facial rash, followed by dropsy, and had to be left in hospital in Canada. The mate, who took over, was then laid up with sciatica and the second mate failed to take depth soundings, causing the vessel to go aground. Fortunately the ship was pulled off at high tide by a steamboat, avoiding an expensive embarrassment, or worse.

With a total of 19 crew deserted and a further three discharged, it was fortunate for the *Aurora* that she had a favourable following wind for her eventual return to Bristol. Among those who came home was James McGannet, who was suffering 'violent fits'.

There were those who moved in the other direction, from the land to the sea, as happened with 38-year-old able-seaman Antonio Pedro Morai who, having deserted the Portuguese navy, had the misfortune to be recognised and arrested when the *Mountaineer* put into Lisbon.

The cook of the *Hermione* fell overboard and drowned while unfurling the top-sail in 1863. His possessions, handed to the British consul at St Lucas, were listed in the ship's log as: a canvas bag, two cotton shirts, pair of cloth trousers, pair of flannel drawers, a blanket, pair of woollen stockings, pair of braces, boots, Guernsey frock, waistcoat, two cotton handkerchiefs and a Bible. A seaman who slit his throat at Leghorn was better provisioned and, as well as a range of bedding, had two hats, three caps, eleven neck-ties, a sextant and compass and other navigational equipment, a silver watch, gold ring and 4 francs 4 centimes in cash. Other on-voyage casualties included 23-year-old Matthew Bennet, who died of smallpox contracted in Naples and 17-year-old Charles Hatcher, who fell from the main-beam of the *Venus*. A foreign seaman named Forstrum, from the *Nymph*, who fell to his death down a flight of steps in Lisbon, had £4.13s.6d. forwarded on his behalf to the Swedish consul.

John Chisholm and Henry Nelson took a boat from the *Expedient* and drowned in an accident 'caused by drink'. Henry Francis, boatswain of the *Aurora*, suffered a serious fall and took a fortnight to return to duty. Charles Maber, who fell to his death from the mizzen-mast while shifting the gaff, left only a satin vest and half a pound of tobacco.

John Strapp, chief engineer of the London & South Western Railway, was busy in Dorset throughout 1863 as he supervised completion of the 'doubling' of the 1846-built single-track into separate up and down lines. Sidings at Wimborne and the Poole Junction side-line to Hamworthy, which remained single track, became construction yards.

Thomas Pride VC, RN, captain of the afterguard – men working poop sails – was born in Wareham and died in retirement in Parkstone. He was awarded the Victoria Cross as a result of the combined fleet attack that destroyed the Japanese batteries in the Straits of Simonosaki on the night of 5 September 1864 – British gunboat diplomacy having followed the Japanese abrogation of international treaties.

The first Poole lifeboat, the 32-ft *Manley Wood*, based at North Haven Point with a crew of 12, came on station on 19 January 1865 at a 'grand demonstration' on Poole Quay. The Sandbanks side of the harbour entrance and Shell Bay opposite also had primitive navigation lights, which had been established by Trinity House in 1848. Pilot and coxswain Richard Sutton Stokes lived in a fisherman's cottage, but his crew, when the mortar was fired, had to be brought by horse-brake from the Antelope Hotel in the High Street at Poole.

Stokes and his crew first went into emergency action on 11 February 1866. With steam paddle-tug the *Royal Albert*, owned by Mrs Charlotte Fayle, needed to tow the *Manley Wood* into Poole Bay in the teeth of a south-easterly gale, conditions were such that, unable to reach the ship said to be in difficulties, the lifeboat returned to Sandbanks. When Exeter brigantine the *Elizabeth* ran ashore on Christchurch Bar the lifeboat was pulled along the coast by road but was not launched. Her first rescue took place on 8 January 1867 when the Prussian brig *Antares*, stuck on Hook Sands, off Sandbanks, with a cargo of Portuguese cork, was later towed into Poole.

Victorian steamers established the route from Poole to Cherbourg, among them the SS *Albion*, a Liverpool-registered iron paddle-steamer built in Glasgow in 1860 and displacing 152 tons. Although she only plied across the English Channel for the summers of 1865 and 1866, she can be regarded as the forerunner of such modern successors as Condor and Brittany Ferries.

The same family firm of railway constructors who had built the Somerset & Dorset Railway and were promoting the Poole & Bournemouth Railway into Bournemouth West Station, also founded the Poole & Cherbourg Steam Packet Co. Charles Waring fronted the concern while his brothers, Henry and William, beavered away in the background. Some 700 of the 800 steam company shares were quickly sold, bought 'mainly by inhabitants of this town *[Poole]*' and financing the purchase of another iron-paddler. Iron-paddlers the *City of Paris* and the *Spicy* replaced *Albion* in 1867, when the major attraction of the 'pleasure season' was the Paris Exhibition. Although some excursions seem to have been successful, many travellers were disappointed with the chaos that accompanied even a less ambitious trip, such as to Portsmouth. Poor timing and ignorance of the tides having prevented the promised landings at Bournemouth and Cowes, those waiting to join the trip were left on the shore.

In 1866 Sir Ivor Bertie Guest built a National School in his estate village at Canford for a maximum of 100 children.

Portsmouth featured in *Spicy*'s route when she embarked on regular Monday and Thursday visits from Poole to Cherbourg in October 1867, lucrative cargoes being delivered to the naval port before she returned to Poole.

On 16 November 1867 the Guernsey brig *Contest*, with ten crew and a cargo of granite, became stuck on the bar off Shell Bay. At low tide 36 labourers were taken out to her to throw the stone overboard before the *Royal Albert* tug attempted to pull her free. When the line broke and the sea threatened to break up the brig it was decided to abandon ship. Of a total of 46 men waiting to be carried to safety by the Sandbanks lifeboat *Manley Wood*, 12 were taken off on the first call and a further 24 on the second. Now dangerously overloaded and swamped by the sea, the lifeboat was so low in the water that she nearly came to grief. Finally, however, she was able to turn around, taking off the rest of the crew on her third return to the *Contest*.

In 1867 Parliamentary reform resumed with the passing of the Representation of the People Act. This ended the borough's privilege, exercised since 1453, of returning two members to the House of Commons, reducing the number to one.

The *Spicy*'s triangular route from Poole to

Portsmouth and Cherbourg seemed set to become the norm for the glorious summer of 1868. Despite perfect operating conditions, however, the company failed to fulfil its commitments and even local pleasure trips to Bournemouth and Swanage frequently ran late or failed to appear.

If by September 1868 the *Spicy* was facing an 'improbable future,' October saw the matter settled. All services stopped, its operating company went into receivership and the *Spicy* sailed 'in disgrace' for Portsmouth, where she put up for sale. George Curtis of Poole drew up the auction particulars:

> *The Iron Paddle-Wheel Steam Ship* Spicy. *100 horse-power. Gross tonnage 230. Registered tonnage 145. Length 164 feet. Beam 22 feet 7 inches. Depth of hold 10 feet. Draught of water* [when] *loaded, 7 feet. Fitted with every accommodation for passengers and goods.*

In 1868 Canford House saw its most significant arrival. What Sir Ivor Guest lacked in charisma was more than made up for by that of his wife, Lady Cornelia Spencer-Churchill (1847–927). The key character at Canford, the family's driving force, was not Lord Wimborne, as he became in 1880, but Lady Wimborne, who will return to our story.

On 15 December 1868 the lifeboat *Manley Wood* pulled the French lugger *Augustine*, from Pont L'Abbé, off the Hook Sands and towed her to safety in Poole Harbour. Although none of this crew was lost, a second French vessel, the *Jeune Erneste*, of Bordeaux, went aground on Poole Bar. By the time the lifeboat had turned around to go to her aid, the vessel was inundated and there was no sign of her crew, who were presumed drowned.

In 1869 the National School, built in Hamworthy at the expense of Lord Wimborne, catered for a total of 102 boys and girls. In 1889, shortly after the arrival of Revd Edmond Sellon as rector, its average attendance was 82 and the mistress was Miss Annie Green.

Brownsea Island was in limbo during the 1860s. Enmeshed in bankruptcy proceedings, it failed to realise its £50,000 reserve, and was sold for £30,000 in 1870 to George Augustus Frederick Cavendish-Bentinck MP (1821–91).

The vicar, Revd Theophilus Bennett, listed 'the happy inhabitants of this island' for the national census in 1881. The population, in two main clusters at either end of Brownsea Island, totalled 270, the western community of Maryland providing the labour force for Branksea Pottery. The 19 dwellings at Maryland, home to 117 men, women and children, included 'the Island Inn and Store' (Mr and Mr G. Petts and two servants) and the Infant School (B. Byles and wife). Cavendish-Bentinck, Member of Parliament for Whitehaven, had brought numerous art objects to the island, the finest of which, an elegant Italian pink marble pozzo, or well-head, became his gravestone in St Mary's churchyard.

Sixteenth-century Italian pozzo well-head over the grave of the Rt Hon. George Augustus Frederick Cavendish-Bentinck on Brownsea Island.

The heart of old Canford Magna, beside the highway that skirts the entrances to Canford House, was also evolving into what is now Canford village. The ornate rusticity of the cottages owes much to the skill of Victorian thatcher John Hicks of Lockyers, at Kinson, who created the splendid little porches. Though both porches and cottages have since been tiled, they retain some of their charm.

Samuel Pettet was stationmaster at Poole for the London & South Western Railway, his daily chores including the running of a shuttle of coaches between the London Hotel and the out-of-town stations across the water at Hamworthy and at Poole Junction, at the inland end of the peninsula. As well as operating an omnibus service to connect with 11 trains in each direction per day, Pettet had to cope with a disruptive tide of navvies and construction traffic for the Poole Junction Railway, which was at last being built from New Poole Junction at Broadstone to Towngate in the town centre, with a quay tramway to the waterside.

Louis French, recognising the prospects for business in Broadstone, established its first grocer's shop in 1870, which in 1880 became the Post Office. In 1872 the children at Lord Wimborne's National School totalled 220. It was an auspicious year, with New Poole Junction – as Broadstone Station was

Upton House, the Tichborne family's second home in parkland beside Holes Bay, featured in the Victorian Tichborne Trial.

Upton House at the time of writing, the focal point of a country park.

originally known – opening on 2 December. Positioned as the station was at the point where the railway intersected the road from Poole to Corfe Mullen, it soon led to a property boom that transformed the poor heathland hamlet of Canford Bottom into the new town suburb of Broadstone. In July 1883, reflecting this, the station was renamed Poole Junction and Broadstone. In 1889 the Railway Hotel was built and William Griffin opened the nearby Temperance Restaurant.

Branksome Dene, the seaside villa built by the Guest family of Canford Manor on their coastline at Branksome Park, became the home of Sir Joshua Walmsley (1794–1871), Member of Parliament for Leicester until 1857 and a close friend of railway pioneer George Stephenson. In 1872 his son, Colonel Hugh Mulleneux Walmsley of the Ottoman Imperial Army, wrote *Branksome Dene: a Sea Tale*, a smuggling and shipwreck adventure set in the chine below. At the time of writing Branksome Dene has become Zetland Court, the Royal Masonic Benevolent Institution's retirement home.

Upton House, set in parkland beside Holes Bay, featured in the events that gave rise to two momentous actions in the London courts, of unprecedented length, which culminated in the great Tichborne Trial of 1873. The story started with Henry Seymour (1776–1849), High Sheriff of Dorset in 1835, whose illegitimate daughter found herself at the centre of this Victorian scandal. Born in France, Henriette Felicité Seymour (died 1868) was married to Sir John Francis Tichborne (1784–1862), who had succeeded his brother, Sir Edward Tichborne Doughty (1782–1853). Sir John was the tenth baronet whose eldest son and heir was Roger Charles Doughty Tichborne (born 1829).

Roger was brought to Upton House for the funeral of his uncle, Sir Henry Joseph Tichborne (1779–1845), the eighth baronet. While Sir Edward Doughty was keen to sell Upton, young Roger fought the plan, preferring the maritime location of the Doughty home at Upton to Tichborne Park at Cheriton, on the Hampshire Downs. The family did not make Tichborne their home until 1848.

When Roger refused to join his family at Tichborne and announced that he was leaving the Army to go travelling, he was offered Upton House as his home. 'We earnestly hope you may be comfortable at Upton,' Lady Doughty wrote, 'and I shall always cherish a hope the day may come when you are a settled and happy man.' Roger finished his military service at Canterbury and also made three visits to Paris before his last outing in the Dorset countryside, which saw him riding to hounds in December 1852.

John Moore, son of the butler from Upton, accompanied Roger Tichborne to Le Havre, from where, on 1 March 1853, they left in the French sailing ship *La Pauline* for Valparaiso. Here they received news that Sir Edward Doughty had died, the title passing to Roger's father, which meant that Roger was now the heir to Tichborne lands and fortune. John Moore, who had been taken ill, was left in Santiago while Roger went on to Peru, crossed the Andes to Buenos Aires and thence to Rio. Here he took to drinking heavily, taking arsenic to counter 'spasms of the heart' which had him 'raving and foaming at the mouth like a mad dog'. On 20 April 1854 he sailed from Rio on *La Bella*, with a cargo of coffee, bound for Jamaica and New York. Though wreckage of a ship's boat from *La Bella* was seen off the coast of Brazil four days later, they were never heard of again.

Although Roger was legally declared dead, Henriette, the Dowager Lady Tichborne, refused to accept that she would never see him again. On 14 May 1863, nine years later, she placed an advertise-

Baffling pose of the 'Tichborne Claimant' as a contemporary porcelain statuette.

Posing as the vanished Sir Roger Tichborne, this gentleman was in fact Thomas Castro, found guilty of impersonation by an Old Bailey jury in 1874.

ment, in English, French and Spanish, in *The Times* offering 'a handsome reward' for 'any clue' of Roger Charles Tichborne or any survivors of *La Bella*. In August 1865 she had placed in Australian newspapers a detailed advertisement to follow up information that survivors had been picked up and taken to Melbourne.

As a result, from Wagga Wagga, emerged 'the Big Butcher' Tom Castro, who claimed to have been 'in a shipwreck'. He spoke colloquial Spanish and wrote a 'My dear Mother' letter. Now 'the Tichborne Claimant', some of his details rang true, although Upton had become 'Hermitage'. He was prepared to 'face the Sea once more' if Lady Tichborne would 'send me the Means of doing so and paying a fue *[sic]* outstanding debts.' Much was made of his deteriorated spelling and handwriting skills.

Castro was able to convince Roger's mother that he was her son, and likewise the family doctor and solicitor, old servants and those with whom he had gone punt-gunning in Poole Harbour as a boy. The bush ranger from Australia was also able to cast flies into the River Test as well as any member of the gentry. The *Poole Pilot* newspaper championed the case of the Tichborne Claimant.

A phalanx of other witnesses, including members of the family, were adamant that he was not Roger. Many had a financial interest in the matter. The title had gone to his brother, Sir Alfred Joseph Tichborne, the eleventh baronet, who died before his son and heir, Sir Henry Alfred Joseph Tichborne (1866–1910), the twelfth baronet, was born. The two resulting cases dragged through the High Court and Old Bailey from May 1871 to February 1874.

It finally emerged that Thomas Castro was not Sir Roger Tichborne but one Arthur Orton, son of a Wapping butcher, and therefore guilty of impersonation. He was sent to prison for 14 years. Dartmoor prisoner No. 10539 was released in 1884, having earned full remission for good behaviour. Arthur Orton, alias Thomas Castro, alias Roger Tichborne, died in poverty in 1898 and was buried in Paddington Cemetery, his coffin bearing the name 'Sir Roger Charles Doughty Tichborne'. The Tichborne family let Upton House from the time of the trials for the remainder of the century when, in 1900, it was sold to William Llewellin.

The quay tramway, constructed over the winter of 1873–74, ran eastwards as far as the Fish Shambles. Beside it stood the kilns of East Quay Works, where James Walker produced tiles, which in 1873 was acquired by Weybridge entrepreneur Jesse Carter (1830–1927), whose teenage son and heir was Charles Carter (1860–1934). Soon they were producing 'Carter's Red' floor tiles and setting about a land reclamation project.

The cutting of the direct line through Branksome and Parkstone in 1874, providing each with a station, also gave a boost to a chain of brickworks and potteries and their associated clay and sand pits. Henry Sharp's Bourne Valley Works became Sharp, Jones & Co. George Jennings, who founded the South Western Pottery in 1856, took the opportunity to construct sidings southwards into his clay pits and works at Parkstone. As a sanitary engineer, he specialised in the production of drainage pipes as well as bricks and terracotta products. Robert Rogers was the brick and tile manufacturer at Lilliput.

Henry Ralph Willett died unmarried in 1857, his Merley estate passing to a cousin, Willett Lawrence Adye, who split it up and sold Merley House in 1875. It became a second home to the Guest family of Canford House, Lady Wimborne retiring there after she was widowed. Merley's history is commemorated by the Willett Arms, a rustic thatched hostelry, until it burnt down and was replaced by a red-brick roadhouse.

Canford Cliffs was famous for one thing from about 1875 through to its demolition in 1890. The east Dorset place-name then applied to a length of wild and desolate 100ft high sandy cliffs between Flag Head Chine and Canford Cliffs Chine, rather than to a prosperous community.

What became the talking point was Simpson's Folly which, according to the *Harmsworth Magazine,* was 'built by an old sea captain, named Simpson without the consent of the owner of the land *[the Guest family of Canford House]* or the highway commissioners'. Simpson had used concrete for the walls, which were several feet thick and braced together with strips of iron. Simpson's Folly, erected at the foot of the sandy cliffs, stood on a rise above the beach and was protected from the waves by an outer wall, though this was soon undermined. Simpson lived in his folly for just five weeks, the next and last occupant being the Revd Hugh Pearson.

The *Bournemouth Graphic* reported:

Immediately on erection of the concrete wall, the sea commenced to scour away the base and sides, the result being the structure was soon undermined, and a portion of the front fell out... The 'Folly' then remained standing for some years, and was visited by hundreds of people, each of whom must have felt prompted to leave some inscription, as before the final collapse came the walls were covered with texts and proverbs.

Once a correspondent to the paper had been handed a religious tract as he walked by the Lansdowne in central Bournemouth. It started: 'Dear Reader, If you ever go to Bournemouth you will find a house built upon the sand...'

Not that its demise had been quite that obvious at the beginning:

It was surrounded by a sea wall of such large proportions that to a casual observer it might seem that nothing could undermine the foundations, as the walls stood out seeming to bid defiance to waves of the roaring sea as well as to the raging elements.

The ruins became dangerous but the sea's attack then reached an impasse. It seemed as if the bulk of this great square, classical edifice would stand as a monument to the strength of concrete well into the next century. Poole Town Council, as the local authority, asked the Board of Trade, which was responsible for the Coastguard service, to deal with the matter. They passed the responsibility back to the town and told them to take action in whatever way seemed appropriate. Finally, in 1890, there was no alternative:

Mr John Elford, the Borough Surveyor, with about 200-pounds of gunpowder, destroyed in a few minutes what had taken three to four years to build and what even the sea could not batter down in twelve years.

For years, however, there were great slabs of debris – a smaller heap of eroded concrete protruded from the beach at the water's edge until 1961. My father took me to see it and quoted the Biblical injunction against building one's house on sand. Both Simpson and Pearson were remembered, by name at least, but then the promenade was extended across the site and what remained became hardcore for the new sea wall. Simpson's Folly was a one-off, although inland the late-nineteenth century Sway Tower, on the sands of the New Forest, still stands as proof of concrete's enduring use as a building material. The last landscape change of 1875 came about with the laying out of the wooded heathland southwards from Parkstone as Branksome Park. Wide streets amd villas in lavish grounds soon made this the best address in Dorset, though many of its well-heeled occupants felt the need to add to the snob-value by having their friends address mail via Bournemouth rather than Poole.

With the opening of the direct line between Bournemouth Central and Hamworthy Junction the area was provided with Branksome Station. Henry Bury of Branksome Towers laid the foundation-stone of All Saints' Chapel – to cover parts of Kinson and Parkstone parishes – on 22 December 1875 but died before the £3,750 project was completed and consecrated on 20 September 1877. The Bury family continued, however, to fund the building for more than half a century. The west porch was added in 1928 in memory of barrister Francis George Bury (1856–1926), who was awarded the CBE in 1918 for his work as treasurer of King George's Club for the Overseas Forces.

On 12 March 1876, in the surf between Canford Cliffs and Bournemouth Pier, the ketch *William Pitt* was reported to be dangerously close to the beach. The sole man aboard was rescued by the lifeboat *Manley Wood*, which the tug *Royal Albert* then towed back to Poole.

Simpson's Folly, built in concrete below Canford Cliffs by a retired sea captain in 1875, had already been undermined by the sea when this photograph was taken in 1881.

Having become increasingly unstable, Simpson's Folly was blown up in 1890, leaving a heap of eroded concrete visible at the water's edge until clearance of wartime and other debris in 1946.

Mrs Augusta Webster (1837–94), born in Poole, was the daughter of Vice-Admiral George Davies (1800–76), who showed great heroism in saving lives from shipwreck. In 1860, under the pseudonym Cecil Home, Augusta published *Blanche Lisle, and Other Poems*. Her abiding concern, however, was to act as an advocate for social justice.

Collected essays from *The Examiner* were reprinted in 1878 as *A Housewife's Opinions*. By now writing under her own name, some examples of her strident advocacy of female rights and equality were turned into leaflets by the Women's Suffrage Society. Hardly the average Victorian housewife, in 1879 she put herself forward for the Chelsea seat on London School Board and won it with 3,912 votes to spare.

In 1874 architect David Brandon began the restoration of Canford Magna Church. Italian mosaicist Antonio Salviati (1818–1900), whose works appear in cathedrals across Europe from Erfurt and Aachen to St Paul's and Westminster Abbey, visited Dorset in 1876 to undertake a commission by Sir Ivor Guest to relay the chancel floor as the pièce de résistance. The estate's clerk-of-works was Robert Tawse.

At the other end of the scale, the quaintest of the church treasures is a wooden offertory collecting box, with a handle for passing along the pews, inscribed 'I.G. 1679'. A board hanging beside the bell-ropes in the tower bears the doggerel verse:

It is not good to hear Men Wrangle
It is not good to hear Bells Jangle
For there is no Music Play'd or Sung
To be Compared with Bells well Rung.

The last rescue by Sandbanks lifeboat *Manley Wood* took place on 27 March 1879, when the iron-hulled sailing ship *Martaban*, from Greenock, went aground on the Hook Sands. In the early hours of the morning it was found that six of the crew had already left in one of the ship's boats. The master and the other ten men stayed put and refused to leave until the afternoon, when they eventually accepted the offer of help. Despite being abandoned, the *Martaban* was later refloated and towed into Poole by the *Royal Albert* for the tug's standard fee of £5. This was the last active run for the *Manley Wood*, which in 1879 was briefly renamed *Joseph and Mary* for a new benefactor, before being retired and replaced by a second *Joseph and Mary*, a 34ft vessel, in 1880.

The British School, for the boy children of Poole's Nonconformist denominations, was opened in Chapel Lane in 1880. By 1889 it had an average attendance of 221 pupils under master James Reynish.

Former allotments at what in 2005 is Delph Wood were purchased in late-Victorian times by Thomas Horwood, who lived in Moorland House beside the corner of the Ridgeway at Broadstone. He proceeded to landscape the land, digging a lake and planting the trees and shrubs of what became Delph Wood.

In 1882 the Sandbanks lifeboat *Joseph and Mary* was renamed *Boy's Own No. 2* on being moved to East Quay, Poole, where a new lifeboat station had been built at a cost of £165. The new name was for its collective benefactors. George Andrew Hutchison (1841–1913) of Leytonstone, founder editor of the *Boy's Own Paper*, collected cash from lads and their families from across the land. Hutchison, who had already donated *Boy's Own No. 1* to Looe, in Cornwall, lectured across the country on behalf of the Royal National Mission to Deep Sea Fishermen.

In keeping with the ethos of its namesake publication, *Boy's Own No. 2* had carried out the daring midnight rescue of nine stranded seamen before she was even named. On the night of 1 June 1882 the lifeboat was called out to the Milkmaid Bank, south-east of Shell Bay, where the Swedish brigantine *Otto*

'Life at The Sandbanks,' was the caption to this postcard view in 1914, before the largely uninhabited peninsula dropped the definite article and became known as Sandbanks.

and a load of timber were heaving and rolling. With such an auspicious start, the *Boy's Own No. 2* was hailed as 'the pride of Poole' at the opening ceremony for the new boat-house on 27 July 1882.

The boom of the signal mortars at Studland announced the plight of the coal-carrying German brig *Victor*, no longer quite on course from South Wales to her home town of Neustadt. Her bow bulwarks and figurehead washed away, the large vessel was being battered by the waves as *Boy's Own No. 2* waited for worse. Instead, the wind abated, and the fortunate *Victor* proceeded on her way.

The second Poole Bridge, constructed with iron girders, was built in 1885. That year also saw the beginnings of Poole Park, with lawns, gardens and lakes across 60 acres of empty shoreline between Poole and Parkstone. The project was brought to fruition in 1889.

The next wave of democratic reforms, under the Redistribution of Seats Act, 1885, saw Poole lose its identity as a Parliamentary constituency, the borough being merged into the Dorset East seat.

Lady Wimborne's brother was that statesman of high Toryism, Lord Randolph Churchill (1849–95), who founded the Primrose League. On 12 August 1885 he was the speaker at the Great Conservative Fête at Canford House, where more than 3,000 people swarmed across the lawn to surround Lord Wimborne as he welcomed the Guest family's famous guest (intended pun, then and now), who was gratified that so many of the ladies were wearing pink – Churchill's colours at his recent Woodstock by-election. Churchill then delivered a resounding speech in which he assured the gathering that he was not being seduced 'by the Jingo Party' whatever they might have read to the contrary in the *Daily News*. He was not trying to make war with Russia over Afghanistan and the Indian sub-continent. The remark was a reference to the popular song: 'We don't want to fight, but, by jingo if we do, We've got the ships, we've got the men, we've got the money too.'

A heckler managed a perfectly timed 'Quite right' when Churchill claimed the *Daily News* portrayed him as 'an incompetent idiot'. He responded that he was not going to sacrifice 250,000 lives in order to gain a few thousand Conservative votes at general elections. In a rousing finale he urged adoption of 'Tory realities' in place of 'the illusion of Radical politics'.

In 1885 the Western Loop was cut from Corfe Mullen to Broadstone so that Somerset and Dorset line trains could bypass Wimborne and have a direct approach from Blandford and points beyond into Poole and the Bournemouth conurbation.

Heatherlands, the suburb bounded by Rossmore to the north and Ashley Road to the south, was created as an ecclesiastical parish on 22 January 1886. It had formerly been part of Kinson parish.

The 3-acre Parkstone Park, laid out around a fountain in 1888, had a mature look by 1901.

Poole Park, laid out between 1885 and 1889 between old oaks and with new monkey puzzles, plus a view that was originally across to pastures beyond Parkstone Bay (centre).

The tennis-courts in Poole Park, opened in 1909, at the close of the Edwardian era.

✦ CHAPTER 12 ✦

Victorian Values

The main-line railway through the conurbation, almost as it remains to this day, was completed through 'missing links' around Bournemouth in 1888. It was now a direct route from Poole to Brockenhurst and in this milestone year the population of Poole doubled its historic size and passed through the 12,000 barrier. The direct line avoided the inland loops of Castleman's Corkscrew (later known as the 'Old Road'). All of these lines have since been closed, and the track been lifted, as a result of the rationalisation of the railways by Dr Richard Beeching in 1964.

In 1888, when the church of St John the Baptist was consecrated at Broadstone, the correspondent for the *Dorset County Chronicle* looked back to the time when there had been nothing there:

> *A few years since this part of Canford parish presented a wide view of heath common, the prospect being broken by the railway station only. Recently, however, the station has become an important junction and what was once a bleak common is now a growing village.*

The cost of providing the church was shared by Lord Wimborne, in his capacity as lord of Canford Manor, and Canon Dawson Damer. It would later expand to keep pace with the growing population, having an aisle added in 1909 and the lady chapel in 1929.

Victoria Park – generally known as Parkstone Park – on 3 acres between Commercial Road and Station Road, was opened in 1888 with a fountain as the centrepiece to the flower-beds, lawns and paths.

Broadstone brick-maker and builder Elias Sharland gave land for a Methodist church on the main street in the centre of the suburb, in 1889, and its first service was held at Whitsun in 1890. The old 'tin church' of St Saviour's at Newtown acted as a chapel of ease to St Andrew's Church in Kinson. When it was damaged by gales in 1887, William Peace gave land for a replacement, built in Early English style. The entire £2,900 bill was met by Lord Wimborne and St Clement's was consecrated in time for Christmas 1889. Branksome still formed the southern third of Kinson civil parish.

Population growth was also marked in 1889 by the provision of an isolation hospital, with 94 beds, in Ringwood Road, Newtown.

Poole's pilots in 1889 were Thomas Brown of Pile Court, John Fisher, George King and James Stone of Baiter, Thomas Hart and James Tilsed of Lagland Street, John Stone of Thames Street, Francis Wills of East Quay Road and Thomas Wills of Thames Street.

Kelly's Directory for 1889, usefully augmented by the invaluable Ordnance Survey town plan of 1888, also lists the coffee bars and public houses of Victorian Poole and Parkstone:

The Angel Inn, Market Street (Giles Foot)
Ansty Arms, Towngate Street/Longfleet (Henry Blandford)
Antelope Hotel, High Street (Joseph Horne)
Bear Inn, Market Street (William Earley)
Bee Hive, Parkstone (George Stickland junr)
The Bell Inn, Fish Street (John Thomas Bryant)
Bell and Crown, High Street (Charles Phillips)
Bentinck Arms, Brownsea Island (Miss Mary Janet Noble)
Brewers' Arms, Towngate Street (George Macey)
Bricklayers' Arms, Parkstone (Chichester Mawditt)
Bridge Inn, West Quay Road (Henry Tucker)
Bull's Head Inn, High Street (Henry Merrick)
Coffee Rooms, Market Place (Samuel Greenham)
Crown Tavern, Market Street (Charles Dore)
Fox and Hounds, Little Canford (Mrs Nellie Smith)
Garibaldi Arms, Strand Street (unspecified)
George Inn, Longfleet (William Brown)
Globe Hotel, High Street (Alfred Harmer)
The Greyhound, Market Street (Mrs Edith Mary Young)
Harbour View Inn, East Quay Road (Joseph Rose)
Haven Hotel, Sandbanks (William Becknell Mullens)
Holm Bush, Lytchett Minster (George Keeping)
Jolly Sailor, Quay (Jasper Dear)
Junction Hotel, Hamworthy (James Baker Clift)
King and Queen, East Quay (William Budden)
King's Arms, High Street/Quay (Thomas Filmer)
King's Arms, Highmoor (Mrs M. Pike)
King's Head, High Street (Alexander John Colombos)
Lion and Lamb, Thames Street (Thomas Dunevan)
London Hotel, High Street (unspecified)
Longfleet Coffee House (George King)
Lord Nelson Inn, Quay (Alfred Maidment)
Market Place Coffee Rooms, Market Street (Samuel Greenham)
New Antelope, New Street (Charles Stephens)
New Inn [since renamed King Charles], *Thames Street (James Pomeroy)*
New Inn, Longfleet (Frederick William Barnard)
New London Tavern, Lagland Street (Henry Stoke)
Newtown Coffee House (Mrs Maria Monk)
Old Inn, West Street (George Legg)
Old London Tavern, Lagland Street (unspecified)
Parkstone Hotel (Charles Hayball)

Peter's Finger, Lytchett Minster (Richard Hancock)
Ponsonby Arms, Hamworthy (Job Fish)
Poole Arms, Quay (Noah Coombes)
Portmahon Castle Hotel, Longfleet (Adolphus Humphry)
Portsmouth Hoy Inn, Quay (Mrs Mary Ann Hayward)
Potters' Arms, Hamworthy (George Young)
Pottery Hotel, Newtown (Silas James Brown)
Railway Hotel, Broadstone (Thomas Collingwood)
Railway Hotel, Longfleet (Charles Edward Wilson)
Red Star Coffee Rooms, High Street (James Hibberd)
Red Lion, Hamworthy (Henry Pearce – who could boast of being born on the day of the Battle of Waterloo, Sunday 18 June 1815)
Rising Sun, Fish Street (Tom Soper)
Royal Oak and Gas Tavern, East Street (Samuel Hart)
Royal Oak Coffee Tavern, Bourne Valley (John Foster)
St Clement's Inn, Thames Street (George Diffey)
Sea View, Constitution Hill (Walter Tucker)
Seamen's Coffee Bar, Quay (Alfred Ennis)
Shipwrights' Arms, Ferry Road, Hamworthy (Tom Hart)
Shoulder of Mutton, West Howe (Harry Toms)
The Sloop, Parkstone (Thomas Chisman)
Sloop Inn, Hamworthy (William Noah Hiscock)
The Star, West Street (Mrs Susan Elizabeth Langdown)
Station Hotel, Towngate Street (unspecified)
The Swan, Lagland Street (Mrs Fanny Medley)
Three Crowns, Nile Row (unspecified)
The Vine, Market Street (George Richard Samuel Pearce)
Welcome Coffee Tavern, Parkstone (James William Scrivens)
Wheat Sheaf, West Quay Road (Thomas Perry)
White Hart, High Street (Joseph Hoskins)
Willett Arms, Merley (Robert Menzies)
Woodman Tavern, Poole Road, Branksome (Hiram Cox)
Yeoman Inn, Market Street (William Chalker)

Businesses around Poole included those of iron-founder Edward Howell at the Waterloo Foundry, John Albert Chinchen making bricks and tiles at Gravel Hill, and miller William Henry Yeatman at Canford Mills. William Carter ran Kinson Pottery Co. at Hamworthy Junction and Newtown and Job Hibberd was a brick-maker, also at Newtown, where George Lee had gravel pits.

Bourne Valley Pottery, Bournemouth Gas Works and the Hygienic Laundry covered hundreds of acres around the new railway viaducts where 0-4-0 tank engines *Pioneer* and *Mars* worked the adjoining clay pits. These were around Mount Talbot to the north and Aspen Road to the north-west, with linking lines crossing Sheringham Road and Alder Road, at its junction in the dip with Fisher Avenue (now Herbert Avenue), before following Northmere Road. Outgoing products from Bourne Valley Pottery went eastwards, across Cromer Road, on a siding that joined the main line between Branksome Station and the northern bridge across Bourne Valley Road. *Pioneer* was delivered from makers Hudswell Clarke on 28 June 1899. Both engines had a long history, *Mars* being sold to British Periclase Co., West Hartlepool, in 1942, while *Pioneer*'s final outing was along the road to the Parkstone breakers' yard of Trent & Co. in 1948. Dick Legg was the last driver.

Mrs Mary Ann Bolt was a shopkeeper in Old Orchard, which Olive Knott described as 'Poole's East End'. Mary Witheridge and her 'spinster sister', Agnes, offered higher-grade competition. Hilbert Waters was the fishmonger, James Greenslade and Joseph Walden were fruiterers and William Nobbs was the cobbler. Thomas William Lambert sold wardrobes, while John Wills was another shopkeeper in Old Orchard.

Mrs Rebecca Long and Mrs Jane Tanner were Mrs Bolt's direct counterparts in cobbled Lagland Street, where William Henry Dudford, George Marsh, Harry Lawrence and James Stone also had shops. George Greenslade was the greengrocer and William Hillyer the poulterer. Thomas White had a marine store in Lagland Street and Richard Cartridge was the 'beer retailer', while Charles Cluett supplied heating oil. Mrs Eliza Johns was the 'provisions dealer' in New Orchard. Angelo Tagliabue was the general dealer in New Street.

As urban expansion cut off town centres from their countryside, alternative open spaces were set aside for air and exercise, and Poole has superb examples of these Victorian green lungs. Parkstone Park was the focal point of lawns and tree-lined paths around a terracotta fountain, while Poole Park covered 60 acres of former meadows and marshes around the inner bay of the former Baiter backwater. On land donated to the town by Lord Wimborne, waterlogged areas were turned into 'pretty little lakes with willowy islands'. The opening ceremony for the completed parkland, including 'a splendid cricket ground', was conducted by the Prince of Wales – the future Edward VII – on 18 January 1890. In a further burst of civic pride, to mark the event, timber merchant John Joseph Norton presented the town with its first museum collection, housed in rooms at the Free Library in Mount Lane.

The Ordnance Survey map of 1890, at a scale of 6 ins to the mile, shows a Martello Tower on the clifftop immediately east of Canford Cliffs Chine, beside the boundary of a pine plantation which stretched northwards to West Lodge and beyond. Martello is a corruption of Mortella, the circular fort in Corsica, isle of Napoleon's birth, which defied the English in 1794. A decade later, though England's coast was defended by Martello Towers, there were none westwards of Seaford Head in Sussex, though they exist in quantity on the Channel Islands. The explanation for the tower at Canford Cliffs was that C.W. Packe, former MP of Branksome Dene, had it built for 'a smoking room and summer house'.

The gazebo became a folly in the grounds of Canford Cliffs Hotel, which was built by Dr A. Smith in 1905, and in 1936 was converted into its staff quarters. Wartime took its toll and the site was later redeveloped, though 'Martello Towers' survives as a name and there is also a Martello Park to the north-east.

The Plymouth schooner *Mountblairy* ran onto the Hook Sands, off Sandbanks, on 'the misty morn' of 26 October 1891. Tug and tide saved her, with a well-timed tow back to Poole for repairs, but this vessel's reputation as a survivor finally ended on the rocks – with horror and heroism – in Ireland nearly four decades later, in October 1929.

The boom of signal mortars from Studland summoned the Poole lifeboat *Boy's Own No. 2* into the bay in the early hours of 11 November 1891. As rowing out of the harbour in the adverse conditions and against the tide was impossible, the lifeboat was towed to the ship in distress – the wind, blowing towards land from south-south-east would anyway have made it impossible to leave the harbour entrance. Offshore they found the Norwegian brig *Solertia*, which had rammed into the Milkmaid Bank with a cargo of Russian pit-props and roof timbers intended for delivery to Poole. Eight crewmen were taken off by the lifeboat, along with a Customs' officer, and put ashore on Poole Quay at dawn – a long night for all concerned.

Whilst visiting his cousins in 1892, playing with them near the Guest family's palatial seaside mansion at Branksome Dene – which they called 'the Beach House' – an 18-year-old fell 20ft from a rustic bridge across a chine. Found unconscious on the path below, he was carried back to Branksome Dene, where he remained comatose for three days. It was more than three months before his ruptured kidney had healed sufficiently for him to leave his bed. Convalescence followed at Canford House.

More than a century later that young man won a national poll to find 'the Greatest Briton' – Rt Hon. Sir Winston Churchill (1874–1966), eldest son of Lord Randolph Churchill. By 1895 he had recovered completely and joined the Army for his first real adventure, serving with Spanish forces in Cuba.

Two false claims are made on a red-granite tombstone beside Canford Magna Church, which reads:

The Right Honourable Sir Henry Austen Layard GCB, the Discoverer of Ninevah. Sometime a Member of Parliament, H.M. Ambassador at Constantinople. Born at Paris 5 March 1817. Died in London 5 July 1894.

Firstly it is not his grave in the churchyard at Canford. Layard was cremated at Woking – the first and, at the time, the only crematorium in the country – and his ashes are there. Secondly, the four palaces he excavated and described in *Ninevah and its Remains*, published in 1848–49, and *Ninevah and Babylon*, in 1853, were not Ninevah at all but proved to be the Assyrian city of Calah, 20 miles away. In 1869 Sir Henry Layard married Mary Evelyn Guest of Canford House and transformed its west wing into Ninevah Court, to house his antiquities.

Another player in the Canford story was a veteran of the Indian Mutiny, Montague Guest (1833–1909), who went into politics. Liberal MP for Youghal from 1869 to 1874, he then represented Wareham, from 1880 to 1885, as a Liberal-Unionist. He was appointed Provincial Grand Master for Dorsetshire, by royal appointment at the hand of HRH Albert Edward, Prince of Wales, with whom his connection extended beyond Freemasonry to close friendship. Ironically, Guest died while visiting Edward, then Edward VII, at Sandringham for the King's birthday party on 9 November 1909. He is buried in Canford Magna Church.

Local Government Order No. 31,582, which came into effect on 30 September 1894, established Branksome as a legal entity. It was formed by detaching part of Kinson Urban District which, according to *Kelly's Directory*, 'was transferred to the Rural District of Poole, and the name of the Urban District and its constituent parish was altered to that of Branksome.' Independence for Branksome was short-lived as:

... this was in turn superseded by the Poole (Extension) Order 1905, which came into operation November 9th, 1905, by which Branksome now forms part of the municipal borough and civil parish of Poole.

Branksome suburb was expanding fast. Its first Baptist chapel, with 250 seats, was built in 1896, and that in York Road, seating 130, in 1899. There were also Methodist chapels, two Salvation Army barracks, and a hall for the Plymouth Brethren. Some 8 acres were laid out for Branksome Cemetery, in Upper Road, where the first graves date from 1904.

Carrying a cargo of cedar from Cuba to Bremen, the Norwegian barque *Brilliant* ended its journey on the Hook Sands, at dusk, on 12 January 1895. It was the worse combination of weather for being on the water in Poole Bay, a near-gale from east-south-east being accompanied by swirling sleet and snow. Into the teeth of this blizzard the Poole steam-tug *Telegraph* towed the lifeboat *Boy's Own No. 2* to Poole Bar. Here, the Swanage lifeboat was already in attendance and had lost its coxswain in the process. Separate approaches had to be made for taking off each crewman in turn.

Even this was hazardous in the extreme and the ship's boy broke his leg when it became entangled in a rope and was cut free by a colleague. Captain Bjercke crushed his ribs and was swept into the sea. Despite these and a series of lesser injuries, all ten Norwegians were saved.

West side of the upper High Street in the 1890s from house furnishers Hunt & Son at No. 132 (left), *furniture dealers Bayley & Sons on the North Street corner* (centre), *and late-eighteenth-century houses from No. 136 through to No. 140* (right).

The northern end of the High Street in 1900, north-eastwards into Longfleet, with the Port Mahon Castle Hotel (left) *at No. 190 and Henry Burden's grocery wagon outside his shop at No. 203* (far right), *near the Kingland Road junction.*

Jesse Carter expanded his pottery empire in 1895 by purchasing the Architectural Pottery in Hamworthy. Jesse's son, Owen Carter, who had already succumbed to the influence of William Morris and his Arts & Crafts Movement, set up his own potter's wheel behind the family home at West End House. His 'artistic' designs went into commercial production at the White Works in Hamworthy before migrating back across the water and evolving into the Poole Pottery range at East Quay Works.

The next owner of Brownsea Island, after the departure of the Cavendish-Bentinck family, was Captain Kenneth Robert Balfour (1863–1936). With his wife, Margaret Anne, he watched helplessly as their Branksea Castle home was gutted by fire on the night of 26 January 1896. Restoration followed in 1897, though the profile of the building was somewhat softened by the removal of several turrets and other Gothic features.

With Margaret Balfour's health worsening after years of chronic illness, Kenneth Balfour put Brownsea Island up for sale by auction at The Mart, beside the Bank of England, on 13 July 1899. When Margaret died on 23 March 1901 Kenneth embarked on a Parliamentary career as Conservative member of the Christchurch constituency, which included Bournemouth, from 1900 to 1906. He moved into Dorset to Higher Kingston at Stinsford.

Two coal ships, the brigantine *Hildred* and barquentine *Albert T. Young.* were close to being claimed by the Hook Sands on 23 February 1896. It was time for the typical sandbank-shoal remedy: on being driven inshore by south-easterly winds, such vessels were 'lightened' by labourers brought out from Poole to shovel out once-valuable cargo now regarded as dead weight.

Poole took delivery of an already historic lifeboat in May 1897. Designed by naval architect George I. Watson, she had taken part in competitive trials at Montrose, in 1893, and had then been stationed in Blackpool. Though water ballast-tanks and a drop-keel made for extraordinary stability, she was never intended to be self-righting.

Naming lifeboats after their financial benefactors can lead to some unlikely-sounding baptisms. Freemasons in full regalia, standing in the rain, watched as 'this Watson craft' was inducted into service as *City Masonic Club* on 26 August 1897. Lady Wimborne carried out the honours on their behalf, accompanied by her brother-in-law Montague Guest (1839–1909), Provincial Grand Master for Dorsetshire from 1877 to 1902. Lord Wimborne chaired a celebratory meeting in the Guildhall.

Over three days, between 23 and 25 November 1898, the *City Masonic Club* and her 72-year-old coxswain, John Hughes, notched up 48 hours on duty. They attended the *Velocity* and then the schooner *Fier*, her crew having already been taken off by the Swanage lifeboat *William Erle*, as the vessel was driven from distress on the Hook Sands to a 'written-off' state on the beach near Flag Head Chine. Even that was not the end of the story as an enterprising and skilful Poole carpenter salvaged, repaired and re-launched her for her next and final sinking, between Antwerp and Newcastle, on 23 November 1903.

Meanwhile, on the evening of 24 November 1898, Poole's *City Masonic Club,* having already provided a stand-in crew for the Swanage lifeboat to rescue the crew of the French barque *Bonne Mère,* had then returned to sea for her fifth rescue of the series. The Poole boat's departing service to the limping *Bonne Mère* was to follow her to Southampton in case of further mishaps. In all, under the command of a man who nowadays would have been compulsorily retired a couple of decades earlier, the Poole lifeboat had recorded its longest endurance record in terms of both time and distance.

In the late-nineteenth century golf courses were

coming into vogue. The 250-acre links of Dorset Golf Club, beside what is now the former railway line at Broadstone, extends for more than 6,000 yards between patches of heathland and glades of silver birch. Owned by Lord Wimborne and designed by Tom Dunn, it was opened by leading politician Arthur James Balfour in 1898, four years before he became Prime Minister. For a time it was virtually the private recreation-ground for Canford House, where Lady Wimborne encouraged fellow females to take up their clubs. In 1914 the bunkers and greens were reconstructed by H.S. Colt – 'Clearly designed by Providence for a golf course,' commented one early user.

Though only a handful of people realised it at the time, Sandbanks was at the centre of development of the dominant technology of the twentieth century. Sailing into Poole Harbour in his ship-sized yacht *Electra*, Guglielmo Marconi of Bologna (1874–1937) adopted what the map called The Sandbanks (always with the definite article). Apart from a few new red-brick villas, notably Sandhills, there were only two relatively historic buildings on the peninsula. The southern tip was dominated then, as now, by the Haven Hotel and, nestling in the northern sand dunes, was the Coastguard Station.

Although German physicist Heinrich Hertz (1857–94) – who gave his name to the measurement of radio frequencies – had proved the existence of electro-magnetic waves in 1886, no one had sent messages over points a hundred yards apart until 1895, when Marconi took up 'the Hertzian challenge'. In November 1897 he set up the world's first wireless transmitter above the multi-coloured sands of Alum Bay on the Isle of Wight. Marconi, needing somewhere to transmit to, initially sailed *Electra* into the dependably flat waters of Poole Harbour, then realised that only a land-based position with an uninterrupted line of sight would be suitable for the next stage of the operation.

He set up his first 125ft aerial landwards of Sandhills. On 3 June 1898 Lord Kelvin paid a shilling for the privilege of sending, from Alum Bay, the world's first commercial radio-telegram, which was successfully received at Sandhills on Sandbanks. Madeira Hotel, latterly Court Royal miners' convalescent home on West Cliff, in Bournemouth, was Marconi's first mainland workshop and laboratory. For both financial and practical reasons he soon moved this to the Haven Hotel at Sandbanks, setting up another 100ft aerial between it and Sandhills, then a third to the north-east of the buildings.

Hotel owner Eugene Poulain spurned the offer of shares in Marconi's new company – a century premature in his fear that their value would collapse – and regretted the fact for the rest of his life. From struggling with both economics and electricity on Sandbanks, Marconi went on to notch up a host of radio firsts, culminating in the transatlantic triumph of sending waves over the horizon to another continent. Transmitted on 12 December 1901 from beside the Poldhu Hotel, above Poldhu Cove, in Cornwall, these were received by a kite-flown aerial, in gusting winds, 2,100 miles away above the Barracks Hospital at St John's, Newfoundland. The first deciphered transmission consisted of 'dot, dot, dot' – Morse code for the letter 'S'. Marconi's diary records signals being received at 12.30, 1.10 and 2.20 local time that afternoon. By December 1902, inaugurated by a message from the Governor-General of Canada to King Edward VII, the Marconi system of 'wireless telegraphic communication' was in operation between Cape Breton and England.

The Scott family of Sandbanks, who ran the ferry service across the harbour entrance to South Haven Point, have been credited for coining the descriptive name 'Shell Bay' for the desirable sands across the water.

On 17 July 1899 naturalist John Clavell Mansel-Pleydell (1817–1902), who owned 9,000 acres around Winterborne Whitechurch, made a major discovery in Poole Harbour when he found a 'single small clump' of the cord grass *Spartina townsendii* growing on 'Owre *[Ower]* mud-flats'. He sent a tuft of this maritime grass to H.J. Goddard, of Tottenham Road in Longfleet, Poole. The 'Whatcombe Herbarium' label that accompanied the specimen, inserted into Goddard's copy of the second edition of Mansel-Pleydell's *Flora of Dorsetshire*, published in 1895, has survived. Goddard, who in later life was the author of *Grasses of Great Britain*, worked for Dunns Farm Seeds Ltd and collected and identified native grasses from 1875 to 1936.

From 1899, Goddard wrote, he 'kept an eye open' for *Spartina* year by year until the summer of 1907. Then it appeared 'all at once' in 'hundreds of spots, in fact nearly every mud-flat' around the Poole side of the harbour, in locations ranging from Lytchett Bay, Lake and Holes Bay in the west, to Whitecliff and Salterns on the other side of the quay. Once described as 'very rare' it had now become 'very common'.

The significance of this was explained to the Royal Commission on Land Erosion by Lord Montagu of Beaulieu, who stated that there had been a similar rapid spread of the grass – known locally as sea-rice or rice-grass – on the Hampshire estuaries. The plant, which had been accidentally introduced from the Argentine by ships unloading ballast, was over-running the mud-banks, solidifying and raising them. Some 6,000–8,000 acres of *Spartina* salt-marsh had established itself in Southampton Water and the Solent. Half a century later, in Poole Harbour, the Nature Conservancy calculated that there were 1,057 acres of this cord-grass, providing extensive roosting areas for waterfowl and causing their winter numbers to increase enormously.

In Poole Bay, however, nature remained as elemental as ever. In 1900 the Hook Sands gripped

Bournemouth tramcar No. 30 (centre), *en route westwards to Poole Park through Lower Parkstone along Bournemouth Road, as it passes shops in Parkstone Terrace* (right) *in 1912.*

Bournemouth-based tramcars Nos 5 (left centre) *and 17* (centre) *in 1913, passing in the northern High Street between Port Mahon Castle Hotel* (left) *and Frank and Ralph King's cycle store on the opposite corner at Kingland Road* (right centre), *along from the shop fronts around Caleb Snook's Longfleet Post Office at No. 201.*

Tramcar No. 12 at the Tram Terminus, outside Davis the tobacconist (left) *and the Port Mahon Castle Hotel in the northern High Street, looking north-eastwards to the new spire of St Mary's Church in Longfleet* (centre), *c.1916.*

Quayside Custom House (left) *and warehouses* (centre), *all built after a fire in 1813, beside the Helmsman at the junction with the High Street* (right).

The central High Street north-eastwards from the Amity Hall (right), *with a 'Sale This Evening' sign, and the Globe Hotel* (centre right), *opposite the junction with Towngate Street* (far left), *in 1900.*

but then released the fully-loaded collier *Matin,* which was able to steam free. Equally fortunate, in 1902, heading into Poole with a cargo of Fenland potatoes, was the ketch *Little Jessie,* which seemed to be held fast but floated free with the incoming tide. This was becoming a regular occurrence and two vessels received help from Poole lifeboat *City Masonic Hall* early on 4 December 1904. The schooner *Carrie Bell* was able to wave the lifeboat men away and successfully deliver her a cargo of limestone to Poole. Following her, however, the ketch *Zenobia* also ran into the Hook Sands and, assisted during the afternoon in setting kedge-anchors, was able eventually to prise herself free.

Poole & District Electric Traction Co., formed in 1899, worked throughout the following year to lay nearly 4 miles of tramlines from the Old Town to Constitution Hill and Parkstone's fashionable villas. The system, consisting mostly of single track with passing places, opened on 6 April 1901. Linkage with the Bournemouth rails, at County Gates, enabled through-working by Bournemouth Corporation Transport across the entire coastal conurbation from Poole to Christchurch, which continued until its closure on 7 July 1935. The following day the routes were taken over by the motorised omnibuses of Hants & Dorset Motor Services. The local tram shed (next to The Retreat in Ashley Road, Parkstone) became the bus company's Parkstone depot.

Boer War volunteer Corporal H. J. Knight from Poole, fighting with the 1st Liverpool Regiment in South Africa, was gazetted with his Victoria Cross on 4 January 1901. He became Captain Knight and enjoyed a long retirement before his death in 1955.

Local green-glazed bricks putting a late-Victorian gloss on the Poole Arms, otherwise dating from the seventeenth century, facing the quay from beside Hosiers Lane (left).

Wealthy socialites Charles (left front) *and Florence van Raalte* (centre) *with party guests, at Branksea Castle, c.1905.*

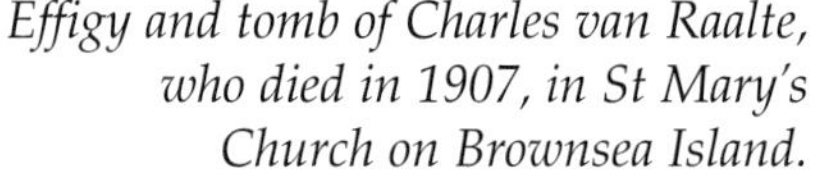

Effigy and tomb of Charles van Raalte, who died in 1907, in St Mary's Church on Brownsea Island.

Poole men on a club charabanc outing, posing for a photograph as they stop to buy steamer tickets at Sydenham's Library, en route to the steamer from Bournemouth Pier in 1922.

✦ CHAPTER 13 ✦

Suburbs and Suffragettes

Edwardian postcard view of cobbled Carter's Lane (left) *and No. 74 High Street – 'the Old Thatched Cottage' on the west side – which was demolished in 1919 to make way for Woolworth's Penny Bazaar.*

The northern end of the High Street, north-eastwards up Longfleet Road (centre right)*, from the old Toll House and George Inn* (centre left)*, drawn by T.J.B. Price in 1949.*

By 1901 there was another Churchill in Parliament. Winston Leonard Spencer Churchill had arrived. The Guest family at Canford had changed their politics from Conservative to Liberal, and on 19 February 1901 young Winston's Aunt Cornelia – Lady Wimborne – was in the gallery of the House of Commons to hear his maiden speech.

She was the strong woman behind the new century's rising star. In 1906, when Winston became Colonial Under-Secretary, Lady Wimborne picked up the tab for him to entertain ministers from all the territories of the British Empire at a dinner at London's Ritz Hotel. Opposing High Church ceremonials in the Church of England, she denounced them as papist, and founded Cornelia's League of Ladies, which had 40 branches nationwide. When Frederick Smith, 1st Earl of Birkenhead and one-time secretary to Lady Wimborne, decorated his office with religious pictures, Cornelia condemned them as 'Romish!', ordering his instant dismissal.

Wealthy socialite Charles van Raalte (1857–1907) arrived on Brownsea Island in 1901 and in 1903 added to the historic confusion over its name – traditionally Branksea – by changing it to Brownsea after guests kept leaving the train at Branksome by mistake. This choice of two names continues to the present day, and I have followed the example of the Ordnance Survey map by referring to Branksea Castle on Brownsea Island.

Charles van Raalte, struggling against the political tide, stood as the Unionist candidate in Poole, fighting the East Dorset seat at two elections, but failed to swing it away from its traditional Liberal tendencies. Chancellor of the Exchequer David Lloyd George imposed a super-tax to finance his social security programme. Van Raalte, feeling depressed when he left for a holiday in India in 1907, then caught pneumonia and died in Calcutta. His embalmed body was returned to England for burial on the island, in a new memorial chapel attached to the south side of St Mary's Church, which was completed in 1908.

The Church of St John the Evangelist, in Ashley Road, was built in 1903 at a cost of £5,260, providing seating for a congregation of 450 from the Anglican parish of Heatherlands, between Upper Parkstone and Branksome.

Though it would be another two decades before it took to the water, the present Floating Bridge link between Studland and Shell Bay came about as a direct result of the failure of the Branksome Park & Swanage Light Railway project, proposed in 1904. The project had been promoted by Studland landowner Walter Bankes of Kingston Lacy House, Sir John Burt of Purbeck House in Swanage, and Lord and Lady Wimborne at Canford House, who between them owned virtually the entire route from Canford Cliffs and Sandbanks to Ulwell and Swanage. Bournemouth Electricity Supply Co. was to have supplied the motive power and the harbour entrance would have been crossed by a cage-and-chain bridge suspended between two high towers – modelled on the Middlesbrough transporter bridge at Teesside.

Though the initial capital of £68,000 was subscribed by the wealthy backers and their associates, costs spiralled to an estimated £266,000, by which time opposition had also mounted. The bridge proposal, the weakest link, was challenged by borough councillors in Poole and also by the Harbour Commissioners, who effectively held the trump card and, playing their statutory role, killed off the project in 1906. They went on to receive growing opprobrium for recognising too late that this was to be the century of the motor car. In 1914 they acknowledged the need for an 'ambitious vehicle-carrying ferry service between Poole and Purbeck', but, with western civilisation about to implode, nothing could be done until after the First World War.

Suburban Poole briefly enjoyed administrative self-rule until, in 1905, Branksome urban district was absorbed into an expanded borough of Poole and the Town Council's writ ran eastwards to what was then the Hampshire border at County Gates, Westbourne. Seawards, the new boundary embraced Branksome Dene Chine, below Bournemouth's fashionable West Cliff. Formerly in the parish of Canford Magna, the emergent Broadstone suburb – no longer called Canford Bottom – became a separate parish in 1906.

Parkstone School for Boys and Girls was founded by W.E. Brennand in 1905. Poole Grammar School also dates from this time, though originally a secondary school, in Mount Street (now South Road) with additional ground – in Kingland Road – given by Lord Wimborne in 1907. The century was embracing enlightenment and learning on an unprecedented scale. Hundreds crowded and queued for public education lectures in Amity Hall and additional meetings were held in Emerson Hall to cater for the burgeoning demand. Magic lantern shows were being upstaged by the new offerings of 'Kinematography' as Amity Hall doubled as Poole's first occasional cinema once the film circuit reached the provinces.

In Purbeck a clay-carrying railway was built across 5 miles of almost uninhabited heathland in 1905, linking lines around Norden clay pits with those from Newton pits to the northern tip of Goathorn peninsula. The Goathorn Railway had the same 3ft 9in gauge as its Middlebere predecessor and was operated from Eldon Sidings by vintage locomotive *Tiny*, built by Stephen Lewin in Poole, and a new engine, *Thames*. The line terminated in a 250ft timber pier, which reached the channel of South Deep and was usually served by Henry Burden's boats from Poole. One of its wagons was provided with a corrugated-iron roof and became a school train, taking children to a classroom at Goathorn or primary school in Corfe. Workers and their wives also used the truck to reach Corfe Castle on Saturdays.

Poole Batonic Brewery (proprietor A.B. Candy) manufactured ginger beer and hop beer in brown and cream stoneware jars before the First World War. The business operated from Brown Bottom at Park Gates East on a site, just below the Sloop Hotel, which became a petrol station. The stalls beside it were established by 'Happy' Carter, whose horse-drawn wagonette ran a regular delivery service between Park Gates and Sandbanks.

Black Tulip, a steam-yacht operating in Poole Harbour, became a mobile floating store in 1900. Owned first by J.R.H. Knight and then by Robert Knight, she was based at their Woodside Boatyard, Lilliput, and remained in service until 1955.

Salterns, Lilliput, which she described as a 'maggot-knot of dwellings' beside Poole Harbour, was the birthplace of writer Mary Butts (1890–1937). Disturbed at the way rural England was changing from the cherished Edwardian watercolour vision of her childhood into the harsh mechanised sprawl of the suburbanised '20s and '30s, she departed for a mad fling in Paris, returning to seek the security of old England and finding it, to an extent, with husband Gabriel Aitken in Cornwall. She was at her happiest, however, back in Dorset, at remote South Egliston, on the Purbeck coast between Kimmeridge and Tyneham Cap.

Winston Churchill was back at Canford House for a Liberal Party rally there on the August bank holiday in 1906. Ivor Guest, who had also taken part in the South African War, presided as 15,000 people strained to hear the Under-Secretary of State for the Colonies. It was hardly vintage Churchill. He went on, and on, about the problems of the day, against the background of internecine warfare in his own party. The arguments were complicated by a constitutional impasse. Campbell-Bannerman's Liberal administration found itself impotent in implementing its programme in the face of implacable opposition from the Tory House of Lords.

In South Africa, Winston Churchill could make progress, as he tried to manoeuvre a collection of disparate colonies into the next dominion. Winning the Boer War was insufficient in itself to establish British supremacy, the majority of settlers being of Dutch origin. Churchill was adept, however, at the techniques of divide and rule, and vigorously and skilfully promoted self-government for Transvaal and the Orange River Colony.

Locally, as well as nationally, political passions were on a knife-edge, Tories storming the platform in the Guildhall and coming to blows with the town's Liberal leaders. Rioting crowds reacted by stoning the windows of prominent aldermen and councillors. Temperance and teetotalism also provoked strife, mayoral denouncements of the demon drink being followed by attacks from licensed victuallers. The argument swung like a pendulum. In 1911 free civic beer was downed to the strains of 'God save the King' to celebrate the completion of the Edwardian decade, while in 1912 all drinks – mineral water as well as alcohol – were banned from Poole Park on Sundays.

The Cornelia and East Dorset Hospital in

Dorset-born Poole councillor Samuel Whittle (centre left) *at the Antelope Hotel, during his week of wearing a kilt in order to win a wager, shortly before his death in 1907.*

Longfleet Road was erected at a cost of £3,750 in 1906/07 on land donated by Lord Wimborne, who also gave £1,000 towards building costs. The name perpetuated that of the Cornelia Cottage Hospital in Mount Street and of Lady Wimborne herself, born Lady Cornelia Henrietta Maria Spencer-Churchill.

In order to win a bet, Poole councillor Samuel Whittle wore the kilt for a week, shortly before his death in 1907. The great uncle of Mrs Dorothy Battrick, 'he had no Scotch connections at all' but came from a family of Wimborne farmers who settled on the shores of Holes Bay, where the Whittle's Way wharf carries their name. Mrs Battrick explained:

> *The Scot attire was donned on Samuel's acceptance of a wager, to walk so dressed from the Antelope Hotel to the top of the town, starting at twelve noon, every day for a week. He was at the time a member of Poole town council and the wager was won from a fellow member.*

Lieutenant-General Sir Robert Baden-Powell (1857–1941) – as he was known after being knighted in 1909 and before he was created 1st Baron Baden-Powell – brought 20 boys to Brownsea Island in 1907, where, from 1–9 August, divided into four patrols, they camped on the south-west side of the island overlooking the Purbeck heaths. Though they played games they were treated as unarmed boy soldiers at this, the world's first Scout camp, the Scout movement being formed the following year for lads who were 'Trusty, loyal, helpful, brotherly, courteous, kind, obedient, smiling, thrifty, pure as the rustling wind.'

Arthur Prinnor, who had helped organise the Brownsea camp, went home to Broadstone and formed a Scout pack. Patrol-leader Victor Watkins had the distinction in 1911 of becoming the first King's Scout in Great Britain, taking the title, with only minutes to spare, from an equally qualified contender from Birmingham, confirmation of his winning of the swimming and life-saving badges at Bournemouth Baths being cabled to London immedi-

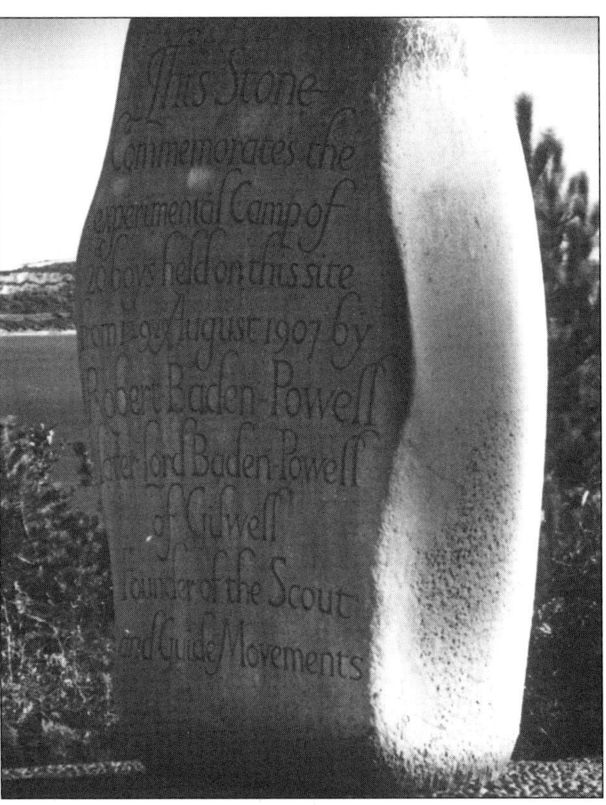

On the southern slopes of Brownsea Island, 'This Stone Commemorates the experimental Camp of 20 boys held on this site from 1–9 August 1907 by Robert Baden-Powell later Lord Baden-Powell of Gilwell, Founder of the Scout and Guide Movements'.

ately. Broadstone Scouts were based in Red Barn, Tudor Road, before taking over the old chapel which had been replaced by a new Congregational Church.

On 21 October 1908 Bridgwater ketch *Conquest*, bound for Cardiff with wheat loaded at Poole Quay, was towed out of Poole Harbour by a tug. While preparing to raise sails as they entered Studland Bay, the *Conquest*'s captain realised they were heading directly into a south-easterly gale and, on discussing the matter with the pilot, decided to turn back and ride out the storm in the harbour. When, on signals from the ketch, the tug changed direction, the line parted and the *Conquest*, drifting helplessly, was driven directly towards the Hook Sands, where she ran aground.

Although the *City Masonic Club* came out from Poole Quay and put eight lifeboatmen aboard to pump water from her damaged hull, it was a losing battle and it became clear that the *Conquest* would break up. The lifeboat took off the pilot and the four crewmen, who were suffering hypothermia.

On 31 July 1909, while staying with his Aunt Cornelia at Canford House, Winston Churchill spent Saturday visiting the corner of the Guest estate that was being suburbanised as a dormitory for Poole and Bournemouth artisans. With the two towns fusing into one beside the railway from Westbourne to Parkstone, Churchill's public appearance was to declare

Branksome Liberal Club open. As President of the Board of Trade he had just spiked a threatened miners' strike.

The Branksome celebrations were disrupted by suffragette protesters; Lady Wimborne, who had given an acre of land for the club, having insisted that separate accommodation should be provided exclusively for women. Far from placating the protesters, this had incensed them, and led to the prolonged chant: 'We don't want a room, we want a vote!'

The suffragettes from suburbia also shadowed Churchill when he returned to address the Radical Fête and Demonstration at Canford on August Bank Holiday Monday in 1909. Mrs Emmeline Pankhurst and her daughters led the protest, at which the police had to prevent an army of estate workers from throwing pig-nets around the agitators and giving them a ducking in the River Stour. Winston had a Liberal budget to defend, and memories of his father's great speech, 24 years before, to live down. Then Lord and Lady Wimborne had been stalwart Conservatives and it was Lord Randolph Churchill who had hammered away at the Liberal radicalism that Lady Wimborne and her nephew now extolled.

In 1910 Lady Wimborne went too far, even for her. By ignoring rules on expenditure and openly violating the laws against bribery, she ensured the election to Parliament of her third son, Captain the Rt Hon. Frederick Edward 'Freddie' Guest (1875–1937). When it was established that votes in the East Dorset constituency had been bought, Freddie's poll was declared void and he was disqualified.

In the resulting by-election the family's substitute, Henry Guest, was duly elected in his place. When the country went to the polls again, however, in the second general election of 1910, Freddie Guest's name was back on the ballot paper for East Dorset, and he, of course, won. Winston again did his bit at the hustings in Poole. Freddie's two young sons and baby daughter, with their nanny, were also pressed into service in a donkey cart with posters urging 'Vote for Daddy' and 'Daddy for Ever'. H.W. Little, who retired to Bridport, told me of a torchlight procession in support of the Liberal cause which began in Upper Parkstone, turning at Bourne Valley Potteries and proceeding through Lower Parkstone to Poole Quay 'where a number of participants ended up in the water'.

Further nepotism impacted on Winston's Parliamentary dealings, perhaps in response to urgings from Aunt Cornelia, when he tried to push Freddie's virtues to a reluctant Asquith, in a bid to have him made Civil Lord of the Admiralty. The Prime Minister, however, could not be moved.

Eminent naturalist Alfred Russel Wallace (1823–1913) lived at the Old Orchard in Broadstone and is buried beneath a fossil tree-trunk from South America in Dunyeats Road Cemetery. Awarded the Order of Merit in 1910, he is remembered as the man who might have been Darwin. Both men had been thinking along the same lines for many years and in 1858 together published a paper *On the Tendency of*

Suffragettes being ejected by a policeman after disrupting Winston Churchill's speech at the Liberal Party rally in the grounds of Canford House in 1909.

Parkstone Bay, south-eastwards from the 'People's Park' – as Poole Park was known – to pine-clad Parkstone, above Model Farm (left) *and Edenhurst, which was being developed fast in 1905.*

Species to form Varieties, of which only two copies survive. It is Charles Darwin's work *On the Origin of Species*, published the following year and packaging the theory of evolution for general consumption, that endures.

Wallace himself was not reticent about going into print, his published works including *Travels on the Amazon* in 1853, followed by writings on such diverse subjects as geography, animals, vaccination (against it), land nationalisation (in favour) until, in 1903, he ventured beyond the planet with *Man's Place in the Universe* and, in 1906, posed the question, as relevant today as it was then, *Is Mars Habitable?*

Although, between the adventure and the foresight, Alfred Russel Wallace championed the odd lost cause, his overall contribution to knowledge was immense in that he acted as a catalyst, encouraging others – notably Charles Darwin – to expand the frontiers of science. His ghost, it is said, was regularly seen by two of the next occupants of the Old Orchard, namely the batman of Brigadier-General Julian Dallas Tyndale Tyndale-Biscoe (1867–1960) and the General's wife, Agnes. After her death in 1968 the Old Orchard was demolished and bungalows built in its place.

One of the major constraints on extensive suburban development was alleviated in 1910 with the building of a water works and pumping station between the Somerset & Dorset Railway and the River Stour, in meadows at Corfe Mullen.

On the evening of 11 January 1910, 14 fishing boats from Poole found themselves in difficulties, when a sudden gale blew up in the bay. As their crews included almost all the men who usually manned the port's lifeboat, back in the Old Town a reserve crew of veterans and trainees mobilised the *City Masonic Club* and took her to the harbour entrance. They then stood by in case of difficulties, counting the fleet home as they struggled through heavy swell and strong currents to return to the safety of the harbour.

Poole received its first self-righting lifeboat in May 1910. At a length of 37ft 6ins, with double drop-keels and a crew of 12 oarsmen, she was named the *Harman* in memory of George John Harman, of Kensington. On 4 June 1910, as the mayor delivered his speech and Miss Daisy Harman prepared for the naming ceremony, a maroon, discharged accidentally, exploded overhead, the launching team responding by removing the pin securing the boat to the slipway. Miss Harman was forced to jump clear as the lifeboat slid prematurely into the water.

In 1911 the expanding community of Canford Cliffs received its own church 'in the glen', donated by the Revd Hugh Pearson. The emergent suburb was still part of the ecclesiastical parish of St Peter's, Parkstone, and it was as the Chapel of the Transfiguration that the pebbledashed timber building was licensed. A separate parish of Canford Cliffs with Sandbanks was created in 1945.

In 1911 the motor car was pitted against a mainstay of biblical transport by Mayor Herbert Carter, who lived in The Hermitage, in Hermitage Road on Constitution Hill, with a viewpoint tower overlooking Poole Harbour. Carter alternated the transport for his duties, as appropriate, between 'a Baby Peugeot' and Jeremiah the donkey, acquired complete with harness and cart for £8.10s.0d. Carter having decided on a race to establish the fastest and most reliable means of transport, Jeremiah was given a head start – a whole day with a night's rest at Corfe Castle – as the family set off by car for a picnic at Chapman's Pool, in the Isle of Purbeck. As the donkey trotted across Corfe Common the Peugeot headed towards Kingston Hill, where it overheated, causing it to take an inordinate time to reach Worth Matravers, where 'Jeremiah ambled past the finishing post, winner by a few lengths'.

The two sons and daughter of the Hon. Frederick Guest, with their nanny, urging 'Vote for Daddy' through the streets of Poole and Wimborne in the elections of 1910.

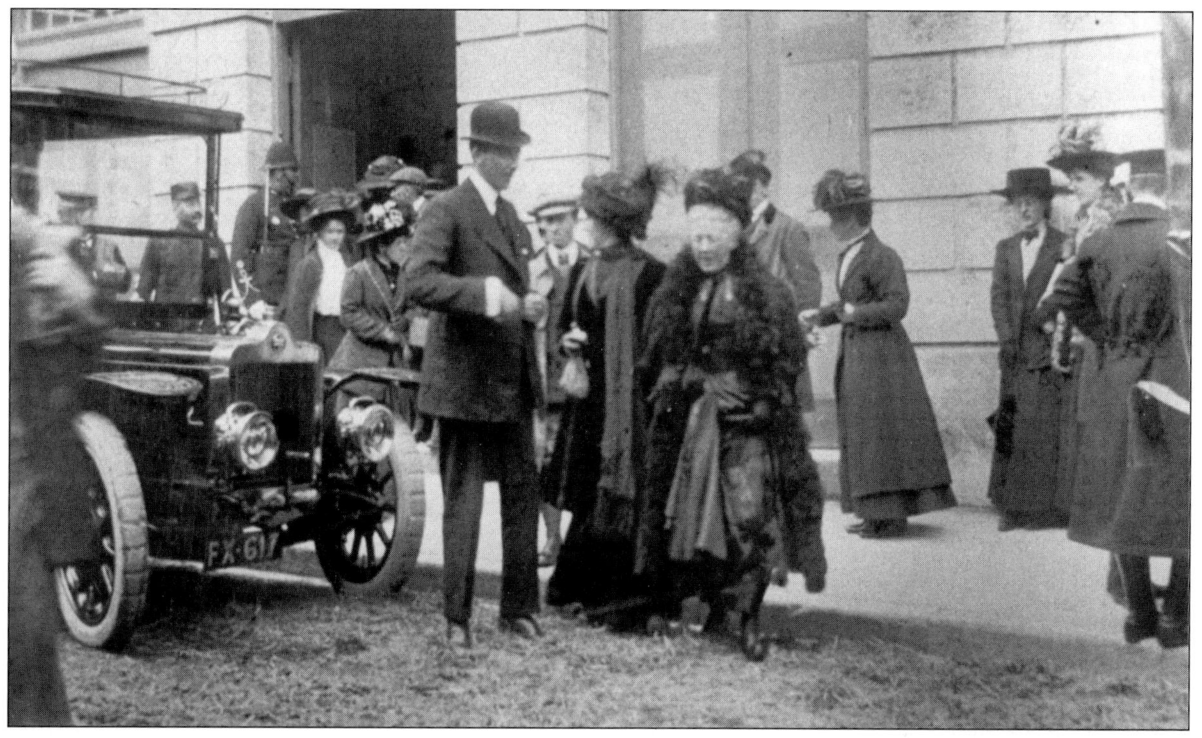

A stressful day for Lady Wimborne (centre) *at Shire Hall, Dorchester, her son's winning result in the first election of 1910 having been successfully contested.*

Lady Wimborne and sons Freddie and Ivor at one of the declarations in the double elections of 1910.

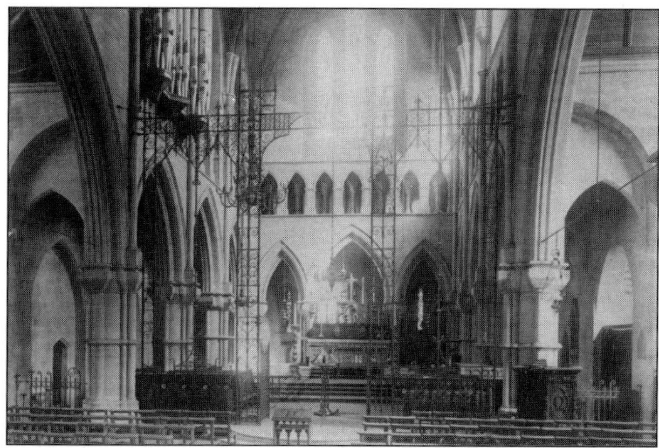

Elaborate wrought-iron rood-screen and Victorian Early English style arches and colonnades in St Peter's Church at Parkstone, looking eastwards into the chancel and glimpsing the organ (top left) *given in 1888 in memory of Revd S.E. Pontifex.*

Cottage at Darby's Corner, the turning for Broadstone, which has become a roundabout.

Where Dorset met Hampshire, at County Gates, in 1905.

A pedlar beside the bollards in Barber's Piles (centre), *looking south-eastwards from West Quay Road to the tower of St James's Church, in about 1915.*

Boats and play at Sandbanks in 1904.

Poole's historic tendency to Puritanism reasserted itself in 1913, when an alliance of Nonconformist aldermen, councillors and magistrates led a rates strike – refusing to pay local property taxes – in protest at the introduction of Anglican religious instruction into state schools. Opt-outs were conceded for conscience cases.

Describing the Fish Shambles on the eastern quay as 'insanitary and unsuitable for the demands of the present time,' the Town Council decided to demolish and rebuild it, at a cost of £734.10s.0d., as estimated by builders E.P. Pearcy, of Parkstone. In November 1913 work began on the replacement, in blue and red Staffordshire engineering bricks with locally-made terracotta and tile dressings. A bell turret was added, and an eight-day copper clock fitted to face the main length of the quay from the western gable, there being 'no public clock in that part of the town.' The bell, which had come from the earlier building, was traditionally rung to alert the town to the arrival of cheap fish when shoals of mackerel and sprats were brought ashore.

The Fish Shambles had an office and 20 shuttered stalls inside a rectangular building 63ft long by 26ft wide. In each of the end walls were ten more open stalls, while the long sides of the building sported verandahs, to shelter fishermen and sailors. The new building was opened for business in May 1914 by Mayor G.C.A. Kentish.

✦ CHAPTER 14 ✦

War and Want

Granny Cousins, last of the Old Town's knockers-up, on call at dawn to wake workers.

Harbour boatman Benjamin Pond in the 1920s.

One of the better aspirations in that last summer of peace, which ended on 4 August 1914 as the lights went out all over Europe – to paraphrase Foreign Secretary Sir Edward Grey – began with the purchase of a house in what was then Sandy Lane. In what is now Canford Cliffs Road, known as Compton Acres and boasting the finest collection of urban gardens in the land, Thomas William Simpson had arrived. His was the idea of creating 'a necklace of interlinking private grounds', while Bob Boothby later helped in realising their vistas and variety. They decided on separate themed designs and plantings, of which the inspiration for the architecture and flora would be drawn from all corners of the globe, from Rome to Tokyo. Delayed until after the Armistice, work began on the £200,000 project in 1919.

With all his energies put into the design of the gardens, Simpson never moved into his new house. Instead, as he recalled at the start of the next war, the plantings were intended to block any sign of surrounding suburbia, with Brownsea Castle the only building in sight:

> *What strikes the visitors to the gardens of Compton Acres is their entirely restful dignity and peace, even as much as their colourful glory. It is difficult to realise that they are but a comparatively recent evolution from wild moorland to sylvan walks, smooth lawns, noble terraces, lily ponds, fountains and tumbling rills usually found only in gardens of great age. In this year of grace 1939, I am impelled to carry my memory back*

Between the wars, Thomas William Simpson set about linking a series of themed gardens in Canford Cliffs by creating Compton Acres.

over at least half a century when, with my brothers, I was wont to chase the elusive lizard and butterfly over this very same spot.

At the outbreak of what was to become the First World War Poole had a total of 62 fishing boats registered to the port under the Merchant Shipping Act of 1894 and carrying the identification letters 'PE'. They totalled 373 tons and were worked by 130 men and boys. The port also had 61 registered sailing and steam vessels totalling 1,740 tons.

Volunteer soldier Lieutenant Sidney Clayton Woodroffe VC (1895–1915), from Branksome Park, was posthumously awarded the Victoria Cross, the nation's highest award for valour, for an action with the Rifle Brigade on the Western Front. The announcement was made on 6 September 1915.

The Navy's armed trawler HMT *King Heron* was driven on to the ledges off Old Harry Rocks during storm-force winds on 13 November 1915. Poole's lifeboat *Harmar* had to make two attempts to reach the vessel due to a heavy sea and surging tide. Another naval trawler towed her upwind so that the lifeboat could lift off the ten sailors, and then re-attached the line to take *Harmar* back home to Poole.

On 22 October 1916, the Royal Navy drifter HMT *Fame* was blown on to the Hook Sands by a south-easterly wind. Seven sailors were taken off by the Poole lifeboat *Harmar* as the stricken boat rolled over and began to break up.

Herbert Carter, writing in 1916, records that sailing vessels formerly involved in the Newfoundland fisheries were still to be seen at Poole Quay, including one of only 80 tons. He also tells the story of the locally owned *Mountaineer*, which was found floating in the Atlantic in circumstances reminiscent of those of the *Mary Celeste*, the American brig, bound from New York to Genoa which, on 5 December 1872, was found in the North Atlantic by a British brig, her crew and the ship's boats missing but the vessel otherwise in perfect condition. Herbert Carter's story of the *Mountaineer*, almost identical, reads like a maritime myth. Although adamant that it was true, he failed to name any of the missing men:

One fine summer day she left Poole for Labrador. Some weeks later she was found with all plain sail set, almost within sight of the American coast, her galley fire still smouldering, a meal spread in the cabin, but with no soul on board. The mystery remains unsolved. Neither boat nor men ever reached shore, nor was any reason discovered for the abandonment of a well-founded craft which continued trading for many years after the incident.

Captain Freddie Guest of Canford, MP for East Dorset, became aide-de-camp to Field-Marshal Sir John French, commander of the British Expeditionary Force in France. Although he could not save his boss from Lord Kitchener's wrath and the butcher's bill that had been paid for the limited advances on the Western Front, in 1917, as Lloyd George's Chief Whip, Freddie was in a position to do a favour for his cousin, Winston Churchill.

Having lost the Admiralty portfolio as a result of the debacle following his Gallipoli landings in the Dardanelles, Winston could well have stayed out of Government indefinitely. Eventually, partly due to Freddie's insistence, he was back in the war as Minister of Munitions.

Then – like mother, like son – Freddie Guest was caught up in a scandal following revelations that honours were being sold. He was more than just naïve – as with his overturned election back in 1910 – believing his mother's maxim that everyone had their price, it never occurred to him that there was anything unusual in such a system. He then tried to form alliances with just about anyone who had a vote in the House of Commons – coalitions were variously suggested with Conservatives, Unionists, Asquith's breakaway Liberal faction and, failing all else, the Labour Party. When the press could no longer take this seriously, Freddie and a few friends bought the *Daily Chronicle* to turn it into a Liberal newspaper and provide themselves with a platform.

Being a port town, Poole found itself on one of the new front lines of the twentieth century when, during the winter of 1916–17, Admiral Henning von Holtzendorff turned his force of about 130 U-boats – only 60 of which were at sea at any one time – into a decisive weapon. By April 1917 they were not only responsible for sinking a total of 860,000 tons of shipping, but had forced hundreds of neutral merchantmen to stay in port, their crews refusing orders to sail. Oil tankers were a particularly attractive

Classes I and II of Branksome Heath School in Livingstone Road, Parkstone, in 1921.

and easy target, with the result that the Royal Navy's fuel supplies from Hampton Roads in the United States were reduced to such low levels that the battleships of the Grand Fleet were allowed to sail at full speed only in an emergency. Disguised Q-ships joined the hard-pressed destroyers in the Channel and nets were also laid in an attempt at preventing submarines operating between their home bases of Zeebrugge and Ostend and the main killing grounds in the South-Western Approaches. Only the deployment of convoy systems staunched the mass destruction.

Boat builders at Hamside included William Allen and Ashton & Kilner; R.A. Newman & Sons and Ephraim Smith were in Hamworthy; G.W. Bromby and the Dorset Iron Foundry Co. Ltd were in West Quay Road. The importance of shipbuilding was recognised in the middle of the First World War, in the winter of 1916, when 35,000 skilled workers were released from military service and brought home to the factories and yards. Plans for cruisers and battlecruisers were cancelled and their steel used to replace some of the losses in the merchant fleet. A total of 1,163,000 tons of 'derelict and obsolete vessels from harbours and roadsteads around the globe' were acquired and reconditioned, in an attempt at plugging other gaps. Despite such efforts, in which 'the booming waterfront at Poole' contributed as best it could, the shortages widened and worsened, a further four million tons of merchant shipping being sunk in 1917.

As a small-scale shipbuilding port, Poole also played a role in the conversion of drifters and trawlers into auxiliary Royal Navy minesweepers and wreck-clearing vessels. Bolson & Co. won an Admiralty contract to construct a steel lighter for carrying ammunition to ships in harbour and also, in August 1918, had the distinction of launching Britain's first ship built from reinforced concrete. In the words of the *Daily Mirror*, at a time when the German war effort was running out of steam, its sailors fearing they might be sacrificed to a lost cause, the new 'concrete fleet' would 'further dash the sinking hopes of the Huns'.

This and another concrete vessel, a tug, failed their sea trials and turned out to be the first of the few. Richard Blomfield, who arrived at Sandbanks from Wimbledon in 1918, remembered the naval gunfire rocking the windows that was immortalised by Thomas Hardy in his poem 'Channel Firing'. Wartime and postwar Poole experienced severe shortages, its population, tired and hungry from years of conflict, then suffering its worst losses as an influenza pandemic swept the globe in the winter of 1918–19, local victims including the editor of the *Poole and Dorset Herald* and his wife.

When Edward Patrick Morris, 1st Baron Morris (1858–1935), Prime Minister of Newfoundland, visited Poole to try to revive the long-distance fisheries, times had moved on. As Richard Blomfield puts it in *Poole Town and Harbour*: 'One might as well have tried to bring back the sailing ships too! There

Japanese warships put into Poole Quay after difficulties in towing a former German U-boat, in 1919, which they were escorting to the Far East.

was simply no longer any commercial incentive to base fisheries at Poole.'

An echo of past dangers came at dawn on 8 January 1919, when the lifeboat maroons signalled that the surrendered German submarine U-143 was aground on the Hook Sands, a southerly gale blowing onshore and waves breaking across the boat. U-143 was en route to Japan – a British ally in the First World War – as part of German war reparations. Travelling down the Channel, she had come into Poole Bay with engine trouble while her two escorts, the Japanese destroyers, *Kanran* and *Kashiwa*, stood by offshore, not daring to venture closer into disturbed and shallow waters.

From Portland the Royal Navy sent drifter HMT *Wild Oak* to give assistance, but her draught also proved too deep for making a close approach and in mid-morning she went into Poole Harbour to tow the lifeboat *Harmar* out against the strengthening gale and surging tide. They then had a mile to go before the crew could row towards the distressed U-boat, which was now being rolled by the rising water. Meanwhile, the tug *Commerce* approached from the east and prepared to pass lines to the submarine, for attachment by lifeboatmen. When these proved useless the destroyer *Kanran*, with stronger cables, also attempted an approach. By nightfall all efforts had failed but the Japanese crew aboard the submarine stubbornly refused to abandon the boat.

During the night another series of distress rockets summoned the *Harmar* westwards towards the harbour entrance, between the Hook Sands and Sandbanks, where the motor schooner *Zwaluw*, from Antwerp, had dragged her anchors and was being driven ashore towards Canford Cliffs. Hours were spent in saving her nine crewmen, who eventually reached Poole Quay at 03.30 hours on the morning of 9 January 1919.

By this time, still determined not to act on their own initiative, the Japanese seamen aboard the U-boat had at last made radio contact with Tokyo via the destroyers. On being told that drowning was not compulsory, the *Harmar* was recalled, although it was another 12 hours before the lifeboat – again towed by the *Wild Oak* – could go out again. The 28 submariners were taken off in fading light at 17.50 hours. One of the destroyers had entered Poole Harbour so that the men could be transferred in the calmer waters of Brownsea Road. As for U-143, she was pulled off by tugs after the gale had abated, on the next optimum sequence of tides, a week later. In vindication of German engineering she was undamaged apart from a few dents.

Russell-Cotes Nautical School, a Dr Barnardo home which trained boys for life at sea, had been established on a 34-acre viewpoint site at Constitution Hill at the end of the First World War. Endowed by the former mayor of Bournemouth, Sir Merton Russell-Cotes, on 8 May 1919 it received a royal visit from the Duke of York, later King George VI, who laid the foundation-stone.

Naval uniforms were worn on Sundays and

A field gun from the Western Front, standing as a war memorial in Poole Park in the 1920s.

practical maritime touches in the grounds included multi-mast flagpoles for the teaching of signalling and a 20ft high ship's bridge. Rocket-fired lifesaving apparatus and a make-believe wreck were used to teach shipwreck survival skills. There was also a large outdoor swimming-pool, cricket and soccer pitches, and 8 acres of vegetable allotments, used as a market garden.

On being demobbed, Cyril Carter (1888–1969) joined the family firm in 1920, with the result that three generations now sat around the boardroom table. Jesse, Charles and Cyril reorganised Carter & Co. Ltd, for trading purposes, as Carter, Stabler & Adams. Although 'CSA' in company shorthand, to 'both the trade and the public' they were known as Poole Pottery. They officially became Poole Pottery Ltd only in 1963, on what is now Dolphin Quay.

Moorland House at Broadstone, renamed Delph House, became the home of Miss Margaret Kennedy (1896–1967), who married David Davies in 1925. A county court judge, he became Sir David Davies (1889–1964), and served as a National Insurance Commissioner. In 1920 Miss Kennedy had given various parcels of land, for community purposes, as a memorial to those who died in the First World War, at a time when German prisoners of war were building a brick wall beside the railway path at Broadstone.

Margaret Kennedy was working on *The Constant Nymph* – made into a silent film by director Adrian Brunel – which immortalised the activities of bohemian artist Augustus John (1878–1961) and his entourage at Alderney Manor. This crenellated Victorian Gothic house, with 60 acres of grounds, stood on what is now the corner of Alderney Avenue and Ringwood Road, on the same side as St Barnabas Church, opposite Alderney Isolation Hospital. In 1911 Lady Wimborne, of Canford Manor, rented the house to John, whose wife, Ida Nettleship, had died in 1907.

Between here and his London studio, John painted many of his most famous canvases, including 'Spanish Flower Girl', 'Mother and Child', and 'Seraphilia', as well as finishing his acclaimed portraits of Lloyd George, George Bernard Shaw, Admiral Lord Jackie Fisher, Princess Marthe Lucia Bibesco of Romania and Thomas Hardy. On 21 September 1923 John met Hardy for lunch at Kingston Maurward House, Stinsford, where the aging author commented on his portrait: 'I don't know whether that is how I look, but it is how I feel!'

Local society was bemused by the Welsh impressionist artist. Resentment of his wartime pacifism became outrage at his multiplicity of lovers, as Augustus John and second wife Dorelia set the pace for the artistic milieu of the 1920s. Hedonistic debauchery around the bonfire, with John providing powerful solo performances of highwayman ballads, would continue until the sun came up over an orchard strewn with exhausted bodies. This frenetic lifestyle, as Christopher Wood noted in 1922, adversely affected John's work: 'He is unquestionably the greatest painter in England today, and if he hadn't drunk so much he would have been greater than Leonardo da Vinci or Michaelangelo.'

W.B. Yeats had a more positive view: 'He is himself a delight; the most innocent wicked man I have ever met.'

John's elder daughter, Elizabeth Anne 'Poppet' John (1912–97), who was born at Alderney Manor, posed with her sister, Vivien, for some of the most beautiful child portraits ever drawn. She went on to marry Derek Jackson in 1930, followed by Villiers Bergne in 1942 and Willem Pol in 1952.

The Constant Nymph, the best-selling novel of 1924, satirised one of the key members of the Alderney set, Dorelia's fancy-man, Henry Lamb, as the character Lewis Dodd, played on stage by Noel Coward in 1926. The sequel was *The Fool of the Family* in 1930. On Lady Wimborne's death in 1927 Augustus John's lease was terminated, Alderney Manor was demolished and the artist and his sycophants moved to Fryern Court, near Fordingbridge.

Another section of society also challenged the established order. What was later described as a 'Red mirage' of radicalism swept Europe after the Russian Revolution. Including near rioting by the unemployed and a strike by teachers, unrest at Poole caused a detachment of Royal Marines to be landed at Poole Quay, with a destroyer standing by offshore, to protect the Royal Naval Cordite Factory on Holton Heath.

A 'liberty march' through the High Street in July 1921 drew unemployed men. They gathered around a poster which paraphrased the famous words from a speech by David Lloyd George at Wolverhampton on 24 November 1918, adding a crucial question mark – 'A Land Fit for Heroes?'. They demanded free school lunches for their children and won their

The relaying of tramlines in the northern High Street in 1914, between Burden & Sons, grocers and wine merchants (left) *at No. 203 and the Port Mahon Castle* (centre right), *in a view westwards to Towngate Street* (centre).

Bournemouth tramcar No. 33, preparing to head for Fisherman's Walk at Southbourne – an hour away in the 1920s – from the extended tram system, seen from Holmes's Temperance Hotel, Joseph Gritten confectioner at No. 176 High Street, and Wallingford & Padley saddlers (far right).

case, by courtesy of Christian charity rather than state welfare, after intervention by the Guild of Hope.

Mrs Eileen O'Callaghan Foott and her daughters, Kathleen and Louie, moved to Parkstone after the First World War. Louie Foott (1894–1982), a spirited wartime member of the Women's Legion Motor Drivers, soon left home and fell in love with Sandbanks and a cabin she found beside the beach. From this shack she ran a fleet of Ford motor cars (named after Henry I through to Henry VIII and then after his six wives) in a taxi service which soon became the mainstay of Eugene Poulain's Haven Hotel and the peninsula's handful of wealthy residents. She regularly pulled delivery vans out of the sands 'as they became stuck whilst bringing provisions to the Haven Stores,' to quote her biographer, Alan Bennett.

Soon she acquired Shell petrol pumps and a Fiat coach, and ran a 'Gypsy Service' from a Romany camp beside Good Road, via Rossmore Road and Albert Road to Ashley Road shopping centre until, in 1928, as Rossmore Bus Co., she registered routes across Monkey's Hump and through Heavenly Bottom to County Gates. Mrs Louie Dingwall, as she became on marrying ex-soldier Archibald Dingwall, achieved the double feat of swimming across the harbour entrance to Shell Bay, and from Sandbanks to Brownsea Island. She later became one of Britain's most colourful racehorse trainers.

Harbourmaster Captain Hubert Ware Chislett, together with Warne Julyan, during his time as mayor in 1921, revived maritime beating-the-bounds ceremonies in Poole Harbour at locations including such deserted spots as Russel Quay beside the Wareham Channel at Arne, where boatmen 'had been accustomed to land freely for centuries'. A later chairman of Poole's Beating-the-Bounds Committee, H.M. Rigler, then a Sea Scout, recalled being one of the youngsters who were 'whipped across the hand' to impress upon them 'the lawful rights of the Port of Poole's citizens'.

Off Sandbanks, the Hook Sands continued to add to its succession of strandings, though most vessels floated free. The Belgian collier *Fernande* ran into the shoals in fog on 21 April 1921, but with the aid of two tugs and by using her own engines was able to resume a planned journey to Portland Harbour. Both the *Sidney* in mid-October 1922 and the *Pioneer* at the end of that month also floated free, though the latter was then beached and caught fire.

Ivor Churchill Guest, 2nd Baron Wimborne and 1st Viscount Wimborne (1873–1939), Freddie's elder brother from Canford, was reaching the peak of his political career. Having come early to high office, as Postmaster General in 1910 and succeeded his father in 1914, by the end of the decade he was His Majesty's Lord Lieutenant in a troubled Ireland about to face partition and civil war. In recognition of his efforts he was created Viscount Wimborne.

Returning to the home front, he was a spent force, though useful as a mediator between the National Government and the Labour Party in the negotiations that ended the General Strike in 1926. Hilaire Belloc immortalised poor Ivor and his mediocrity:

Grant, O Lord, eternal rest
to thy servant Ivor Guest.
Never mind the where or how
Only grant it to him now.

Moortown Aerodrome, a private airfield at Canford Magna, was established by Captain the Rt Hon. Frederick Guest PC, CBE, DSO, MP of Canford House. In 1921 he was appointed Secretary of State for Air, moving into Winston's seat as his cousin went another rung up the ladder to become Colonial Secretary. After giving up the aviation portfolio, Freddie continued to use his airstrip into the 1930s when he became a Squadron Leader in the Auxiliary Air Force, in an Avro DH9a with No. 600 (City of London) Bombing Squadron. Both Winston and Freddie became Conservatives, the latter being returned to Parliament for Plymouth's Drake division in 1935.

The Victory Palace cinema in Parkstone opened in 1921 with a contemporary newsreel showing the Turkish massacre of thousands of Armenians – genocide as recreation which was ahead of its time. On becoming the Regal, in 1937, starlet Marie Lohr was first through the door as Charles Laughton appeared on screen in 'Ruggles of Red Gap'.

Crime-writer Edgar Wallace (1875–1932), all-time master of the pure thriller, set his novel *Mr Justice Maxell*, published in 1922, in Branksome Towers at Branksome Park, which elegant home, together with its lodge at County Gates, the last vestige of the seaside estate – had been demolished in time for the centenary celebrations of Wallace's birth.

When Lady Wimborne moved to Merley House in 1923 Canford House was bought by the Church of England Trust and Canford School was founded by Revd Percy Warrington. Lady Wimborne's answer to the problems of the decade, culminating in the Great Depression, has echoed down the decades and was used to devastating effect in television's 'Days of Hope': 'How about emigration?'

The Poole Corporation Act of 1919 provided for the acquisition of Poole Bridge from its private shareholders, with a £16,000 deal eventually completed in 1923. Free passage across a toll-free bridge brought an additional commitment in its wake. The townspeople found themselves owning a poorly maintained structure that was overdue for replacement. This, it was estimated, would cost £33,591.

Another natural barrier was also receiving attention. Isle of Wight businessman Frank Aman bought Alum Chine Hotel, Bournemouth, and galvanised his sons – engineer Gerard and stockbroker Arthur – into

Newly operational ferry in 1926 crossing the harbour entrance from Sandbanks (right) *in a view north-west to Brownsea Island* (background).

The Floating Bridge and its chains, at Sandbanks, 1928.

A crane on the Hamworthy side of the water (top left) *with demolition of Poole Bridge in progress, in 1927, and aggregates piled on Poole Quay* (foreground).

reviving the scheme for a road link across the harbour entrance from Sandbanks to Shell Bay. Their influential patron was pioneer motorist John Walter Edward Douglas-Scott-Montagu, 2nd Baron Montagu of Beaulieu (1866–1929) , chairman of the Bournemouth–Swanage Motor Road & Ferry Co., incorporated by its own private Act of Parliament in July 1923.

The scheme took three years to come to fruition. Ferry No. 1 (until *Bramble Bush Bay* the ferries were unnamed), steam-driven with coal boilers, was such an instant success, when it came into service on 15 July 1926 that Gerard Aman adapted it to accommodate 15 cars at a time instead of 12. In two months it carried a total of 12,000 cars and 100,000 passengers.

The ferry company then proposed a suspension bridge, with a main span of 600ft, with cars rising to its 120ft road height via circular ramps. The plan, which went out for public consultation in 1929, received insufficient support and in 1930 was blocked in the House of Commons.

The third and present Poole Bridge – which opens from the centre – was constructed by Cleveland Bridge & Engineering Co. Work started in 1924 and the opening ceremony was performed on 9 March 1927. The town's dolphin emblem appears on each side, facing the waters, in Della Robia ceramic tiles.

With a pair of gold scissors Mayor Harry Carter cut a blue ribbon, speaking of his pride at having achieved 'the hopes and aspirations of all the years', reaching 'the high point of my mayoralty'. He and Alderman Ballard – 'who is responsible for this great undertaking' – had achieved free access between the town and its main industrial area. It was also 'a fine structure from the engineering point of view'.

Poole Town Band then led the crossing into Hamworthy with a procession of robed municipal officers, members of the Dorset Constabulary and

The borough coat of arms, featuring scallop shells and a dolphin in glazed tiles, to finish off the new Poole Bridge in 1927.

Fire Service, and what must have been every fit Boy Scout and Girl Guide in the borough. Construction workers had done themselves out of a job but could celebrate an accident-free project. Fog-horns blared and then the bridge mechanism clanked into action and its carriageway was raised to allow the passage of *Excel*, the harbourmaster's launch, followed by the lifeboat *Harmar*, and a flotilla of fishing boats, steam-tugs and rowing-boats. They circled Holes Bay at high water and retreated back through the opening just before time and tide trapped them on the mud.

'Up on the hill' was the name given to the shopping centre at Upper Parkstone by the populace of Lower Parkstone between the wars. It must have been in common usage as two of my informants, Jack Lawley and Harold J. Steele, each used it without a second thought.

In the mid-1920s a graceful older world reasserted itself in Poole Harbour. A fleet of Danish schooners, acquired by an Italian company, made regular visits to Poole for Purbeck ball clay and by 1933 *Fratelli Garre*, *Willi Taaks* and their sister ships were carrying 35,000 tons of clay a year to Civitavecchia, Leghorn and Savona.

On 21 February 1927 the *Daily Express* published allegations that explorer, author and lecturer Frederick Mitchell-Hedges (1882–1959) had staged a bogus highway robbery. Living at Bridge House, Sandbanks, he was said to have carried out the stunt 'to draw attention to a device known as the Monomark' with almost paranormal claims and 'gain himself fraudulent notoriety'. The headlines ran: 'Robbery on the Ripley Road. True story of the great midnight hold-up. A pure fake'. The incident was said to have happened on the night of 14 January 1927, when Mitchell-Hedges, with his driver Colin Edgell, were on a car journey from the National Liberal Club in London to their homes beside Poole Harbour. On the outskirts of Ripley, Surrey, they were stopped by a person who said a man was ill and in need of assistance. This, they claimed, was a trap. A skirmish then took place in which the attackers tied

Poole Bridge open for maritime use, seen from the quay in 1973, in a view to the south-west that includes Sydenham's timber yard (left) *and the twin chimneys of Hamworthy Power Station* (top right).

Banks Road, Sandbanks, was constructed between 1924 and 1926 in a scheme to relieve unemployment.

up the chauffeur with a rope before making off with Mitchell-Hedges's attaché case which, he said, contained 'four reduced heads of human beings' obtained on his travels, and various documents.

Mitchell-Hedges claimed to hold several world records for the capture of giant fish and to have discovered a new race of people in Panama in 1921. He credited himself with discovering the ruins of the vast Mayan lost city of Lubaantum in 1924. By accident, or design, newsworthy events seemed to follow him around – for example, as he arrived back at Paddington Station from Venezuela, a snake, 18ft 6ins long, escaped from his carriage. A *Daily Mail* reporter and Lady *[Richmond]* Brown were able to put it back in its box but when it eventually reached London Zoo seven men were needed to deal with it.

Mitchell-Hedges's financial affairs also attracted attention and he was declared bankrupt in 1912. As one might expect, his books, with such titles as *Battle with Giant Fish, The White Tiger, Land of Wonder and Fear, Battling with Sea Monsters* and *Danger My Ally*, were pure gung-ho stuff. Undaunted by his troubles of either 1912 or 1927 he was soon off again, to Central America in 1930, and Tanganyika and the atolls of the Indian Ocean in 1950.

An era ended on Brownsea Island in the mid-1920s with the death of Florence van Raalte, widow of Charles van Raalte, who had died two decades earlier. The new owner, Sir Arthur Wheeler (1860–1943) 'decided, in view of probable development on the island, to dismantle the castle.' The first stage, to empty the building, was carried out when a 2,714-lot country house sale took place in Branksea Castle over nine days in June 1927. A total of £22,300 was raised, the top price of 3,500 guineas being paid for the tapestry panel 'Winter', by French dyers Gilles and Jehan Gobelin and dating from about 1450, which had been illustrated in *Country Life*.

Branksome Chine in the 1920s, still a wild ribbon between the villas, before it was tamed and turned into a municipal park.

On 19 October 1927 the Prince of Wales – the future King Edward VIII – visited the town and placed a wreath on the war memorial, near the salt-water lake in Poole Park.

Informal parking arrangements among the cabins at Branksome Chine, including the thatched beach café (left centre), *when it was bought by Poole Corporation in 1927.*

Built in 1932, the solarium (near right) *at Branksome Chine, became the new beach café.*

Aristotelian translator William Adair Pickard-Cambridge (1879–1957) retired to Brimlands in Water Tower Road at Broadstone. He was from a musical family at Bloxworth, where he ensured the survival of old-style Christmas singing in St Andrew's Parish Church. His *Collection of Dorset Carols* was published in 1926.

The architect Elisabeth Whitworth Scott (1898–1972) was the daughter of surgeon Bernard Scott and a cousin of Sir Giles Gilbert Scott, designer of Liverpool Cathedral, while her grandmother was a sister of distinguished nineteenth-century architect G.F. Bodley. In 1928 Elisabeth, who went to Redmoor School in Bournemouth, won a competition to design the new Shakespeare Memorial Theatre at Stratford-on-Avon. As an example of English architecture it only served to prove how unimaginatively brick-work could be used, its existence and future still being in contention into the next century. Thankfully, Elisabeth Scott created nothing else of similar note and retired to Mount Pleasant Road in Poole.

From 1928 to 1934 Purbeck stone was carried along the Goathorn Railway by steam engines *Tiny* and *Thames* for building the Training Bank, a mile-long protective spit along the southern side of the Swash Channel. The trains comprised ten clay-carrying trucks, each of which held 3 tons of stone. From Goathorn Pier the loads were taken out at high tide and dumped from barges, on to the 10-ton blocks already laid, to form the core of the causeway. Devised to direct incoming tides into the harbour entrance to scour-out silt, this public works project provided jobs during the Depression.

Though intended to aid navigation, in November 1932 the Training Bank nearly claimed its first victim, the motor yacht *Glencora* from Southampton. Holed on running into the boulders, she sank in the shallows. The two crewmen climbed into the rigging, which fortunately remained above water, and spent most of the night there before being taken off by the Poole lifeboat *Harmar*, towed to the scene by Commander Charles Euman, the harbourmaster, in his motor launch.

The Wall Street Crash and subsequent Depression saved Branksea Castle and Brownsea Island from the development plans of owner Sir Arthur Wheeler, who sold the 600-acre property to Mrs Mary Florence Bonham Christie (1864–1961). For the islanders, however, relief was short-lived, and Mrs Bonham Christie, having decided to dispense with the services of the 20-strong community, embarked on a mass eviction which saw them departing for the mainland on the island's *Branksea* ferry-boat in 1929.

In 1929 the economic crisis also provided the opportunity for Poole Corporation to buy Branksome Chine and entomb its informal wooded gardens with concrete culverts and a municipal corporate identity. In 1930 the transformation was declared open by the Rt Hon. Margaret Bondfield (1873–1953). From a country cottage childhood in Chard, Somerset, she had worked her way through radical politics into an unlikely and unique position as the country's leading female trades unionist. As Minister of Labour, she was the first woman to sit in the Cabinet in Ramsay MacDonald's government.

A solarium, built beside the promenade and sands in 1932, failed financially and was turned into a beach café.

But for Margaret Bondfield and the influence of her male colleagues from the Labour Party's urban heartlands, Poole seemed set to become Dorset's Detroit, the Ford Motor Co. being keen to build its European 'Motown' at Hamworthy. Combined rail and sea access points were among the essential requirements and specifications included sidings, blast furnaces and a power station, with 'electric unloaders' for such raw materials as coal, coke and ore, which would arrive by ship at a harbourside

The Battrick family of Brownsea, on the eve of the island evictions in 1929, with Dorothy and Jack (centre) *sitting between parents Hannah and Freeland Battrick before their last journey on the boat* Branksea (offshore).

pier. At the centre of the visualised waterside complex, looking southwards to Arne and Purbeck, would be the 'administration block'.

The plan was scuppered, however, as far as Dorset was concerned. In 1930 the plant went to Dagenham Marshes, beside the River Thames, as a result of the introduction in Parliament of the Distribution of Industry Bill.

On 8 July 1930, between Holes Bay and Sterte Road, north-west of West View Road, the Sterte House estate was auctioned for building land. At that time the bay curved inland as far as the railway line to the north of White House Laundry, operated by Albert Fryer Roberts.

Branksome Gasworks Football Club, known as the 'Lights', fielded workers from Bourne Valley, Poole. Formerly based at Eastlake, Parkstone, their latterday home ground was beside Alder Road. The team, which played for the first 73 years of the twentieth century, over the winter season of 1929 made it through the Football Association's amateur cup competition to the final on 12 April 1930 at Upton Park – West Ham United's ground. Here their winning spree came to an end as they lost to Ilford.

That day the 'Lights' fielded George Joyce, Bob Saunders, Harry Cobb (captain), Frank Turner, Herbie Phillips, Tom Gillingham, Bert Smith, Tom Pettey, Percy Lovell, Harold Cornibeer and Cyril Tapper. Tom Pettey scored the only Branksome goal, bringing his total for the season to 60.

Novelist and dramatist Sir Hall Caine (1853–1931), whose home was on the Isle of Man, had an English residence at Branksome Park. World traveller Percival Christopher Wren (1875–1941) also moved to Poole, where this former British cavalryman and sometime trooper with the French Foreign Legion took advantage of the comparative peace of Westwood House, Talbot Woods, to complete the most famous of his novels, *Beau Geste*, in 1923.

Wren had a number of other addresses in the conurbation, including Frerem in Penn Hill Avenue, Parkstone (1924–25), Cintra, Ipswich Road, Westbourne (1927), and Marlborough Cottage, Marlborough Road, Canford Cliffs. In the mid-1930s he moved for the last time to the Cotswolds, to Amberley, near Stroud, in Gloucestershire.

Branksome Gasworks Football Club in 1929/30, when they reached the final of the English Amateur Cup, losing to Ilford at West Ham United's ground.

Researcher Brian Carter, who supplied this information, insists, incidentally, that Wren was born on 1 November 1875, not 1885 as given in biographical reference books.

The Municipal Buildings at Park Gates East, which occupy the traffic island between Commercial Road and Sandbanks Road, were the grandiose scheme of town clerk Charles Lisby and borough engineer and surveyor Ernest John Goodacre, with the support of Mayor John Arthur Rogers and his successor, Herbert Spencer Carter. Poole Corporation had bought the 3.75-acre site in 1923 for £4,400 – for which it had to get loan consent from the Ministry of Health against considerable opposition from Poole Ratepayers' Association and the National Citizens' League, this being £1,000 more than the district valuer was prepared to authorise. Preliminary architectural drawings were prepared in 1926 after Goodacre's appointment as borough engineer and the entire budget was £62,500.

Construction, by Branksome builders Whitelock & Co., began in the spring of 1931. Lord Mayor of London Sir Phene Neal laid the foundation-stone on 16 May 1931. Architectural concrete and reconstructed stone castings were produced by the Vinculum department of Tarmac Ltd at Ettingshall, Wolverhampton, and Crittall metal windows, made in Southampton, were used throughout. The imposing frontage faces the northern entrance to Poole Park, the two lofty main storeys displaying relatively restrained neo-classic lines. The central feature of the balcony, the arms of Queen Elizabeth I, who granted Poole its crucial charter, was surmounted by the town's arms in coloured faience produced locally by Carter, Stabler & Adams Ltd. Stone panels displaying historical events were designed by Percy Wise, headmaster of Poole Art School, in Mount Street. Inside, the central feature was a circular council chamber of 'majestic proportions' beneath a glass dome.

The Municipal Buildings were to transform the town's administration. The official opening, by the Earl of Shaftesbury as Lord Lieutenant for the county of Dorset, took place on the afternoon of 21 May 1932, a Saturday. Following the presentation of a bouquet to Lord Shaftesbury by Miss Denise Goodacre, the borough engineer's daughter, the Lord Lieutenant addressed the public from the balcony, after which those officials and contractors 'closely identified with the erection of the building' were 'presented to his Lordship'. In the evening there was dancing in Poole Park to music by Poole Municipal Military Band. The building was then flood-lit for two hours.

Municipal Buildings, built beside the northern gates into Poole Park (near right) *in 1931, drawn by Sheila Sturdy in 1949.*

Emily II *passing the Boat House at Lake in 1937.*

Though meetings were still held in 'smoke-filled rooms' there was now adequate air space between floor and ceiling. The opening of Hamworthy Park saw increased opportunities for outdoor air and exercise for the growing estates in the west.

Another of Ernest Goodacre's pet projects was the new solarium and café at Branksome Chine, which promised 'Continental sun-bathing' with 'two halls for ladies' and gentlemen's dressing accommodation' and a 'Vita-glass' sun lounge between them which guaranteed 'the full benefit of ultra-violet rays'. Above, there was to be space for 'concentrated' open-air sun bathing, on the flat roof.

Young people were also flocking to Poole for reasons of both sun and sentiment. In the summer of 1932, 500 Scouts were allowed by Mrs Mary Florence Bonham Christie to camp on Brownsea Island, to celebrate their silver jubilee.

It was the year in which Canford made its administrative exit after more than 1,000 years of recorded history. Poole, its upstart tithing incorporated as a borough in 1248 and given county status in 1559, had at last eclipsed its parent parish. The borough had already absorbed Branksome, Hamworthy, Longfleet and Parkstone. Under the Dorsetshire Review Order of 1933, Poole's boundaries were extended northwards to the banks of the Stour to take in the rest of the parish of Canford Magna, including Broadstone, but excluding parts beyond the river which went to Pamphill. In area the borough doubled in size to 24 square miles, while its population increased from 61,000 to 65,000.

Offshore, in 1933, along Poole Harbour's measured mile, Hubert Scott-Paine (1891–1954) seized the world water-speed record. As founder of the British Power Boat Co., in 1927, he designed, built and raced *Panther I* and *Panther II*, and then *Miss Britain I, II* and *III*. Scott-Paine then turned his talents to creating the first motor torpedo boat for the Admiralty and an equivalent high-speed air-sea rescue launch for the Royal Air Force. Involved in the flying and designing of aircraft and sea-planes since 1910, he had financed and built *British Challenger*, which had won the Schneider Trophy in 1922. Poole Harbour was adopted by the Royal Motor Yacht Club for both its racing and social activities.

In 1934, when Brownsea Island was swept by fire for three days, though it seemed that as well as the pine woods and rhododendrons, buildings at the eastern end would also be destroyed, the wind changed direction just in time. Clouds of smoke had reached Poole and the peaty marshland continued to smoulder for weeks. The experience was so traumatic for owner Mrs Bonham Christie that she banned all public access for the rest of her life.

Bacteriologist Major Sir Robert George Archibald (1880–1953) retired to Lowne Hame, Spencer Road, Canford Cliffs and in 1934 was knighted for a lifetime's services to medicine. Back in Edwardian times, with the Royal Army Medical Corps, he had made the tropics his speciality, and was seconded to the Sleeping Sickness Commission in Uganda. Military matters intervened and he was mentioned in despatches during the Blue Nile Operations of 1908 and the Mediterranean Expeditionary Force landings in the Dardanelles in 1915. From the Gallipoli diversion he returned to Africa, with the Darfur Expedition to Sudan, in 1916.

Staying on to continue his work, he made his name there soon after the First World War as director of the Wellcome Tropical Research Laboratories in Khartoum. He went on to run the Stack Medical Research Laboratories in 1928.

A different sort of contribution to world health was made by cigarette magnate Sir Ernest Wills (1869–1958). The director of Imperial Tobacco, based in Bristol, he had his great country home at Littlecote, Wiltshire, and seaside residences at Homestead and Bohemia in Banks Road, Sandbanks.

Evelyn Cecil, 1st Baron Rockley of Lytchett Heath (1865–1941), was elevated to the House of Lords in 1934 and took his title from a redbrick mansion built in 1875 at Lytchett Matravers with a quality view across Rockley Point. A barrister and Member of Parliament – continuously for 31 years – he was assistant private secretary to the Marquis of Salisbury, as Prime Minister, in his two administrations between 1891 and 1902. He then travelled the world both for the International Railway Congress and the Foreign and Colonial Investment Trust, making 'Empire migration' his special subject. At home he was a national expert on young offenders. His lasting contribution to Parliamentary life, however, was in manipulating Conservative reaction to calls for reform of the House of Lords. On arriving there he introduced the Life Peers Bill which passed its second reading in 1935.

Baroness Rockley, Alicia-Margaret Cecil, daughter of the 1st Baron Amherst of Hackney, shared her husband's colonial interests and for two decades was vice-chairman of the Society for the Oversea Settlement of British Women. On her travels she collected plants, the descendants of which flourish in Kew Gardens and Chelsea Physick Garden, which she helped found and then managed from 1900 until her death in 1941. She wrote standard works on the subject, from *A History of Gardening in England* in 1895, to *Wild Flowers of the Great Dominions of the British Empire* in 1935 and *Historic Gardens of England* in 1938, and in 1896, Lady Rockley had received the prestigious award of the Freedom of the Worshipful Company of Gardeners. For years it was said that Lytchett Heath was the place for some of the most interesting 'garden escapes' in the land.

Also overlooking the Wareham Channel, with views across Poole Harbour to Arne peninsula and the Purbeck Hills, the Boat House at No. 75 Lake Drive, Hamworthy, is a remarkable building dating from 1935. It is not a conventional boat-house at all, but rather a house that incorporates a ship which made a major mark on international travel. The Boat House was built around lavish panelling from the captain's quarters and three cabins of the 31,938-ton ocean liner RMS *Mauretania*.

Launched into the River Clyde from Swan Hunter's shipyard on 20 September 1905, she made her maiden voyage from Liverpool on 16 November 1906. In May 1908 she won the prestigious Blue Riband for the fastest transatlantic crossing from Europe to New York, lost it to the *Lusitania*, then regained it in September 1909, holding it until after the First World War. Later, at a more leisurely pace, the luxury liner of the Cunard fleet became known as 'The Grand Old Lady of the Atlantic'. She sailed for the last time to New York on 26 September 1934, the very day her successor slid into the Clyde – a new era dawned at the launch in Glasgow of the *Queen Mary*.

After her withdrawal from service in April 1935, the *Mauretania* was sold for scrap, first being stripped of her finery, of which the Boat House received the choice pickings. The house, behind big picture windows is a mass of luxury fittings, furnishings and port-holes. Maple wood from the drawing-room of a predecessor, the first great ship to be named *Mauretania*, is enriched with gilt-carved sea urchins, leaf courses, dishes and pans and ornamental hanging wreaths. Set into these panels are numerous mirrors and cupboards for books and china.

Flowing art-deco settee frames, with leaf-carved cresting rails and panelled ends, adorn the corners of the ground-floor lounge, which measures 30ft by 22ft and has panoramic views. The first owner of the Boat House was Lloyds broker Tom Cullen, who used it as a weekend retreat and sailed in Poole Harbour, in *Emily II*. His son, Peter Cullen, often came with his family, as did colleagues and friends. Housekeepers Alf and Alice Hatchard and family shared the building from the winter of 1935 through to 1951, apart from times during the war when there were fears of invasion, bomb alerts and preparations for D-Day.

Architecture was also flourishing on the islands. On an appropriately small scale, Mrs Ella Barratt had not only made herself comfortable on Green Island since 1922, reading her books and listening to gramaphone records, but had employed Fred Churchill to run a market garden. In the benign microclimate of the sheltered south-eastern corner of the island they created 'the best soil in Dorset', fertilised by seaweed dragged from the shore by a donkey. To everyone's surprise, despite surges of seawater, the largely landlocked harbour waters are well diluted by the River Frome. The combination made for a highly productive soil and produce included tomatoes, strawberries, raspberries and figs, as well as the Morello cherries flanking the path to Mrs Barratt's bungalow.

In 1935 her nearest neighbours, Lord and Lady Iliffe, were building a house on 35-acre Furzey Island. Designed by Sir Edward Maufe and intended for their daughter, its long verandah faced Green Island to the south-west. Maufe, the architect of Guildford Cathedral, showed a penchant for innovation in using modern materials including silicate blocks, a form of reconstructed granite, and window glass an inch thick.

During the evening of 16 September 1935 a south-westerly gale gathered force with its epicentre swirling around the usually calm waters of Poole Harbour. More than 40 vessels were lifted from their moorings and broke free. Almost all were unoccupied and later recovered from mud-flats and beaches, though two men trapped aboard the cutter *Foxhound*, from Bermuda, were taken off by rowing-boat, the Poole lifeboat *Harmar* having also been swept on to a sandbank, where she remained until refloated a few days later.

Such experiences heightened realisation that Backwater Channel and Holes Bay, forming the innermost northern arm of the harbour, formed a safer place for 'parking boats', the only access point being through Poole Bridge. W.E. Cobb created Cobb Quay and what is now a marina behind Woodlands Avenue at Hamworthy. There the suburban streets protected the pontoons and slipways from the prevailing south-westerly winds and even an easterly gale only has a mile in which to ruffle the water as it approaches from Sterte. By 1980 there was berthing for 700 yachts, plus space for 550 to be laid up ashore, with all necessary chandlery and repair facilities for vessels of up to 100 tons.

Sail and yacht clubs were also functioning on a grand scale in the mid-1930s. The editions of *Kelly's Directory* compiled in 1934 and 1939 list half a dozen operating in Poole Harbour (names of secretaries given in brackets):

East Dorset Sailing Club, Sandbanks Road, Parkstone (C.O. Haythorne and A.J. Adam)
Hamworthy and Bournemouth Sailing Club, Harbour Road, Hamworthy (K.M. Morgan)
Harbour Yacht Club, Salterns Way, Sandbanks Road, Parkstone (unspecified)
Parkstone Sailing Club, Weston's Point and Sandbanks Road, Parkstone (H. Keene)
Poole Yacht Club, 120 High Street, Poole (J. Kerlin)
Royal Motor Yacht Club, Florinda (moored 'clubhouse' yacht), Poole Quay (Miss E. Pearson and F.S. Webber) and then also premises at Sandbanks, built 1935 (S. Dagg, manager)

By this time publican John Henry 'Harry' Davis, born in 1874, had become Poole's champion life-saver of the twentieth century, 32 people owing their lives to him. Harry Davis moved on from seafaring to being mine-host at the Jolly Sailor on the quay. On one occasion, although suffering a recurrent bout of malaria, he heard cries for help and jumped into the sea to rescue a drowning boy. This gallantry was witnessed by the author Arnold Bennett (1867–1931), who wrote to the mayor of Poole that 'not only did Mr Davis rescue the lad from the water, but he applied the proper means of restoration of breathing in a very able manner and with rapid success.' Asked how he came to be such an accomplished swimmer, the hero replied:

All I remember about it is that when I was a kiddie standing on the Quay, a lad pushed me into the water. It frightened me so much that I struck out with my arms and found I could swim. I was a natural born swimmer!

Brigadier-General Henry Huntly Leigh Malcolm (1860–1938) retired to Glenmorag in Haig Avenue, Canford Cliffs, at the end of the First World War. He began his military career with the 42nd Royal Highlanders in 1879 and had a distinguished service record across the African continent, serving at the Battle of Tel-el-Kebir in Egypt, where he was 'twice wounded' in 1882, before recovering to sail with the Nile Expedition of 1884–85, and receiving two mentions in despatches in the Boer War at the turn of the century. He went on to command troops in Ceylon and took a brigade across to France with the British Expeditionary Force of 1915.

His would have been a quiet retirement but for the activities of his daughter who grabbed headlines as 'air-girl' Miss Betty Malcolm (1913–36), burned to death when her aeroplane crashed into a hangar at Alicante, Spain, in January 1936, where she had been preparing for an attempt on the solo record for the flight between England and Australia. Betty's mother, Mrs Edith Malcolm, put the family's grief into words for the *Daily Mail*:

I was afraid that Betty would kill herself, but she would not listen. She pointed to the splendid flights she had made all over Europe since she learned to fly about three years ago, and said she was determined to become famous. Betty would rush off at a moment's notice without telling anybody where she was going and, with only a few things flung hastily into a suitcase, disappear in her plane across the Channel for weeks on end.

Mining engineer Professor Sir John Cadman (1877–1941), of the Wych, in Panorama Road, Sandbanks, was created Baron Cadman in 1937. During the First World War he was a member of the Chemical Warfare Staff and the Trench Warfare Committee. In the 1920s he became the Government's Consulting Petroleum Adviser and was chairman both of Anglo-Persian Oil and the Iraq Petroleum Co., as well as serving on numerous royal commissions and the Television Committee of 1934.

National events from this time also left their mark on local streets. Evidence of the great constitutional crisis of the century, resolved by the abdication of King Edward in order to marry divorcee Wallis Simpson, can be found between Poole and Canford Cliffs. Although cylindrical Post Office pillar-boxes bearing the insignia of Edward VIII are a rarity because his reign was so short, the suburb of Lilliput, which was being developed in 1936, has two.

Bournemouth and Poole shared an epidemic in the autumn and winter of 1936. It began in August when an outbreak of pyrexia – an unidentified fever – was reported from Durley Dean Hotel and households in prestigious West Cliff. More than a 100 people were admitted to hospital in the two towns with what was then identified as 'suspected enteric fever'. Medical opinion then gave it the more ominous title of 'paratyphoid'.

Worse followed. On 24 August 1936 laboratory tests confirmed it as the real thing – typhoid – and the number of cases soared to 700, the disease infecting residents and visitors alike.

With all cases seeming to come from homes and hotels supplied by Froude's Dairy from The Triangle in Bournemouth, who supplied 10,000 households, suspicion fell on the milk. When their equipment and hygiene was found to be blameless, the trail was narrowed to an unpasteurised supply, in particular to milk collected from Merley where, on 8 September 1936, a farmer's wife became dangerously ill and died from typhoid. Dr Vernon Shaw, who himself died three months later from unrelated causes, traced the bacillus to a stream on the farm into which sewage had seeped from a drain at Merley House.

Dr Shaw had found the source. When the 16 members of the household were examined, the carrier was identified as the owner of Merley House, Captain Angus Valdimar Hambro (1883–1957), who had travelled extensively in the tropics. Educated at Eton, he had played golf for England and had been Member of Parliament for South Dorset from 1910 to 1922, serving as Parliamentary Private Secretary to the Minister during the closing stages of the First World War.

A total of 51 people died during the epidemic and those survivors who had become carriers were not released from isolation hospital for more than a year. Typhoid bacilli continued to be found in samples from Poole's sewers into the 1960s and was also found alive, at post-mortem, in the lower intestines and gall-bladders of elderly carriers who had died from other causes. Few in Bournemouth and Poole needed to be persuaded of the wisdom of changing to bland but safe pasteurised milk. The story is also a cautionary tale for our times, showing that even in the clean-living country houses of Dorset the perils of the past can still return to haunt us.

One of the greatest improvements in domestic life for women during the twentieth century, equal in its way to female suffrage, was the implementation of the Midwifery Act of 1936, under which such boroughs as Poole had to establish a midwifery service, paying off the 'Mother Gumps' who had traditionally attended at births. Doctors, though sometimes booked, were more often than not absent from the home delivery, Poole's only public pre-natal service being a clinic with one case worker run as a charity by the dynamic Lady Ommanney.

The new publicly funded Ante Natal Clinic of 1937 provided free maternity packs of sterile accessories and arranged daily visits from a qualified midwife, six of whom were appointed initially, with a further four joining as the scheme advanced. Cots were available on loan and a doctor could be called if necessary, the fees being met by the borough. Then, as now, premature births were prioritised and, if necessary, those mothers visited several times a day. Puerperal fever was a major threat to life in the last decade before the widespread application of basic hygiene practices, and the reason why giving birth in hospitals – where bacteria flourished – was regarded as much more hazardous than home delivery.

Some eminent Europeans arrived in Poole as the war clouds gathered over their home countries. Eddie Frater, returning to England in 1937 from his adopted Czechoslovakia, went into partnership with K. Guttenstein to found Loewy Engineering, originally in Branksome Park, which expanded greatly on moving to Wallisdown Road and was bought out by Tube Investments in 1960.

Intellectuals were also fearful of the future. Leading Dutch playwright Jan Fabricius (1871–1964) came to live in Broadstone, at Caesar's Camp beside Roman Road, in 1938. Although he took British nationality and remained here for the rest of his life, his reputation at home remained as illustrious as ever, the Queen of the Netherlands representing the nation when she attended his funeral in St John's Church, Broadstone.

The dramatist's Broadstone neighbours included wireless announcer Stuart Hibberd and the young Richard Todd (born 1919), who had entered the theatre in 1937 and served in the Parachute Regiment for the duration of the Second World War. It is therefore appropriate that his best known film, from 1962, is *The Longest Day,* which relived the Normandy landings. Christopher Chataway (born 1931) was another local thespian, with the Broadstone Players, before being distracted by athletics and politics. He briefly held the 5,000m world record, in 1954, before becoming one of the first reporters for Independent Television News.

Medical care in the community expanded into other areas, the clinic at Burley Towers offering appointments with a chiropodist and other specialists. Red Cross volunteers prepared patients for treatment and a cleansing room was provided for old people who had no bathroom or who were incapable of bathing themselves. The home help system followed in 1939, with an advertisement for six workers, and the clinic was particularly proud of its 'Blitz Squad', sent into the filthiest of homes with mops and disinfectant. Every other street had its hermit, or recluse, living in extreme cases in large houses that were falling apart and surrounded by impenetrable bushes and trees. In the worst cases there would also be dozens of feral cats.

On 12 January 1939 Poole received a new lifeboat to take over from the *Harmar,* credited with having saved 60 lives during her 40 emergency launches. Her replacement was a 32ft motor vessel built by Groves & Guttridge of Cowes, Isle of Wight. She cost £3,337, which was met by a bequest left to the Lifeboat Institution by Bournemouth benefactor Thomas Kirk Wright, in whose memory she was named at a ceremony on 7 June 1939. Meanwhile, on the morning of 22 January 1939, she saw her first service action when the motor launch *Snapper*, making for Southampton and seen to be in difficulties in a heavy sea off Boscombe Pier, was towed back to Poole by the new lifeboat. Though smaller than her predecessor, the *Thomas Kirk Wright* was an advanced Surf-type inshore vessel with watertight compartments and 83 air-pockets, with a crew of 15 and a range of 44 miles.

'Follow me' signal from a duty operations officer in his launch in Poole Harbour to a Sunderland flying-boat from Calcutta as she taxis to her mooring buoy in 1945.

Swimming training at Sandbanks for newly enlisted Army personnel in the summer of 1940.

A British Airways stewardess accompanying comedian George Formby and actress wife Beryl Ingham as they depart from Poole for the Far East to perform for the troops with the wartime Entertainments National Service Association (ENSA).

✦ CHAPTER 15 ✦

Flight and Fight

Both Henry Harbin School and Kemp-Welch School opened in 1939. As ominous skies gathered over a Europe heading for war, offsetting the political optimism over the airwaves and in the newspapers, there was a graphic reality on the streets and in the playgrounds, where millions of children were competing to collect Wills and Capstan cigarette cards on 'Air Raid Precautions' and the set from Player's of 'Aircraft of the Royal Air Force'. Jack Skinner (born 1921) was collecting the latter at Hamworthy in 1938.

'At that time I never envisaged that by 1943 I would have flown five of them,' he told me at his Queen's Road home, in Poole, 60 years later. Another significant set for him was 'Modern Naval Craft', produced by Player's in 1939. By the end of the year, Britannia still ruled the waves but was facing challenges. The series included both the German pocket-battleship *Admiral Graf Spee* and the British cruiser HMS *Exeter*. Another Hamworthy lad, Revell White, Jack's closest friend, served on the *Exeter* as a gunner during the Battle of the River Plate.

Thousands of children began arriving in Poole, as the London & South Western Railway system became the main conduit for the evacuation of the cities. Bombing, as the cigarette cards predicted and Poland had shown, was inevitable in this war. Everyone, of all ages, had been issued with a gas mask. Overloaded with pupils, the schools had to run a shift system, and it was not unusual to see classes held outdoors in playgrounds and playing-fields.

Southampton, with liner-sized docks and the Supermarine aviation factory which produced the Spitfire, was regarded as a prime target. Besides its children being evacuated to Poole, the war also brought flying-boats to Hamworthy, as Poole Harbour became Britain's major civilian international aerodrome for the duration of the conflict. In August 1939 Imperial Airways and British Airlines were amalgamated to form the British Overseas Airways Corporation. Its chairman, John Reith, had been the founding director-general of the BBC and, until his creation as 1st Baron Reith of Stonehaven in 1940, was Southampton's Member of Parliament . The sea-based fleet of Short C-class Empire flying-boats, with their support facilities, operated from Hythe and Calshot on Southampton Water.

There they not only had to compete for space with ocean-going merchant ships and liners but also battled with difficult cross-winds in an inflexible stretch of water which required south-easterly take-offs. With the possibility of air attacks from the Luftwaffe the Air Ministry decided to disperse flying-boat operations westwards to the quieter and more benign meteorological conditions of Poole's inland sea. Requisitions followed fast, including Salterns Pier and the club-rooms of Poole Harbour Yacht Club, which became the Marine Terminal, while Harbour Heights Hotel was the rest and recuperation centre for pilots and crews.

GJX was the radio pundit code for Poole Airport. The letters, in Morse code, interrupted a continuous tone, at 30 second intervals, and were broadcast from a mobile aerial during wartime. Then, in peacetime, the signal was broadcast directly from the Marine Terminal. The BOAC offices were at No. 4 High Street, Poole, which became Airways House from 1940 until 1948.

Water runways – called 'trots' – were marked out by lines of tyres and extended from the Wareham Channel, between Hamworthy and the Arne peninsula, to Brownsea Roads anchorage between the island and Sandbanks. The war stopped all scheduled transatlantic services planned for January 1940.

A pair of Poole-based flying-boats, *Cabot* and *Caribou*, seconded by BOAC to 119 Squadron at Invergordon, were sunk by the Germans in Bodo fjord, Norway, on 4–5 May 1940. In another action, Flight-Lieutenant Peter Slade Joliffe from Poole was shot down and killed over Norway. That month Hitler marched into the Low Countries, bringing down the Chamberlain Government in London – replaced by Winston Churchill's coalition – and sending 3,000 refugees streaming down the English Channel in an armada of small boats. The Royal Navy shepherded them into Poole Harbour, where Brownsea Island was used as a reception centre.

Pleasure craft from Poole and Weymouth joined Operation Dynamo, in which 330,000 soldiers, two-thirds from the British Expeditionary Force and the remainder French, were taken off the sands of Dunkirk. Among the flotilla that headed to Dover from Poole were Harvey's *Ferry Nymph* and *Southern Queen*, Davis's *Felicity* and *Island Queen*, and Bolson's *Skylark VI*, *Skylark VIII* and *Skylark IX*. Poole lifeboat *Thomas Kirk Wright*, which also assisted in the Dunkirk evacuation, was able with its shallow draught to go in close to the beaches and survived shore-fire from Germans positioned only 40yds away.

As for Poole's fishing fleet, which also turned out in response to the Admiralty's appeal, it was

Model of one of the first self-righting lifeboats in the Maritime Museum and a lifebelt from the Dutch Prinses Juliana, *which was blown up in the Swash Channel, off Sandbanks, by a German mine in June 1940.*

summarily rejected by the Navy. Much to their chagrin, the fishermen, who considered themselves to be Poole's elite seamen, were sent home from Kent by train and their vessels impounded for future reserve use – they were deemed unsuitable for the mass evacuation that was grasping victory from the jaws of defeat. *Island Queen* and *Southern Queen* were sunk off Dunkirk and *Skylark VI* was abandoned but later recovered and returned to Bolson's Shipyard at Poole for refitting as an air-sea rescue vessel.

The war then came to Poole Bay itself. The *Prinses Juliana*, outward bound, was the first boat to be blown out of the water off the Training Bank. Then, on 13 June 1940, the *Abel Tasman*, returning empty from the evacuation of St Valerie-en-Caux, was blown apart in the Swash Channel – together with her crew of 11 from the Royal Navy Volunteer Reserve – when she hit a German mine. Some of these lethal weapons were magnetic, of a new C-type which the Admiralty were keen to investigate.

Harold Cartridge, sent out with the Poole fishing boat *Smiling Through*, secured and towed a mine on a 700-ft line from the Bar Buoy to the sandy shallows of the Milkmaid Bank off Studland. Here, however, 'it decided to explode, though without delivering more than a shock and a shake to Cartridge and his craft.'

Among those who dodged the Luftwaffe and the mines to reach sanctuary at Poole Quay was the London coal-barge *Alnwick*, which arrived on 17 June 1940 carrying from Cherbourg a cargo of fully-armed British soldiers. Crowds cheered and tossed the men packets of cigarettes and bottles of beer. 'Are we downhearted?' one shouted, prompting the determined reply, 'No!' An infantryman of the 51st Highland Division played the bagpipes as remnants of the 154th Infantry Brigade stepped ashore.

A flying-boat flown by Captain Donald Bennett – later Air Officer Commanding Bomber Command's Pathfinders – carried out the daring rescue of General Wladyslaw Sikorski (1881–1943), the commander of Free Polish Forces, who was plucked from the chaos surrounding the fall of France. On 21 June 1940, having landed on a coastal lake at Biscarrosse, south-west of Bordeaux, within sight of German armoured vehicles, Bennett took his highly important cargo to the comparative safety of Poole Harbour. The only fire that came in their direction was from a British cruiser in the Bay of Biscay.

Poole was now in the front line as England stood alone. Local anti-invasion defences were taken over by the 69th Infantry Brigade, comprising the 7th Battalion, the Green Howards, the 5th Battalion of the East Yorkshire Regiment and the 6th Battalion of the Green Howards, who were dispersed into the Dorset countryside. An 'anti-tank island' of pillboxes, concrete obstacles, minefields and flame-traps was established around the Old Town. Obsolete tanks from the First World War, previously positioned as symbolic gate guards or as museum exhibits at Bovington Camp, were also dragged back into service as stationary pill-boxes. One was the tank named Little Willie – as inspected by King George V – which held a machine-gun post at the main cross-roads in Ashley Road.

Check-points were set up and passports issued as the Dorset coast became a 'defended area'. Anti-ship guns of the 554th Coast Regiment of the Royal Artillery, with its headquarters at Conningtower in West Road, Canford Cliffs, were emplaced at Brownsea Island, Hengistbury Head, Mudeford and Swanage. An examination ship was positioned in the Swash Channel and boom defences guarded the harbour entrance. There was also an old steamship, *Empire Sentinel*, packed with explosives as a block-ship, and boats H1 to H6 of the Poole Harbour Patrol. The garrison commander, based in Bournemouth, controlled all troops between Upton and Highcliffe.

Float-plane training for the Fleet Air Arm moved from Calshot on Southampton Water to Poole Harbour, and the Royal Navy Seaplane School was established at Sandbanks.

Prime Minister Winston Churchill, accompanied by General Sir Alan Brooke as Commander-in-Chief Southern Command, visited the Dorset invasion coast on 17 July 1940, inspecting units at Branksome Chine and Sandbanks. Churchill laid bricks at Branksome as a practical contribution to the defences taking shape there. Brooke, unimpressed by the state of readiness in the face of an imminent German invasion threat – which he privately described as 'our nakedness' – nevertheless made such a favourable impression on Churchill that just two days later he was promoted to Commander-in-Chief Home Forces.

Southern Command's Camouflage School was in Shore Road at Canford Cliffs. Signs were being taken down across the land in order, it was hoped, to confuse German invaders, and elaborate artistry disguised the new defences. Position was the first consideration – the Shore Road war-works was set into the sandy cliffs without breaking the skyline – but imaginative murals could do much to hide those defences built in conspicuous or exposed locations. Pillboxes were painted to look like advertising hoardings, parked vans, petrol pumps or thatched cart-sheds.

One of the most noticeable removals of signage, taking away the capital letters of the place-name but leaving the word 'HOTEL' over the entrance, took place at the Sandbanks Hotel. Such buildings were being requisitioned by the military all along Dorset's holiday coast. Sandbanks Hotel became a training centre, each part of the grounds being used for something specific, from motor engineering classes in the car park and press-ups for physical training in the tennis-courts, to bayonet charges into dummy Germans hanging from ropes in the sand-dunes.

The Hamworthy Engineering Co. Ltd, to give it its full title, founded at the start of the First World War, celebrated its silver jubilee at the beginning of the Second World War. Based in Harbour Road, and holding the wonderful word 'Inventions' as its telephonic address, the firm manufactured air compressors, engines, generators, pumps and winches. Its wartime role included, in readiness for a German invasion, the fixing of demolition charges to its own factory floor and to other strategic installations and facilities around Poole.

Essential VIP trips across the Atlantic resumed on 4–5 August 1940 when the Empire flying-boat *Clare* took off for America. At the same time the *Clyde* headed for Cape Trafalgar and then turned south, to Leopoldville in the Belgian Congo, carrying Colonel René de Larminat, who was organising the repossession of French Equatorial Africa. The Free French Army, led by General Carretier, walked back to power and took Brazzaville by complete surprise. The coup was of practical as well as strategic significance – the seizing of the Vichy-controlled French colonies of the Congo basin enabled resumption of the Empire flying-boat services from Poole to South Africa, India, Malaya and Australia.

Air Ministry Under-Secretary Captain Harold Balfour travelled on the *Clare*'s second wartime crossing, on 14 August 1940, and while in Washington bought the three huge Boeing 314 Clipper flying-boats which were to transform air links from Poole.

A German mass bombing force of 220 attacking planes and their escorts devastated the Bristol Aeroplane Co. works at Filton on 25 September 1940. On the way home, however, the raiders were harried by the Royal Air Force, one Heinkel force-landing at Studland and another crashing into Underwood, a large house in Westminster Road at Branksome Park. All but one of the five crewmen were killed. When they were buried in Parkstone Cemetery, next to the graves of British seamen, the *Poole and Dorset Herald* was outraged that 'Nazi murderers and British heroes' had been placed side by side. A week later the newspaper felt utterly let down by one of its readers: 'Someone has put flowers on the grave.' On 12 August 1942 Underwood was again hit by a bomb. A block of flats, called Chatsworth, stands on the site.

Two Spitfires of 152 Squadron from RAF Warmwell were scrambled on 14 November 1940 to intercept a single German reconnaissance aircraft which had crossed the Channel. They spotted it at 24,000ft above the Blackmore Vale, on a course for Yeovil or Bristol. The Junkers Ju 88 turned southwards, to return to France, as the Spitfires attacked. A burst of fire from the rear gunner shattered the windscreen of Pilot Officer Eric 'Boy' Marrs, who had to withdraw from the fray, as Sergeant-Pilot Albert 'Bill' Kearsey kept 'going hard at it'.

The Junkers lost height and became a fire-bomb over Poole. One of its four crewman baled out but

Grounded BOAC Speedbird G-AGEW Hanwell *on the hardstanding at wartime RAF Hamworthy.*

his parachute failed to open and he fell through the roof of Kinson Potteries. The aircraft hit the ground near the end of Herbert Avenue and exploded 50ft from a cobbler's shed at Witcombe in Ringwood Road. Boot repairer Leonard Stainer and his family had narrow escapes, as did their neighbours, while a night-time fire watcher was trapped in his bed by collapsing roof debris. Part of the fuselage ended up on top of Moore's Garage.

Sidney Sherwood and his sons, Fred, Henry and Robert, were killed when a parachute mine landed on their home in Fancy Road, Newtown, in the early hours of 16 November 1940. There were other blasts in Haskells Road, and Cynthia Road, causing serious injuries. Though she was able to shield her daughter, Molly, Mrs Lilian Kitkat was badly lacerated by flying glass and lost an eye.

On the night of 9 January 1941, leaving their garden air-raid shelter after an incendiary attack, Frank and Henry James of Canford Cliffs were blown up by the next wave of German bombers. The attack caused numerous blazes, including a fire at the Fire Station, and left a total of 248 houses badly damaged though only one, a bungalow at Lilliput, was completely gutted.

On 1 February 1941 a new sound came to Poole Harbour – that of the Twin Wasp engines of Pratt & Whitney – much louder than the familiar Bristol Pegasus 9-cylinder radial engines of the Short Empire flying-boats. The arrival was that of the first long-range American-built Catalina flying-boats, named *Guba*, for the BOAC service across the Bay of Biscay to neutral Portugal. The following night was the brightest of the war, a deliberate breaking of the black-out as petroleum slicks pouring from the beach at Studland were ignited in an anti-invasion measure. Partly a test, there was also a psychological motive for the conflagration, German soldiers being particularly fearful of being burned alive.

Having logged 4,000 miles of civilian flights, the Empire flying-boat *Clio* took off from Poole for Belfast on 12 March 1941. There she was fitted out with armour plating, bomb-racks and four machine-gun turrets. Given the military number AX659, she was handed over to 201 Squadron in Scotland and patrolled the Iceland Gap until her loss on 22 August 1941.

The vital Royal Naval Cordite Factory on Holton Heath, making the propellant for shells, was a long-standing target for German bombers, which at night were drawn off course by a decoy factory on the opposite side of the Wareham Channel in heathland at Arne. The trains servicing Holton Heath were another attraction for the Luftwaffe. One, known as the 'Glamour Puffer', carried the workforce of young women to and from Poole and the Bournemouth conurbation.

At 17.19 hours on 21 March 1941, a Friday, the train pulled out of the Holton Heath Station on the homeward run. Just as it crossed Rockley Bridge, heading towards Hamworthy Junction, a stick of six bombs straddled the embankment beside the harbour backwater and blew out all the windows of the ancient non-corridor 'bird-cage' carriages. The train, reaching a semi-protected stretch of sandy cutting, came to a halt and waited for more of the same. The enemy aircraft did not return and the train was able to draw into the platform. Apart from severe fright none of the passengers suffered anything worse than minor cuts.

The air-raid siren having sounded at Branksome almost every day for a month, at lunchtime on 27 March 1941 it was business as usual at Bourne Valley Gasworks. Two bombs from a single enemy aircraft, aiming for the railway viaducts, fell short and landed on the gasworks, the first blowing up the stores and the second smashing through the upper storey above the canteen, where it became wedged, protruding through the ceiling, to the horror of those seated beneath. With only a matter of seconds to begin evacuating the crowded tables before a delayed-action fuse activated the bomb, 33 people were killed. They were named as:

Sidney James Allen (aged 57) of 16 Methuen Road, Bournemouth.
Walter Frederick Bacon (aged 52) of 143 Rosemary Road, Parkstone.
Charles Reginald George Badcock (aged 35) of 17 Washington Avenue, Bournemouth.
William Martin Barnes (aged 37) of 305 Columbia Road, Ensbury Park.
Leonard Reginald Bartlett (also known as Ridout, aged 43) of 5 Alton Road, Wallisdown.
Leslie Norman Batchelor (aged 14) of 52 Kingswell Road, Ensbury Park.
Arthur Luke Brewer (aged 46) of 69 Alton Road, Wallisdown.
Archibald William Cherrett (aged 38) of 158 Kinson Road, West Howe.
Andrew Collin (aged 45) of Mantonville, Dale Road, Parkstone.
Arthur George Dennett (aged 43) of 25 Granville Road, Parkstone.
Leonard George Derryman (aged 43) of 114 Howeth Road, Ensbury Park.
Charles Edward Edmonds (aged 63) of 443a Poole Road, Branksome.
Frederick George Graham (aged 33) of Palatine, Somerby Road, Oakdale.
Cyril Owen Hatch (aged 19) of 58 Braidley Road, Bournemouth.
Ernest Stanley Heath (aged 46) of Cosy Cot, Cornwell Road, Parkstone.
Frederick Arthur George Horne (aged 16) of 68 Kinson Road, Wallisdown.
H.P. House (details unrecorded).
Thomas William Hustings (aged 50) of the Knoll Laundry, Corfe Mullen.
Edward Barren Keffen (aged 57) of 73 Churchill Road, Parkstone.
Frederick Stephen Loader (aged 35) of 37 Denmark Road, Poole.
William James Notley (aged 20) of Roslyn, Foxholes Road, Parkstone.
William Walter Notting (aged 16) of 16 Sandbourne Road, Longfleet.
Charles Edward Phair (aged 36) of 323 Ringwood Road, Oakdale.
Frederick Edwin Randall (aged 63) of 5 St Clement's Road, Parkstone.
Norman John Shirley (aged 17) of 139 Portland Road, Winton.
Joseph Marfleet Short (aged 23) of 15 Oakdale Road, Oakdale.
Reginald Albert Dash Sparkes (aged 43) of Peny Bryn, Roman Road, Broadstone.
Henry George Stovey (aged 63) of 1 Hope Cottages, Archway Road, Branksome.
William George Webb (aged 63) of Mosul, East Howe Lane, Kinson.
Austin George Joy Wilcox (aged 50) of 243 Kinson Road, East Howe.
Edgar George Bennett Wilcox (aged 19) of 243 Kinson Road, East Howe.
Herbert Stephen Williams (aged 26) of 21 Victoria Avenue, Winton.
Herbert Charles Young (aged 60) of Khyber, Wharfdale Road, Parkstone.

On the evening of 10 April 1941 Canford Cliffs and Parkstone suffered a major incendiary raid. Phosphorus devices were blazing on a number of big buildings including Canford Cliffs Hotel, Tennyson Buildings in Ashley Road and Pinewood Laundry at Pottery Junction. Paintings were removed from the blazing hotel as, with no water coming from the hydrants, it was abandoned to the flames. Canford Cliffs had, in fact, come off lightly, as the following morning the Royal Engineers defused eight unexploded bombs in Haven Road.

Empire flying-boat *Cordelia* flew off to Short's factory in Belfast for military conversion on 16 April 1941. Her new life started with 119 Squadron on anti-submarine depth charge trials but, destined to come back to Poole, she returned to BOAC's civilian fleet in September 1941 and, having survived the war, was scrapped at Hythe in 1947.

Cloak and dagger came to Poole in April 1941 when, under the command of Captain Gustavus March-Phillips, an operational guerrilla unit of commandos was formed. Known as the Small Scale Raiding Force, its headquarters were at the Antelope Hotel in the High Street. Instructed by Winston Churchill to create 'a reign of terror down the enemy coast', they were soon trying to do just that. On 13 September 1941, however, a cross-Channel raid by No. 62 Commando was foiled by the Germans as they attacked the Atlantic Wall. Though the commandos managed to kill the seven-man patrol that intercepted them, the wooden boat they were using was hit by a shell as they withdrew. March-Phillips was among those killed.

In the teeth of German airborne invasion in May 1941 Poole flying-boats *Cambria* and *Coorong* evacuated 469 of the 30,000 British, Australian and New Zealand troops garrisoning the island of Crete. A total of 13 flights were made across the Mediterranean from Suda Bay to Alexandria. Back at home, flying-boat *Maia* – formerly used as the pick-a-back mother ship for a Mayo Mercury float-plane – was sunk in Poole Harbour on 12 May 1941. Her attacker, a Heinkel He.111 bomber, was brought down off Arne by anti-aircraft fire.

Take-off for an Empire, westwards into the wind off Brownsea Island, as a Poole-based BOAC flying-boat heads for Africa and Asia at the end of the Second World War.

The town fought back by funding a £5,000 Spitfire – named *Villae de Poole* – which was handed over to the newly formed 411 (Royal Canadian Air Force) Squadron on 22 June 1941. The fighter had a short war, crashing in a blizzard at Chester on 7 December 1941 and killing Sergeant-Pilot S.W. Bradshaw.

The Biting Plan for a commando raid across the Channel to seize the aerial, receiver and cathode-ray tube of a German Wurzburg radar apparatus was organised by Combined Operations, based at Anderson Manor, near Bere Regis, and at Poole. With Acting Admiral Louis Mountbatten in overall command, the raiding party of 'C' Company, 2nd Battalion the Parachute Regiment was led by Major J.D. Frost with technical expertise provided by Flight Sergeant C.H. Cox.

On 27 February 1941, jumping from 12 Whitley bombers, they landed on a 400ft clifftop near Bruneval in deep snow to take their objective completely by surprise. Wurzburg, operating at a wavelength of 53cm (between 558 and 560 mHz), was a coast defence system with a range of about 40km and its parabolic aerial had shown up on air reconnaissance photographs of clifftop fields at Cap d'Antifer. The equipment was dismantled for removal by landing-craft from the beach below and, on being brought back to England, its components were examined by the Telecommunications Research Establishment at Worth Matravers.

The western end of Brownsea Island rocked to countless explosions in the early hours of Whit Monday morning, 25 May 1942. Many of the incendiaries dropped by German Pathfinder bombers aimed at a new Coastal Command flying-boat base at RAF Hamworthy, had landed, with some high explosives, in Rockley Road, Coles Avenue and Hinchcliffe Road. Many bungalows were destroyed and five civilians killed, the fires being extinguished just in time for the newly completed 'Starfish' apparatus of a Major Strategic Night Decoy to come into operation across the water on Brownsea Island.

With design consultants provided by the pyrotechnics department at Elstree Studios the combination of wood, coal, and paraffin, plus water, produced white-hot flashes just like those of bursting bombs which lured the 55 enemy aircraft to unload 150 tons of high explosive harmlessly onto the uninhabited western extremity of the island. That night only one bomb found a military target, making a direct hit on Poole's Home Guard company headquarters in Lindsay Road and causing the unit's first death from enemy action, with the loss of Private W.J. Griffiths.

During the Second World War the Brownsea Island decoy saved Poole and Bournemouth from a total of 1,000 tons of German bombs.

The German raid on Hamworthy and Poole in the early hours of 4 June 1942 was partly thwarted by a different sort of decoy. Incendiaries from the Pathfinder bombers started heath fires in heather and gorse near Rockley Point. Although these drew many of the bombers westwards from the urban area, they nearly created a different disaster.

One of the bombs that exploded on Ham Common ruptured a giant tank of 100-octane aviation fuel concealed in the old clay pits at Doulting's Pier. As a million gallons of fuel formed lakes across the wasteland and the area filled with the stench of fumes, fire teams could only pray that no one dropped a match, let alone a bomb.

Across the water, the swift ignition of half a ton of waste shell-propellant at the dummy factory on the Arne peninsula also drew bombers away from the Royal Naval Cordite Factory on Holton Heath. Inspection by daylight revealed 206 craters, while it was estimated that 50 or more bombs had also fallen in Poole Harbour.

Some of the bombs did find the urban areas of Hamworthy and the densely-packed Georgian terraces of the Old Town. Opposite the Parish Church a grocer's shop was hit, as was Yeatman's Mill on Poole Quay. Bolson's Wessex Wharf shipyard store in Ferry Road at Hamworthy was gutted. The yard manufactured harbour defence motor launches, twin-screw vessels, 72ft in length. Of the 26 people taken to Cornelia Hospital, three died from their injuries – the 55-year-old fire-watcher at Bolson's, Louis Pittwood, six-year-old Victor Park and Mrs Florence Duffy of Green Road.

The Royal Navy's Headquarters Ship for the port, HMS *Sona*, berthed beside Poole Quay, was sunk by a bomb which dropped through the funnel and buried itself in the mud beneath the hull. As it failed to explode, sailors were able to escape by scrambling up the quayside.

On 11 September 1942 a single German bomber ignored the Bofors guns at Canford Cliffs to come in from the bay and drop a stick of bombs that killed six people in adjoining roads at Parkstone. The dead were Revd William Russell and his son Frank at 11 Marlborough Road, Mrs Winifred Phillips and her 11-year-old daughter June at Woodgrove, in Bournemouth Road, Mrs Annie Watts at 12 Earlham Drive and Lois Millard of 453 Poole Road.

In February 1943 the rifle-range shooting by the 2nd Special Services Brigade on Canford Heath was being supervised by author Evelyn Waugh (1903–66), who a year before had published *Put Out More Flags* and *Work Suspended*. As staff officer to Acting Admiral Louis Mountbatten, Commander of Combined Operations, he played a part in assault landing training on Brownsea Island and Studland beach. The confinement and constraints of war perhaps proving conducive to suave sensuality rather than sophisticated satire, Waugh's novel *Brideshead Revisited* appeared in 1945, while his experiences with the Royal Marines were the basis of his *Sword of Honour* trilogy.

From November 1942 onwards aircraft cannon-fire could be heard incessantly on the heathland north of Poole, in the vicinity of Fleet's Corner. The noise, however, came not from the sky but the ground. The local munitions factory, in Soper's Lane at Creekmoor, made the 20mm Oerlikon machine-guns fitted to the latest version of the Spitfire and other fighters. Production continued around the clock and test firing was carried out every day.

On 21 March 1943 Sunderland flying-boat T911 of 461 (Royal Australian Air Force) Squadron was wrecked off its base at RAF Hamworthy when a night flight was aborted and it ran into mud-flats. The squadron, which carried out Coastal Command patrols against U-boats in the English Channel and South-Western Approaches, had 'UT' as its code letters. On 23 March 1943 a civilian Catalina also crashed in Poole Harbour, killing three crewmen as she ran into a mass of flotsam. Ironically, the BOAC flying-boat had just completed an otherwise uneventful return from Lagos, Nigeria, before taking off on the fateful training flight.

Repainted with the white and blue roundels of South-East Asia Command, BOAC Catalina flying-boats *Altair* and *Vega* lifted off from Poole Harbour on 17 April 1943 bound for Trincomalee, Ceylon, where they were handed over to the Royal Air Force. The Sunderland flying-boats of 461 (Royal Australian Air Force) Squadron were also on the move, from RAF Hamworthy to Pembroke Dock, in South Wales.

From May to December 1943 the BOAC trots, hard-standing and workshops at Hamworthy were shared with 210 Squadron of the Royal Air Force, whose military Catalinas carried the squadron code letters 'DA' and operated long-range anti-submarine patrols for Coastal Command.

Among those who received bad news from overseas in May 1943 was Captain Angus Hambo of Merley House. His only son and heir, Major Robert Hambo, born in 1911, was mortally wounded whilst serving in a reconnaissance regiment of the 8th Army in Tripoli.

A Dutch craft, the *Leny*, was blown up by a mine in the Swash Channel on 23 June 1943. Only two of her crew were rescued.

One of those heroes who thrilled the nation with daring exploits in desperate times, Major Geoffrey Appleyard of the commando unit from Poole was listed missing, presumed dead, on 12 July 1943. The 26-year-old officer – known in Combined Operations as 'The Apple' – was deputy commander of the 2nd Special Air Service Regiment, operating in the Mediterranean as the 1st Small Scale Raiding Force, which was taking part in the Allied invasion of Sicily.

Pilot Officer Duff died with seven of his crew when he brought a military Catalina of 210 Squadron back to Poole at 04.25 hours on 24 August 1943. Descending into thick fog, the flying-boat missed the clear waters of the trots in the northern harbour, instead ploughing into the cord-grass salt-marshes around Round Island. Only four crewmen were rescued from this tragic training flight.

On 28 August 1943 one of the most decisive flights of the Second World War touched down in Poole Harbour. The BOAC Boeing Clipper *Bristol*, landing at 14.00 hours, brought home the Secretary of State for Foreign Affairs, Anthony Eden, together with General Sir Alan Brooke, Chief of the Imperial General Staff, and Admiral Louis Mountbatten, Chief of Combined Operations.

They had returned across the Atlantic from the Quebec Conference, which set the location and

Turn-around checks from BOAC maintenance staff for a Short Sunderland Empire flying-boat on arrival in Poole Harbour in 1946, after the forward gun turret (centre left) *has been removed from the bow.*

timetable for launching the Second Front, the decision having been taken to land on the beaches of Normandy, thus forgoing the need to capture a port by towing across prefabricated concrete caissons – confusingly codenamed Phoenix and Mulberries – to make two instant harbours. The provisional date for the invasion of Europe was 1 May 1944.

The next VIP flight of major significance was in another direction, on 11 October 1943, when Field-Marshal Sir Archibald Wavell, Viceroy of India and Supreme Commander Allied Forces in South-East Asia, lifted off for Bombay.

At 20.00 hours on the evening of 28 January 1944, two disorientated Glider Regiment pilots of the British 6th Airborne Division, relieved to spot a double line of flares, proceeded to bring their Horsa down on to the flare-path of the western trot in the waters of Poole Harbour off RAF Hamworthy. The wet nature of the landing came as a surprise.

A BOAC Sunderland flying-boat, waiting for take-off, radioed for a launch to come and rescue the pilots, whose glider, which had been released on a night-flying exercise, was then towed from the Wareham Channel by a BOAC pinnace and berthed on the slipway at Hamworthy.

Round-the-clock production in the three yards of shipbuilders J. Bolson & Son Ltd at Hamworthy meant the completion of one assault landing-craft every day for the biggest armada in history, planned for D-Day. Lines of these LCAs were tethered in Holes Bay. The yards, including the Skylark Shipyard in Harbour Road which had previously made yachts and other pleasure craft, also produced Air Sea Rescue speedboats and Royal Navy minesweepers, as well as carrying out repairs on tank landing ships.

With their work practices revolutionised, one squad being made responsible for the complete production of a single vessel, Bolson's attained their premier position as the largest manufacturer of assault landing-craft in Britain.

On the night of 23 April 1944 houses were damaged and three people killed in an incendiary attack on the northern parts of Poole and at Broadstone. The dead included 50-year-old fire-watcher Arthur Martin and, though most of the blazes were soon brought under control, 13 people were left homeless. Fire-fighting had become particularly dangerous, as recalled by B.T. Condon in 1987:

I was home on leave from the RAF. When the sirens sounded I decided to go down to the ARP Wardens' Post in the annexe of the Broadstone hotel to see if I could be of any help to my former ARP colleagues.

My way took me past Willis the builders' merchants shop, at the side of which was the lorry entrance to their paint store behind it. There I saw Mr Bryant, one of Willis's lorry drivers who lived nearby, and he asked me for my help in reeling out a small hosepipe to fight a fire which had started in the paint store.

Imagine our dismay when we found that we could get no water through the tap, presumably because the Fire Service were using all the mains supply elsewhere. Some of the bombs dropped on that occasion were the fiendish Ibsens [Incendiary Bomb Separating Explosive Nose]. *These were designed with a delayed action fuse on an explosive device which separated from the fire-bomb on impact and exploded shortly afterwards with the object of maiming anyone fighting the fire caused by the incendiary.*

Poole's direct connection with military flying-boat operations ended on 30 April 1944 with the closure of RAF Hamworthy, which became a key part of the concentration area for invasion preparations. Service flying-boats could still be refuelled and oiled in Poole Harbour by BOAC staff. On land, the Sheriff of Poole handed over the Guildhall for use as an American Red Cross Club. This offer of 'ye olde ancient monument' was gratefully accepted by Clarence C. Cline of the United States Embassy in Grosvenor Square.

On 6 June 1944 a fleet of 60 cutters from the United States Coast Guard, comprising Rescue Flotilla 1, sailed from Poole Quay in support of the invasion of Normandy. The 83ft boats, built entirely of wood and crewed by a total of 840 personnel, were credited with saving the lives of 1,437 men and one woman during the Battle of Normandy.

On 23 July 1944 a Mosquito fighter-bomber of 408 (City of Edmonton) Squadron, on a low-level daylight flight over Poole, crashed 200 yards west of Alder Road Drill Hall. It appeared to have been pulling out of a roll across Wallisdown when a wing struck a chimney in Mossley Avenue. Though there was only slight damage to the house, the aircraft exploded shortly after hitting the ground and Pilot Officer Bowhay and Pilot Officer Taylor, of the Royal Canadian Air Force, were killed.

That July an American Liberator bomber hit Furzey Island when it crashed in Poole Harbour, with the loss of all its crew. In August three naval ratings were killed and six injured when ammunition spontaneously detonated in a landing-craft berthed at the HMS *Turtle* shore-base in Poole Harbour, destroying the vessel and damaging nearby buildings.

On 22 September 1944 British VIPs returning from the Ottawa Conference flew back into Poole Harbour aboard a BOAC Boeing Clipper. The party included Chief of Imperial General Staff Sir Alan Brooke, First Sea Lord Admiral Sir Andrew Cunningham and Chief of Air Staff Sir Charles Portal.

A Poole refuse disposal stoker, working at the town's incinerator, literally had a close shave – a superficial face wound – on 30 October 1944 when a cartridge clip exploded in his furnace. The incident highlighted a serious danger and the public was warned to be more careful when disposing of explosives. As well as personal ammunition and trophies there were quantities of unexploded ordnance around those areas of the heath and harbour where wartime training had taken place. Most of the anti-invasion coastal minefields were also still in place.

Given its connections with South-East Asia, Poole's big victory celebrations were reserved for VJ Day, celebrated through the night of 14 August 1945. Parkstone's principal party was held on Constitution Hill, accompanied by flags, fires and fireworks, leading the *Poole and Dorset Herald* to make comparisons between 'Darkest Africa' and 'Peaceful Parkstone'. It was also a time for missing those who would not return. Historian Harry Smith lamented the loss of three of the boys from South Road Boys' School who had helped him excavate Roman Hamworthy between 1926 and 1934 – Flight-Sergeant Ralph Puckett and Flight-Sergeant John Lacy of Bomber Command and Lance-Corporal George Shorto of the Royal Corps of Signals, the latter killed while on manoeuvres in Ulster.

BOAC flying-boats were soon involved in the repatriation of prisoners of war from Japanese camps, the first touching down on 18 September 1945 amid enormous Press interest in the men's sensational stories of degrading and inhuman treatment. Mayor Mervyn Wheatley stood at the top of the steps on Poole Quay to shake hands and welcome them back to dear old Blighty. Postwar reconstruction was now the theme, newly-knighted town planning expert Professor Sir Patrick Abercrombie having co-operated with local architect Miss Elisabeth Scott and Clough Williams-Ellis of Portmeirion fame in drawing up plans for the Bournemouth conurbation. Poole Chamber of Trade, though generally backing such 'progressive proposals', correctly feared that under Clement Attlee's Labour administration the Board of Trade would revert to the stance it had adopted in Ramsay MacDonald's time, that of favouring traditional industrial centres.

Gas engineer Dr Frederick Dent (1905–73), who became assistant director of the Gas Research Board at Poole North Works in 1941, continued in the job until 1952. Dr Dent, who lived in Panorama Road at Sandbanks, advocated the production of synthetic rather than natural gas and pioneered a process of hydrogenated coal and oil in fluidised beds. He was also the first to produce catalytically gasified methanol. As a member of Parkstone Sailing Club he competed in X-class events for over 20 years before buying *Blue Jay*, the 42ft yawl which in 1967 took him into his retirement on Malta.

Immediately after the war, in 1945, James Pitman,

Civilian BOAC flying-boat G-AGJN Hudson (left) *and military UT-G of 461 Squadron* (right)*, with RAF roundel, on their postwar moorings in Poole Harbour.*

managing director of the *Poole and Dorset Herald*, bought Delph House at Broadstone, where he had the estate wall completed, bringing it alongside Golf Link Road. Sergeant Joseph Davies VC retired to Parkstone.

On 13 March 1946 Poole's public health officer, George Chesney, sent a confidential letter to all doctors within the hinterland of Poole Airport, the flying-boat base in Poole Harbour being the major national terminal for the repatriation of troops, prisoners of war and expatriates from India and the Far East. To add to the physical and mental traumas of what had been a long war, sometimes involving inhumane and brutal incarceration in forced labour camps, the returnees were often regarded as potential pariahs. With ships also arriving at Poole from the Far East, 'imported smallpox' was the subject of George Chesney's letter, from the Municipal Buildings:

During the past three weeks four ships from the East have arrived at British ports with cases of smallpox on board. From these ships, up to the present, 19 contacts have arrived in Poole and been placed under surveillance.

The disease, no respecter of medical qualifications, was as likely to prove lethal to those tending the sick:

A medical orderly nursed a case of Asiatic smallpox. It was then found that the orderly, who was himself well vaccinated, had evidence of recent mild attack of the disease. From this incident two cases of haemorrhagic smallpox developed, both of which were fatal.

Chesney also warned local doctors that 'modified smallpox' should be considered in evaluating apparent cases of chickenpox in persons recently returned from the East, and that any case of 'indefinite illness' in such people or their families should also be kept under observation. As well as bringing the threat of smallpox, passengers were arriving within the incubation period of typhus fever, cholera and plague. 'These diseases should be borne in mind', the medical officer warned.

In the spring of 1946 pleasure trips resumed from the temporary landing stage at Bournemouth Pier, which had been 'broken' to prevent its use by German invaders. 'Any more for the *Skylark*?' was the traditional cry, the boat being Bolson's *Skylark-6* from Poole. Newly reconditioned, she 'looked a picture', according to newspaper reports. The second day's boating, on 21 April 1946, saw *Skylark-6* crowded with '60 to 70 passengers' as the two crewmen took her on a 'trip round the bay' just before two o'clock that Sunday afternoon.

Just 15 minutes later the engine failed and the boat became waterlogged, drifting three-quarters of a mile off Alum Chine. There, a beach-hut owner, his binoculars trained on the becalmed boat, saw a man jump off and raised the alarm, which spread like wildfire along the length of Bournemouth beach as thousands watched from the cliffs and the remains of the pier. Jake Bolson, the boat's owner, leaving Poole with one of his men and six buckets, 'saved the situation by keeping the boat high enough out of the water until the rescues were effected.' On being asked to explain why the boat was leaking, Jake Bolson replied:

Jet age endurance test for the RAF Meteor being refuelled by a Lancaster tanker, over Holes Bay (left) *and a half-built Hamworthy Power Station* (centre right), *south-eastwards to Sandbanks* (below fighter) *in 1949.*

> *It's a mystery to me. I cannot for the life of me explain how she came to be holed. I cannot see how something going wrong with the propeller shaft could let the water in.*

No one could have foreseen the disaster which unfolded when the *Skylark-6* was taken in tow by a motor launch. As the bailing ceased the pleasure boat 'half-capsized and then sank'. Amid much panic, with seats and life-rafts thrown overboard, dozens found themselves clinging for their lives, their watches stopped at 2.15. Fortunately the water was calm and all the passengers were rescued by the armada of small craft already swarming around the *Skylark-6*, including a yacht, a BOAC flying-boat launch from Poole Harbour and at least two rowing-boats, each manned by teenage boys. When 20 tried to crowd into one boat a girl fell back into the sea only to be rescued a second time, alive but shivering alarmingly.

Several families, separated during the rescue operation, had an anxious hour or two before they knew everyone was safe. Among those most worried were Mr and Mrs W. Rexworthy of Dalkeith Avenue, Bristol, whose three young children were aged ten months, two years and three and a half years respectively. Mrs Rexworthy, as she told the *Bournemouth Daily Echo* about the rescue, recalled a *Titanic*-like cry of 'women and children first':

> *I handed my baby and the boy to someone on a raft. I was thinking all the time, 'Where has my baby gone?' It was a most desperate worry. Everyone was screaming. We threw everything overboard to try and lighten the boat. I lost my bag and my purse with my money. My husband was one of the last off the boat, and we did not find each other again until we got ashore. I was picked up by a rowing boat. When someone handed me my baby on Bournemouth Pier a policeman kindly took charge of it until we got back on the beach.*

The policeman had taken the baby because the pier presented an obstacle-course of broken stumps and temporary gangways. Despite the tearful reunions and general good fortune of the passengers, a 26-year-old member of the crew was found to be missing. The body of Reg Kent, who had fallen overboard, was picked up by a rowing-boat and put ashore at Alum Chine. By the time the Poole lifeboat,

The end of an era. The hulks of Solent-class flying-boats Solway (left) *and* City of Liverpool (right) *beached at Lower Hamworthy in 1959.*

the *Thomas Kirk Wright*, arrived there was just one man, drifting on a life-raft, to be rescued. He was duly grateful.

The psychopath Neville Heath (1917–46), having carried out a brutal murder in Notting Hill, went to Bournemouth, where, under an assumed name and rank almost guaranteed to arouse suspicion – Group Captain Rupert Brooke – he booked into the Tollard Royal Hotel. There, the handsome and debonair Heath entertained Miss Doreen Marshall, whose body, on 3 July 1946, was found dumped in rhododendron bushes at Branksome Dene Chine. Heath was arrested, stood trial at the Old Bailey, and was hanged on 26 September 1946.

On 17 September 1947 the Poole lifeboat recovered wreckage from a Spitfire that had ditched in the sea. The Town Beam on the quay, a replica of the port's Staplecross wool-scales, dates from 1947, the year in which Poole borough was promised that it would again become a Parliamentary constituency in its own right – taking it out of East Dorset – on the recommendation of the Boundary Commission for the Redistribution of Seats in the House of Commons.

In 1948 Lady Iliffe employed demobbed sailor Alan Bromby (born 1923) on Furzey Island. Having remained there for a decade, he then moved on to Round Island before becoming head warden of Brownsea Island for the National Trust, in so doing completing a hat-trick of almost legendary proportions. The other larger-than-life character associated with Round Island is orchestral conductor Sir Thomas Beecham (1879–1961), who was briefly in residence there for the purpose of writing his biography of 'Old Fred' as he called the composer Frederick Delius. This was published in 1958.

✦ CHAPTER 16 ✦

Boats and Business

House-boat living adopted a naval look after the Second World War, when the Admiralty sold off hundreds of surplus vessels including Motor Torpedo Boat 453, which appeared on a mooring off Hamworthy. Not only was she the honeymoon suite of Guy and Joan Sydenham in 1950, but was also both berth and birthplace of their son, Russel Arne Sydenham, named for Russel Quay on the Arne peninsula, whose birth certificate has the address 'Mooring E12, Wareham Channel'.

Though the birth was without problems, it had been arranged with the doctor that in case of difficulties a flag would be hoisted. Young Russel grew up at sea with Siamese kittens Bosun and Sinbad until, in 1955, Major Dudley Ryder of Rempstone Hall took pity on the family and leased them that offshore extremity of his Purbeck estate known as Long Island.

With their 72ft vessel beached on the western side of the 7-acre island, beside its old pier, the Sydenhams proceeded to collect clays for their innovative experiments in the art of pottery. They produced a pioneering range of slips, glazes and inlays, with graduated surfaces including a stiff glaze applied over a more liquid one. Their products, as diverse as those of any craft pottery in the land, ranged from authentic-looking copies of Bellarmine mugs, named for their Dutch Protestant caricature of the grey-bearded cardinal, to erotic line-ups of terracotta mermaids with smear-glazed torsos.

Poole's links with the water continued to feature the Russell-Cotes Nautical School, on Constitution Hill, which in 1949 merged with another Barnardo nautical home, from Watts, in Norfolk. The combined institution was renamed Parkstone Sea Training School.

On 7 March 1950, the *Karin III*, a 38ft yacht of 14 tons built in 1920 and carrying a crew of five, sailed from Poole Quay to cross the Atlantic. Aboard were her owner and skipper Commander C.I. Payne, of Stourpaine, and his companions Flight-Lieutenant Peter Almack, Dutch yachtsman Jan Bakker, and two Australians.

They put into Madeira, 1,531 miles non-stop from Poole, after eight uncomfortable days riding out a fierce Atlantic storm in which even the *Queen Mary* was forced to hove to. Setting sail for the Bahamas, they were forced off course by another gale, eventually arriving in New York on 18 May 1950.

After the three head sails they had lost had been replaced, courtesy of Rear Commodore Engholme of the Royal Canadian Yacht Club, they then took part in a race from New York to Bermuda, after which, on 2 July 1950, they joined the Atlantic Race for the return to England with a lead of 22 hours 30 minutes. Despite more trouble with the sails they reached Plymouth on 27 July 1950 and sailed on to Dartmouth. The *Karin III* having made an unheralded return to Poole Harbour in mid-August, Commander Payne immediately prepared to put back to sea and the following week won the Poole-Ouistreham race.

As well as yachting, swimming had also returned to the list of permitted pursuits, as the last mines and other wartime obstructions were cleared from the beaches. Channel swimmer Sam Rockett, born in Milborne St Andrew in 1920, had attended South Road School in Poole and learned to swim in the town's Corporation Baths. As a 14-year-old he finished eighth in the men's race from Bournemouth Pier to Boscombe Pier. The following summer he completed the 4-mile swim from Poole Quay to Sandbanks.

In 1941, having represented five counties in water polo, an achievement which passed almost unnoticed, he played for Wales. He achieved national fame when, on 21 August 1950, at 21.00 hours, 24 swimmers attempted to swim the English Channel between Cap Gris Nez and Dover. There, on the shore below Shakespeare Cliff, Sam Rockett was the first to stagger out of the water after a swim of 14 hours 20 minutes, winning the £250 prize money put up by the *Daily Mail*.

Before the age of cheap flights, vacations for the masses were limited to caravans and holiday camps, one of the latter coming to Hamworthy in 1950, when Poole Corporation bought Ham Common and Rockley Point from Brigadier Robert William Evelyn Cecil, 2nd Baron Rockley of Lytchett Heath (1901–76). Here, Rockley Sands Holiday Park was created, on the south-facing shore in the shallows of the western harbour, marketed as 'Sunny, sandy and safe'. Off-shore, water-skiers played what Lord Rockley called 'Riviera rodeo' around the yachts, bringing excitement and thrills as the wartime and postwar flying-boat trots took on a new lease of life.

The Llewellin family of Upton House had been in residence since 1900. Colonel John Jestyn Llewellin, 1st Baron Llewellin (1893–1957), son of William Llewellin and Frances Mary Wigan, commanded the Dorset Heavy Brigade and, as Unionist MP for Uxbridge from 1929 to 1945, held several Govern-

The newly-completed Hamworthy Power Station (centre), *looking westwards along the Quay Channel towards Poole Bridge* (left) *and Poole Quay* (right).

ment posts including that of Minister of Food from 1943 until the Labour landslide of 1945.

Lord Llewellin's final posting was to the colonies, in 1953, as Governor-General of the Federation of Rhodesia and Nyasaland. He never married and his title died with him.

The Poole generating station of the Central Electricity Generating Board – with its Cubist buildings and 325ft octagonal twin chimneys – formed a great postwar landmark. Built on land reclaimed from the southern shore of Holes Bay and opened in 1952, it immediately disrupted traffic from Poole to Hamworthy 'far more than anything the Luftwaffe managed'. The reason was its insatiable appettite for coal which ran at 1,000 tons a day.

Colliers from Humberside were now regular callers in the Backwater Channel, via its access through Poole Bridge, which had to be raised for a quarter of an hour a dozen or more times a day. An unusally numerate reporter for the *Poole and Dorset Herald* did the sums, and also calculated that the level crossings at Towngate closed 100 times a day for three minutes at a time. Poole was effectively closed for eight hours a day, the newspaper proclaimed, making it 'as impregnable to road traffic as an ancient walled town'.

The sailing cutter *Freda*, from the River Hamble, ran into the Training Bank on 7 October 1953. Her four crewmen set off flares and, after four attempts, were rescued at the top of the tide, the Poole lifeboat towing them into the safety of the harbour.

The commando base that had been established during the war as HMS *Turtle*, off Lake Road and Napier Road at Hamworthy, received a new lease of life in 1954. Formerly housing Combined Operations, it was renamed the Amphibious School Royal Marines and was then expanded into the Joint Services Amphibious Warfare Centre, in a project fronted by the First Sea Lord, the Earl Mountbatten, in 1956. Though the joint services role of the Amphibious Warfare Centre was disbanded in 1963, the Hamworthy base continued to specialise in landing-craft operations, clandestine combats and covert reconnaissance for Royal Navy gun-laying.

The postwar projects to renew the nation's housing stock caught up with Poole in 1955. The number of slum properties in the Old Town was roundly estimated at 900, an additional 87 having been more easily classified and counted elsewhere in the borough. Once condemned, closure and clearance orders followed. Rectification took another decade, in the high-rise fashion of the time, as communal back-to-backs and intimate terraces were replaced by 'rabbit hutches in the sky'.

These flat blocks and maisonettes strode across the town from Holes Bay at Sterte to Boyd Road in Branksome. The very last in the programme, the multi-storey Grenville Court, was opened in 1968, by which time, with warnings being heeded that 'society has shot itself in the foot', replicas of the very houses

Keeping watch, from the Dorset Belle, *about to set off from Poole Quay on a spring cruise along the coast in the early 1970s.*

that had been demolished were being built. These copies are now the envy of those who, dispossessed from the originals, were moved sideways as the 4,000 population of the Old Town – out of 100,000 in the borough as a whole – found themselves moved outwards and upwards. Soulless modernity was marketed as 'progress' in an era when the nation had 'never had it so good'. The word 'inevitable' was also over-employed. Once again, the communities who had won the war lost their homes in peacetime.

R.A. Newman claimed a 90-ft motor launch, built in his boat yard, as the biggest 'non-military' vessel

Taking the bus to the boat in the 1970s, from the Arndale Centre, with Colin Burt of Wilts & Dorset Bus Co. (centre left) *being greeted on Poole Quay by Stuart Harvey, of Harvey's Pleasure Boats.*

Poole Bay Fuels in the 1970s, operating from a pontoon off Salterns Quay at Lilliput, with a boatman taking on oil.

Above: *Clambering aboard* Banhart Girl, *off Brownsea Island, in the 1970s.*

Repairs in the 1970s in the shipbuilding yard at the eastern end of the Hamworthy peninsula, beside the Ballast Quay which, although on the opposite side of the Quay Channel, is historically part of Poole's St James's parish.

Boats beached at high tide on the sand beside Shore Road, looking north-westwards to a skyline of masts from Brownsea Island (top left) *to Hamworthy Power Station* (centre right).

Ferry No. 3, in operation from 1958 to 1994, fully loaded as she prepares to cross the harbour entrance, looking south-westwards from Sandbanks to Shell Bay with the Purbeck Hills in the background.

of its kind yet launched from Poole, a claim upated when Bolson's yard produced a steel platform 140ft long and 40ft wide. Towed southwards by a Dutch tug to Lago de Maracaibo, in Venezuela, the raft was used as a pontoon for oil-drilling.

The Housing Act of 1957 was the enabling legislation for the devastation of Georgian Poole. Whole streets were levelled and the Old Town criss-crossed by urban freeways as the 'close clutter of historic passages' was dissected by urban rat-runs. That from Lagland Street to West Quay Road separated families from work, schools, shops and their social life. Old Orchard became a through road and Bowling Green Alley an empty space, which then smashed through High Street shops (23 were eliminated) and swept its trail of rubble westwards behind the Guildhall. Then West Street was devised as the traffic link in the other direction, from Poole Bridge to Longfleet, and subsidised by the Ministry of Transport as an approved 'new main road'.

Slum clearance was also an excuse for creative de-housing, as was the case with the adequately repaired and attractively positioned Garland's Almshouses, dating from 1812 and forming the corner of West Quay Road with Hunger Hill. Given to the town by George Garland, these were allowed to fall into disrepair, despite having been built to last in Flemish bond brickwork. The inmates were provided with cosy bungalows at Hamworthy.

The bulldozers also revealed the past and provided the means for a prank or two. Boys turned up at school with skulls from the old tombs on the other side of the road at Hunger Hill, which was to become a roundabout. Poole Station, reduced to a bus-stop, was also levelled, as was Nile Row in its entirety and a dozen other clusters of properties redolent of Empire and expansion: Wellington Row, dating from 1814 and the great victory over Napoleon; Earl Grey Row, built in 1832. The bigger world had died in little England.

In 1960 former commando Major-General Ferris Nelson 'Chips' Grant (1916–91) became commanding officer of the Royal Marines' Amphibious Training Unit. In May 1941 he had been officer on watch on HMS *Suffolk* in the Denmark Straits, when the *Bismarck* was first sighted on what became her final voyage. Elite Special Forces were back in vogue and the Royal Marines revived their equivalent of the Special Air Services, the motto of the Special Boat Squadron being 'Not by strength but guile'. Among those who trained at Poole was future Liberal Democrat leader Paddy Ashdown, whose first child was born in Poole District Hospital.

Huge pre-war local authority housing estates spread across Parkstone, the principal developments being Alderney West Estate, Bourne Estate, Trinidad Estate (named for an asphalt company rather than West Indian immigrants) and Wallisdown Estate.

Poole lost its Fish Shambles in 1959, demolished by Compton's, following a national trend which left

Though 'PO75' on the sail (top left) *stood for Post Office 1975, this range of commemorative stamps was launched with a 'We are sailing' promotion at Poole.*

Billingsgate reigning supreme. Christopher Hill Ltd replaced their grain-handling building with an 85ft high silo further along Poole Quay. Beyond, across the Backwater into Holes Bay, Poole Power Station with its 325ft high chimneys remained the predominant skyline landmark for the next three decades.

J.&S. Sieger was founded in 1959 by Joshua Sieger to manufacture gas detectors and alarms before such systems became mandatory. Soon the company was employing 300 workers and winning national export awards.

Poole also played a part in the development of modern building materials. Analytical chemist George Osborn (1911–90) invented plastic guttering after an accident at his home, Cherry Tree Cottage, in Merley Ways in which a large length of traditional cast-iron guttering fell on the lawn where his sons were playing. Although no one was hurt, as the former chief chemist of British Drug Houses at Poole from 1947 to 1952 he set about developing an alternative in reinforced plastics. As a result, Osma 'rainwater goods' made their public debut on his riverside house in 1957. Osborn was also credited with the invention of Britain's first non-stick frying-pan, for Tower Brand of Birmingham.

During the war, Osborn was chief chemist for International Alloys, evacuated from Slough's bombs to Aylesbury and commissioned to supply materials needed in the Manhattan Project for the production of the first atomic bombs. Working with William Stross, a Czech refugee, Osborn produced beryllium salts to levels of optimum purity. He wrote 40 research papers and, in 1955, a textbook on *Synthetic Ion-exchangers*.

In retirement, George Osborn gave talks and wrote books on hill-forts and follies, encouraging people to explore the countryside, as he did himself, on a global scale, walking major frontier fortifications from Offa's Dyke to the Great Wall of China. He also followed in the footsteps of Robert Louis Stevenson in the Cevennes, though without a donkey.

Anthropologist Dr Jane Goodall, who attended Uplands School at Poole from 1946 to 1952, started studying chimpanzees in the Gombe National Park, Tanzania, in 1960. At the time of writing her mother, Vanne Goodall, lives in Bournemouth. For the past four decades Jane Goodall has been campaigning for the global survival of the great apes.

In 1960 the Church of the Transfiguration at Canford Cliffs was provided with a parish room, attached at an angle to its eastern end. The work was the start of a £59,050 scheme in which the entire church was rebuilt and expanded to plans drawn up by architect Lionel Gregory. The new church was consecrated on 26 May 1965.

Brownsea Island's long heritage of applied eccentricity ended with the death of Mrs Bonham Christie on 28 April 1961. Her grandson, John Bonham Christie, having presented the island to the Treasury in lieu of death duties, the Government handed it to the National Trust in 1962. The 'secret island' was soon attracting more than 100,000 visitors a year, arriving by ferry from Poole Quay and Sandbanks, while Branksea Castle became a staff hotel for the John Lewis Partnership.

The lifeboat *Thomas Kirk Wright*, on being replaced in 1962, was converted by Paul Neate into a fishing boat. Since restored and repainted in her old colours, the Dunkirk veteran is now the centrepiece of the Lifeboat Museum established by the Royal National Lifeboat Institution at Fishermen's Dock, Baiter, in 1975.

Her successor was the 35.6ft Liverpool-class *Bassett Green*. Built by Groves & Guttridge at Cowes, and previously stationed at Brixham, she was named for W.H. Bassett Green of Winchcombe, near Cheltenham. Her first operational calls, to a succession of leisure craft, started with a yacht that grounded on the Hook Sands on the afternoon of 14 August 1962. Next came the yacht *Margara Della*, drifting in the harbour on the evening of 29 September 1962, in a call shared by the cabin cruiser *Sea Knight*, which was found beside Furzey Island in the early hours of the following morning. The two men who should have been aboard, it was later established, had been ashore bait-digging on Goathorn peninsula when their boat began drifting away. The pair eventually reappeared at Sandbanks, where they had been taken by a passing boatman. The *Bassett Green*, which finished towing *Sea Knight* into Poole at 10.15 hours on 30 September, was put back on her mooring after 13 hours of overnight service.

The Great Winter of the twentieth century was that of 1962–63. A foot of snow falling immediately after Christmas was freeze-dried for weeks in sub-zero temperatures. This permafrost descended on Poole Harbour, which had 'as much ice as the North Pole'. Boating became impossible and Poole Harbour postman Harry Reeve walked across to the southern islands from the Isle of Purbeck. If that

The commissioning party for Environist *attended by* (left to right) *Nick Adams, John Savory, Dr B. Mullins, Joshua Sieger, David May, Mrs Sieger, J. Smit and Sandy Balfour.*

Environist, *locally-made by Coastal Ship Designs and Berthon Boat Co. in the early 1980s, set cutting-edge standards with the latest lines and radar scanner, plus advanced electronics by Sieger Ltd on the Nuffield estate.*

sounds difficult to believe, there is evidence in print, backed by a photograph, in the *Western Gazette* of 1 February 1963. The caption reads:

> *Mrs Joan Sydenham who chose to stay on ice-bound Long Island in Poole Harbour to feed the starving wildfowl. To get this picture a photographer walked a quarter of a mile across the frozen harbour from Arne, seen in the background.*

Harry Reeve brought more than the post to islanders and house-boat owners. He also struggled across the ice-floes with milk, newspapers and provisions.

In 1963, as development pressures continued in a process which was becoming inexorable, Delph House, with its cottages and lake, together with 16 acres with planning consent for luxury housing, was sold at auction.

Pioneer, *leading the new range of 'family cruisers' from NB Yachts in Poole Bay in 1987.*

Coal-age Poole, with gantries on the quay (centre left) *supplying the gasworks in 1962, in a view westwards across the Old Town from the lifeboat station* (nearside shore) *to Hamworthy Power Station* (top right).

Lower Hamworthy (left) *and Poole Quay* (centre), *northwards across the Old Town to Barclays House* (upper right), *with a Truckline ferry approaching the container port and a timber ship outward bound in the 1980s.*

CHAPTER 17

Scandal and Slums

National events had a local link. The twentieth-century scandal which revolved around the relationship between War Minister John Profumo and call-girl Christine Keeler also brought about the downfall of society osteopath and portrait painter Stephen Ward (1912–63), an alleged pimp who, in order to win male friends, provided the smart set with available young women.

Underlying his complex sexuality were experiences he traced back to his time at Canford School. The irony was that, with singular appropriateness, whilst on trial for living off immoral earnings, he brought the school motto, 'Without the Lord, all is in vain', to the attention of the media:

The son of a Torquay vicar, Ward said he wrote a devastating letter to the Home Secretary – exposing what had been Profumo's now famous lie to the House of Commons – because of an incident at Canford School. 'This time I am not going to take the rap,' he protested.

This was a reference to an incident in the school dormitories in which, when a boy was snoring incessantly, Ward was urged, 'Give him a slap, Stephen'. When Ward did not do so, someone else crawled across, and gave him a thump, whereupon the snoring stopped abruptly. The next morning the boy, who failed to wake up, was found to be comatose, with a fractured skull. Ward said in 1963:

All my life I've had a secret fear of something like this happening again. That poor lad was really ill and someone had to be punished. The boy who had crawled over my bed kept quiet. The upshot was that I was taken and thrashed in front of the whole school. I jolly well nearly got the sack as well. Of course, all the other boys thought me a famous fellow. I'd done the right thing and hadn't split. Now, I suppose, they expect me to go along again with this stupid public school convention that good chaps don't tell.

The north-east side of Market Street, from the Guildhall Tavern (right) *and Crown Hotel* (centre), *northwards to the Guildhall* (centre left), *1975.*

Stephen Ward had been easy for the Russians to manipulate, having virtually fallen in love with the Soviet Embassy's second naval attaché Eugene Ivanov, a GRU military intelligence operative. Ward delighted in his company:

Ivanov was about 37, approximately 5 feet 11 inches in height, his face showing slight traces of Mongolian ancestry. Heavy ridges over the brows; a boxer's nose; the total effect quite attractive. I believe I was closer to him than anyone else in my life.

Stephen Ward retained a schoolboy interest in male flagellation, which featured in a series of photographs – allegedly including some eminent people – which Ward entrusted to journalist Warwick Charlton for safe keeping. They were confiscated by Scotland Yard. Charlton described them:

Some of them faded, some comparatively recent. As the story went, the little room in Bryanston Mews West [Ward's flat] *had become a sort of boys' dormitory in which forbidden fruit was being revealed. Of course, this was relatively childish stuff. More adult material was to follow, including some pictures with the heads of the participants chopped off.*

The prime location of the scandal, and where the meetings leading to Profumo's resignation and Ward's suicide took place, was the National Trust owned Clivedon estate, home of William Wardorf Astor, 3rd Viscount Astor. Stephen Ward, who had a cottage there, had introduced Bill Astor to Bronwen Pugh, who became his third wife. Life for the Clivedon set centred on its swimming-pool and nearby Clivedon Reach, where skill at fishing was measured by one's success in landing naked nymphs from the Thames. Lasting evidence of Stephen Ward and Eugene Ivanov having been at Clivedon is a rockery which they toiled to construct on the slope from Ward's cottage to the river. 'How are the Russian Steppes coming along?' Bill Astor used to ask the pair.

The gas holder behind Emerson Road and Poole Quay, almost empty, in 1972.

Demolition of the gasworks behind Emerson Road, in 1972.

Gasworks dereliction in 1972 and football graffiti – 'Man United the Best' – arguably equally valid a generation later.

Market Street from Bowden House at No. 9 (left) *and No. 8* (opposite, white fronted), *south-westwards to Levet's Lane and Church Street* (centre), *in 1969.*

Rebuilding, beside Levet's Lane (left) *and the north-west side of Market Street in 1969, with a mock-Georgian replacement for eighteenth-century No. 2 though the next cluster remains intact from No. 4 through to No. 12* (centre right).

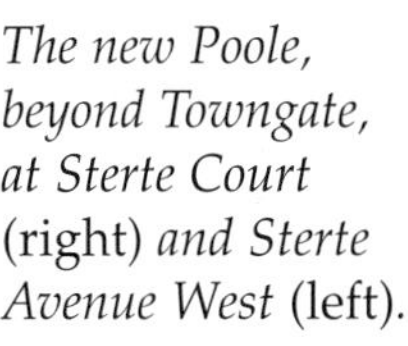

The new Poole, beyond Towngate, at Sterte Court (right) *and Sterte Avenue West* (left).

Hancock's Lane in 1969, southwards between Scaplen's Court (left) *and walls of Georgian brick to a gas-lamp cast with the town's dolphin emblem and quay warehouses in Sarum Street* (centre).

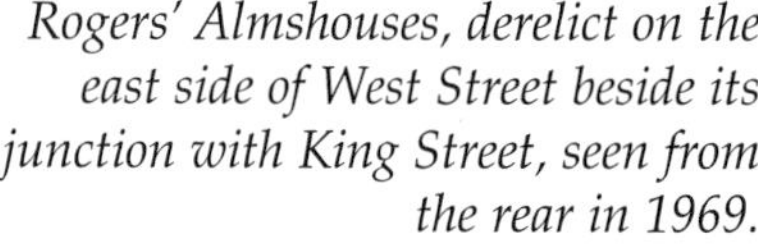

Rogers' Almshouses, derelict on the east side of West Street beside its junction with King Street, seen from the rear in 1969.

Dereliction around the chancel end of St James's Church, looking northwards across Church Street to three-storey Nos. 2 (with blocked shop window)*, 4 and 6, and a glimpse of the Rectory* (centre left), *in 1973.*

Spy writer John le Carré, pseudonym of Parkstone-born David John Moore Cornwell (born 1931), went to Sherborne School and became a Poole schoolmaster. The son of Ronald Cornwell of Mount Road, Parkstone, and then Ambleside in Brownsea View Avenue at Lilliput, he put his Dorset memories to use for his creation of 'Carne School' in the 1962-published *A Murder of Quality*. Whether this is a thinly disguised 'Cerne' or 'carnal' (or both) is for George Smiley to determine. He describes the place as seething with class corruption and as 'a sanatorium of dying souls'. Despite this the school provides an excellent start in life for several of his characters and he returns to it in *A Perfect Spy*.

John le Carré's earliest espionage novel, *The Spy Who Came In From the Cold*, published in 1963, was written in 1954 whilst he was at the British Consulate in Hamburg. From 1960 to 1964 he was a 'Member of HM Foreign Service' which perhaps explains his need for a pseudonym.

In 2002 David Cornwell drew an intimate portrait of his father in a feature for the *New Yorker*, in which he calls Ronnie Cornwell, founder of Poole Round Table No. 12, 'a five-star conman' and admits to a lifelong preoccupation with thoughts of killing him. This 'endured on and off even after his death' in 1975: 'How I got out from under Ronnie, if I ever did, is the story of my life.'

He puts the obsession down to 'exasperation that I could absolutely never put him down'. John le Carré's preparatory school was St Martin's, which he describes as a 'boarding-school gulag' and which removed him both from daily contact with his father's physical and psychological ill treatment of his mother and from a series of scams in which he sought to inveigle his son. These included smuggling, in a whisky-running scheme, during Britain's postwar liquor shortages.

John, sent to Paris to retrieve cash from the Panamanian envoy who was a partner in the venture, was told that the money was in fact owed by his father. He was accompanied by a 'Middle Eastern lady of some age' to Switzerland, where she posed as Baroness Rothschild, her bogus mission being to recover a family treasure chest which included gold dollars, a first-edition Gothenburg Bible, and rolled-up Rembrandt drawings.

Though Ronnie's enterprises seldom prospered – he faced prison and bankruptcy – they must have provided John with first-hand experience of a devious and deceitful life to mould into his fiction. John paints a picture of a prototype 'back-slapping, two-fisted tearaway' who 'throws champagne parties for people who aren't used to being given champagne' and 'opens his garden to the local Baptists for their fête'. He would take on such positions in the community as honorary president of the boys' football squad or men's cricket team, and present their cups, even though he had not paid the milkman, newsagent, or local garage for a year, or even 'the shop that sold him the silver cups'. There is such a character, he says, in every second London street.

One thing I'm particularly sure of is that there is no development to be traced in Ronnie's character, no illuminating moment you can put your finger on and say 'From here Ronnie was bent'. All the evidence I ever heard suggests he was bent from the day he shook his first rattle. And, like a lot of conmen, he was a sucker, as gullible as those he conned and, after the event, as shocked as were his own victims by the baseness of his deceivers.

A 12ft rubber dinghy with an outboard motor, similar to the Zodiac craft made famous by television diver Jacques Cousteau, joined Poole lifeboat *Bassett Green* for inshore rescues. She soon showed her value and versatility, though the first call ended in failure – two men from the speed-boat *Jaime Lewis* were rescued by a pilot boat and a third men swam ashore, but the fourth crewman was missing presumed drowned.

Former Kemp-Welch schoolgirl Ann Sidney, from Parkstone, won the Miss World competition in 1964. Wearing her sash, she was treated to a celebratory trip around Poole with Mayor Tom Sherrin in a borrowed open-top white Rolls-Royce. This was followed by a civic dinner in her honour at the Municipal Offices – bringing the cost of what was cheap national publicity to £253 – which caused a story in its own right when Town Councillor Geoffrey Adams resigned. He protested that funding such entertainments was an abuse of the borough's contingency fund and suggested that those who took part should pay for it themselves.

In 1964 Captain Sir Richard Pilkington (1908–76) of the Coldstream Guards, who had sat in the House of Commons for Widnes from 1935 to 1945 and then for Poole from 1951, resigned through poor health. During the Second World War he had served as Civil Lord of the Admiralty and regularly spent his holidays walking Roman roads. He was replaced as Conservative candidate in the constituency by Oscar Murton.

Parkstone Sea Training School closed in 1964 and its site became Bournemouth and Poole College. It was the start of ten years of frenetic change, with so-called slum clearance schemes removing some of the best Georgian terraces in the Old Town and creating a wide, windy gap at New Orchard separating Market Street from Dear Hay Lane. Towngate Bridge and the George Roundabout did much the same for the area over and beyond the railway tracks, where the Arndale Centre (since renamed the Dolphin Centre) and Barclays House (housing Barclays Bank International) became the new landmarks.

Cold War exiles Prince Carol and Princess Jeanne of Romania were renting Upton House when Chief Constable Arthur Hambleton had it surrounded by

100 policemen, including marksmen, as the Royal Marines cut off a potential escape route from Lytchett Bay into Poole Harbour. The date was 10 July 1965 and the operation was part of nationwide searches following the Great Train Robbery. With suspects and cash being brought to the police station at the Lansdowne in Bournemouth, the Upton tip-off was apparently from someone who knew that Ronald Biggs had been a small-time Swanage crook. Nothing was found at Upton, and nor were there any connections with the Romania royal family but, in another coincidence, police also looked for Biggs at Cranleigh, Surrey, where Prince Carol was in negotiations to purchase Winterfold House.

On 9 November 1965 Dorchester brewers Eldridge, Pope finally called time at Poole's oldest public house and the Bull's Head Inn was converted into offices and a printing works for Southern Newspapers Ltd. Old Fleet Street hands would have seen the irony. The final pint was pulled by E.P. 'Euy' Shorto, licensee from 1938 until the summer of 1965, when Fred Harrad became the manager.

The town's traditional pottery trade was also undergoing changes. Sharp Jones Ltd, formerly at Bourne Valley Pottery and Rock Concrete Tube Works, Branksome, were manufacturers of salt-glazed stoneware drainpipes and sanitaryware, terracotta chimney-pots, bricks, concrete tubes and man-holes. The yards were serviced by the Sharp Jones Sidings, off the railway near the Pottery Junction Roundabout, at Branksome. These had been disused since the firm was taken over by Redlands Holdings and then lifted in 1972 when it was clear that they would not be needed again.

Beatles singer and song writer John Lennon bought Harbour's Edge, a five-bedroom bungalow at Sandbanks, for £25,000 in 1965. He gave it rent-free to Mimi Smith, the aunt who had brought him up, and she lived there until her death at the age of 85 in December 1991. As Lennon still owned the freehold at the time of his murder in New York, his executors sold it at auction in July 1992, to 56-year-old Hampshire businessman Geoff Kaye and his wife Karen, for £410,000. It was then occupied by squatters, its boarded-up windows displaying the slogan 'Love is Life'. After their eviction, in December 1993, the remains of Harbour's Edge were bulldozed and replaced by Kaye House.

The chirpy voice of disc jockey Tony Blackburn (born 1943), the son of a Lilliput doctor, was first heard across the nation from the offshore pirate station Radio Caroline in 1965 and became a sound people either loved or loathed. Its owner has been among the few to emerge with enhanced dignity and popularity from the reality television programme 'I'm a Celebrity, Get Me Out of Here'.

The former library site at No. 4 High Street, presented to the town by Members of Parliament Benjamin Lester and William Ponsonby in 1830, was redeveloped for the new Harbour Office in 1966. Its heraldic relief of the borough coat of arms is surmounted by a bust of Parkstone-born Miss World, Miss Ann Sidney, her head rising from the bosom of a naked mermaid.

Bigger changes lay ahead at the Towngate entrance to the Old Town. A leading player from 1966 onwards was Arndale Developments Ltd and its successor, Dolphin Developments Ltd, which borrowed Poole's Dolphin Brewery logo. Both were chaired by Sir Christopher Benson (born 1933), knighted in 1988 for services to the Civic Trust, Royal Opera House and other public bodies and charities.

Disaster threatened the harbour fisheries and wildlife in April 1967 when the oil tanker *Torrey Canyon* rammed the Cornish coast. Part of her cargo was ignited by napalm bombs dropped by Royal Navy fighters but the bulk of the spillage drifted up the English Channel and fouled Devon beaches. Dorset appeared to be next but the weather changed and northerly winds took the slick towards the French coast. Preparing for the worst, Poole Harbour had been blocked between Sandbanks and Shell Bay with a 1,000-yard boom costing £15,000. The idea of the Wilson Government's chief scientific adviser, Sir Solly Zuckerman, the urgent work was completed almost on schedule.

Whether it would have worked, however, is in question, the force of tide at the Haven proving problematic. Some of the buoys anchoring the 75ft sections of the boom dragged their moorings. Once these were properly secured the force and movement of water began to tear the fabric of the boom. Although nylon ropes were used to reinforce and secure the sections, there was little confidence that they would hold. It was to everyone's relief (except the French) that the wind changed direction and the boom was dismantled.

In 1967 the old walled gardens beside Merley House were turned into a bird sanctuary by retired builder John Wilmot Hudson, who created aviaries and a flamingo pool and planted tropical shrimp-plants to create a setting among the mellow brick-work for a multitude of exotic species. Merley Bird Gardens, which opened on 23 May 1968, with a collection including lyre-birds, parrots, macaws, parakeets, pheasants, pelicans and penguins.

In December 1968 another Noah's Ark was on the move. Guy and Joan Sydenham 'island hopped' in the harbour, eastwards from Long Island to Green Island, between Ower and Goathorn. Owned by Tim Hamilton-Fletcher, here the Sydenham flock of hens and golden pheasants had the run of 18 acres. The family of potters established their Quay Pottery on the northern tip of the island and a cedar cabin, known as Greensleeves Studio, was built in 1971 at the end of a 100-yard avenue of sweet chestnut trees planted by naturalist Charles Xavier Hall early in the twentieth century. They provided a dependable crop of edible nuts.

Guy Sydenham, born in 1916, looked back on their time on Long Island as a 'two-decade idyll'. It was marked by such harmless fun as dressing up as pirates to raid neighbour Ted Foster on Round Island, with the odd bizarre incident such as a huge bonfire on the salt-marsh which burned itself free of the island and floated like one of Drake's fire-ships amid clusters of moored yachts. Guy Sydenham recalls in *A Potter's Life*:

> *Green Island was a Mecca, too, for artists and craftsmen, other potters interested in our salt-glazing operations, and lovers of nature and the open and free way of life. It was a delight to see, sometimes, their uninhibited young children running free and nude through the trees and sunny glades, dappled in sunlight and exalting in their youthful freedom.*

The creator of a magic world for both young and old, John Ronald Reuel Tolkien (1892–1973) spent his holidays at the Miramar Hotel in East Overcliff Drive, Bournemouth, in the 1950s and early 1960s. He then retired with his wife, Edith, to a bungalow at No. 19, Lakeside Road, Branksome Park. She died in 1971 and Tolkien returned to Oxford, where he had been a superb historian of the real world, as Professor of Anglo-Saxon from 1925 until 1945, when he became Merton Professor of English Language and Literature.

It was in Oxford that his mind-children were created and discussed over drinks at meetings of 'The Inklings' in the back bar of the Eagle and Child in St Giles. His cronies included C.S. Lewis and the poet and novelist Charles Williams – an elitist but productive literary clique. Tolkien's death occurred in Bournemouth on 2 September 1973, when he came back to visit his old friends Dr and Mrs Tolhurst.

Poole Quay lost its biggest industrial monument in 1968 with the demolition of the double cranes and associated coal-carrying overhead gantry. These stretched from waterfront fuel stacks between Baiter Street and South Road to the gasworks beside Green Road and Emerson Road. The Southern Gas Board was preparing to close the plant as pipelines were planned to bring natural North Sea gas into Dorset to replace the coal gas supplied since Victorian times.

At the other end of the quay, towards West Quay Road, another landmark moved with the times as the familiar name of Christopher Hill, for decades the town's largest 'corn, seed and cake manufacturer and poultry feed manufacturer', was replaced by that of the conglomerate Dalgety, in even larger letters.

Poole's bureaucracy also provided itself with a palatial new home, the towering upward extensions to the Municipal Offices being re-branded as the Civic Centre.

Her Majesty Queen Elizabeth II and the Duke of Edinburgh opened Poole General Hospital in Longfleet on 11 July 1969. The Friday visit to Dorset lasted six and a half hours and began with the Queen, at 10a.m., stepping off the royal train at Dorchester South Station, where she was received by the Lord Lieutenant of Dorset, Colonel Joseph Weld, before seting off in a maroon Rolls-Royce to Duchy of Cornwall farms and the Atomic Energy Establishment on Winfrith Heath.

At Poole, the centrepiece of the trip, the Queen and Duke were met by Richard Crossman, the Social Services Secretary, on behalf of the National Health Service, and P.G. Templeman, chairman of the Regional Health Board. After a couple of short speeches they toured the wards – 500 beds in a £3 million complex that boasted the best views of any hospital in the land. Richard Crossman remarked:

> *Everyone who met the Queen experienced a lifetime's moment of excitement. You saw it in their faces. Those who went untouched by the royal hand – meeting me instead – were visibly disappointed at the time and would remember nothing later.*

At 5.30p.m., the official part of the visit over, the Queen and Duke were driven to Wimborne Station to rejoin the royal train. They attended a country house dinner and ball at Cranborne Manor hosted by Lord Cranborne, returning to the nine-coach train in the early hours of the morning. It was then moved southwards, towards Poole, stopping for the rest of the night near Broadstone. Wimborne Station having closed in May 1964, the royal visitors were its last passengers. At 6.30a.m. the train was on the move again, heading for Windsor via Broadstone and Poole.

The next major opening, by Lord Parker as Lord Chief Justice of England, was of the new Law Courts in Sandbanks Road on 9 September 1969. These took the pressure off the Municipal Offices and saw Malcolm McGougan, Recorder of Poole since 1954, adequately housed for the last gasp of his ancient office – dating back to Giles Escourt in 1568 – which was abolished by Parliament in November 1971. His Honour David Pennant (born 1912), of Ettrick Road, Branksome Park, took over as county court judge in what was then the Crown Court.

Furzey Island had passed to Lady Iliffe's eldest grandson, during whose time the rhododendrons became a jungle. In 1969 it was sold to Birmingham businessman H. Newton Mason for £40,000. He carved out lawns on each side of the house, which regained its south-facing views across the South Deep to the conifers of Goathorn peninsula, and entertained his staff at a number of lavish functions.

Heathland habitats around Poole and in south Dorset generally continued to be destroyed on an unprecedented scale for housing, forestry, agriculture, aggregates and clay mining. Canford Heath

The fourth Floating Bridge, Bramble Bush Bay *came into service in 1994 and is the first to carry a name, seen in a view westwards from Sandbanks to Furzey Island* (top right) *in Poole Harbour.*

Bramble Bush Bay *coming into Sandbanks, from the Isle of Purbeck, fully loaded with four lanes of cars and vans.*

Bramble Bush Bay *loading at Sandbanks, looking southwards to the slipway* (centre right) *on the opposite side of the ferry route across the harbour entrance, at Shell Bay.*

became a virtual new town, its name now applying to a suburb rather than a wildlife refuge, particularly after the opening of Canford Heath Middle School in September 1970. Two war heroes graced this brave new world. Wing Commander Donald Bennett, who flew flying-boats from Poole Harbour before leading the Pathfinders of Bomber Command, was master of ceremonies for Carlton Homes, claimant to Poole's first 'metric measured' construction project.

Donald Bennett was upstaged by the best known representative of The Few, disabled Battle of Britain survivor Group Captain Douglas Bader (1910–82), who lost his legs in a flying accident in 1931 and whose story was told in both words and on celluloid in *Reach for the Sky*. Bader was brought to Poole by

Dorchester brewers Eldridge, Pope to open the new Fighter Pilot public house. There he had a little bit of fun with the carpet, which showed four propeller blades, rather than the three of the Spitfires he had flown. He left with an enhanced reputation, the DSO and bar, and DFC of his war record having been upgraded to a Victoria Cross by the town's publicity machine. The error has been perpetuated in the book *Poole's Pride Regained*, though it pointed in the right direction, Bader being created a knight in 1976.

Measured from its drawings at 23ft in height, and looking like a veil across a corpse as surrounding houses were reduced to their footings, the smoothly flowing lines of Towngate Bridge opened for use in the spring of 1971. Down below, in a phrase from the *Poole and Dorset Herald*, was 'a hideous derelict piece of wasteland' likened to 'a huge bomb site'. Pedestrians were banned from using the modernistic structure, which vaulted the railway line and its level-crossing bottlenecks.

Cars could now enter the Old Town unimpeded. To the south-west, through the middle of the Georgian terraces, New Orchard, a wide highway in place of the narrow streets, was completed in 1971. It cost £46,000 to take the new road system to Hunger Hill, where mass demolitions included burial-ground mausoleums, Garland's Almshouses, the former Poole Brewery and Nile Row. Redevelopment followed with First National Commercial Properties Ltd, in a joint venture with Poole Corporation, advertising 73,000sq.ft of office space served by a multi-storey car park for 575 vehicles.

'Pastiche Poole' was another theme, a few of the demolished buildings being replaced by replicated history. Some designs won the qualified approval of Sir John Betjeman and one – the 1969-built flats at Guildhall Court in Market Street – received an award from the Department of the Environment. Restoration of the nearby Guildhall, now standing next to a windy wasteland, was undertaken by Poole Corporation in 1971. It became a museum, while some of the old businesses in the area were given a new lease of life on the Nuffield estate or in the mushrooming industrial district around Fleet's Lane on the other side of the new Fleet's Bridge flyover. Here Dorset Way replaced Dorchester Road as the town's main east–west link for through traffic.

British Seagull marine engine makers moved from 'a back street in Poole' to a huge factory near Ringwood Road. Boat builders F.C. Mitchell, after half a century at Lilliput, boosted exports to £200,000 and launched the Brownsea Class of cruiser in 1971. Dorset Lake Shipyard, in Lake Drive at Hamworthy, which had built 360-ton minesweepers for the Admiralty, took on 'as bread money' the task of 'care and maintenance' of the long lines of United States landing-craft which had been moored beside the Wareham Channel since General Charles de Gaulle pulled France out of the NATO alliance. They remained a conspicuous contribution to the scenery until being declared obsolete in 1977. Rotork Marine Ltd acquired waterside sheds and assembled the next generation of shallow-draught hulls in reinforced polyester.

Lord Shackleton (1911–94), leader of the Labour opposition in the House of Lords, lived at Arrowsmith Road, Broadstone. He was the son of Sir Ernest Shackleton, the heroic Antarctic explorer who led his men to safety across South Georgia in an epic of survival. Lord Shackleton shared his Broadstone home with Dr Eric Courtin, who discovered a burglary there in December 1971. Their losses included Sir Ernest Shackleton's pocket watch and a silver casket, engraved with the *Nimrod*, the ship which had taken him to the Antarctic, presented to him when he was given the freedom of the London Borough of Lewisham.

A 200-ton former United States naval vessel, acquired by Plesseys in 1970 as a floating laboratory, was refitted at Poole during the winter of 1971/72 for her new research role. Named *Sono* and registered in Guernsey, she carried out sonar and other top-secret anti-submarine detection trials for equipment devised for the Admiralty Underwater Weapons Establishment at Portland.

The Prince of Wales, aboard the minelayer HMS *Scimitar*, en route between Plymouth and Portsmouth, put into Poole in 1972 for what John Hillier and Martin Blyth itemised as 'crab cocktail and Dover sole' followed by 'drinks in the bar' at the Antelope Hotel. In *Poole's Pride Regained*, the authors quote the licensees, Charles and Mary Dowland, as saying that being British, the regular customers showed 'only polite interest'. Hillier and Blyth also record the 1972 heroics of the Special Boat Section from Hamworthy in dropping down on the *Queen Elizabeth II* in mid-Atlantic after Cunard's luxury liner had been held to ransom, by telephone from New York, over a terrorist bomb threat. Unaccustomed to airborne assaults, the men dropped by parachute into a choppy sea and were picked up by lifeboats from the ship.

That was heroism. There were no terrorists and no bombs but no one knew that at the time, least of all passengers Fred and Bertha Rowe, who remained unaware of the drama unfolding around them until hearing about it from the wireless on the BBC World Service. On returning to Poole, borough alderman Fred Rowe treated the Royal Marines involved to a reception in the Municipal Offices. Fred Rowe always did things in style. He is remembered for turning up at a Tudor-themed fancy-dress event in medieval chain-mail, seated on a white charger replete with post-Raleigh Churchillian cigar.

As Michael Dawney told me, on hearing that Fred Rowe was aboard *Queen Elizabeth II* at the time, sending in the Special Boat Section 'could be regarded as overkill'. Such larger-than-life characters were a joy of the twentieth century. Fred Rowe told his fellow councillors that they were 'duty bound' to give the Corps of Royal Marines the Honorary Freedom of the Town and County of Poole 'while it still exists as such'. This was achieved in Poole Park on 5 September 1973, the honour being accepted by their Commandant-General, Lieutenant-General Sir Ian Gourlay.

Cutting-edge modern architecture came to Poole in 1973, when the Arndale Centre was about to be overlooked by the nine storeys of Barclays Bank International. Three hexagonal towers, each 138ft high and joining on single sides, rose above an enlarged George Roundabout at Towngate. At their centre a rectangular hole was being filled by a core building even higher, at 145ft. There was 435,000sq.ft of office space taking shape, with 1,600 parking spaces for the 2,000-plus staff being relocated or recruited. Barclay's international wing then traded under the abbreviation DCO, which stood for the politically incorrect 'Dominion, Colonial and Overseas'.

Residents of Serpentine Road were less enthusiastic about the effects on daylight and parking, Mrs Joan Clements at No. 21 resisting to the point of a compulsory purchase order and beyond. She was also dicing with danger, as was demonstrated after lunch on 29 June 1973, when a semi-dismantled crane belonging to contractors John Laign began to topple as it was lowered from the roof of Barclays House. This unbalanced a 60-ft mobile crane standing in the road, which fell across Mrs Clements' home. It was a Friday afternoon and she was out, although her companion, 81-year-old Mrs Ellen Simmons, was there, doing the ironing. She was unhurt and unfazed. Typical of a generation that had weathered two world wars, Mrs Simmons told the media that she was more worried about possible adverse effects on the apple crop in the garden.

Next door at No. 23, Millie Sheppard had a timely reason for not being at home – she was celebrating her seventy-seventh birthday and had taken her blind younger sister, Freda, 73, to visit a third sister for tea. The Sheppard sisters were rehoused at the Dolphin Hotel as a legion of insurers and lawyers debated liability. Freda Sheppard emphasised her personal reason for needing the terraced house rebuilt as she rejected offers of somewhere new:

We've lived there since 1910 and that's a long time. Now I can't see I have to move around by feel. So I feel safe there because I know every nook and cranny in the place. Please make them put my home back just as it was.

The training of Royal Marines drivers, vehicle mechanics and other technicians was transferred to Poole from Eastney in 1973. A bizarre court case that year featured unpaid Poole hotel bills and a fraud in which the American astronaut Scott Carpenter was lured into 'travelling to London to discuss a £1 million deal to raise a ship from the bottom of the sea off Dorset'. He spent £1,400 on hosting a conference at the Hilton Hotel but did not press charges against the instigator of the scam, the inventor of the 'black box' flight recorder (which in fact is orange). The 55-year-old scientist, Alfred Watson, who lived a double life as a confidence trickster, pleaded guilty to six charges of fraud. He had spent 27 of the previous 29 years in prison, during which time he obtained a doctorate and degrees and received frequent visits from government scientists and other experts seeking his advice.

Local government reform, which saw Poole Corporation become Poole District Council on 1 April 1974, coincided with the historic borough's last great land deal. This was with Ivor Fox-Strangways Guest, 3rd Viscount Wimborne (1939–93) for 530 acres of building land on Canford Heath at £7,600,000 – a sum regarded by the district valuer as 'cheap' for another 6,000 homes that would boost the new suburb's estimated population from 4,500 to 20,000. Some of the land was to be sold off for factory estates, or used for roads and 'landscaping', but 340 acres would be left for housing. As these were built and sold, it was hoped, there would be growing profits, the surplus from which would go towards paying for Poole's prestigious new Arts Centre. In the event, however, an international oil crisis prompted a crash in Britain's escalating property prices. Years later the district valuer was still grappling with economics as councillors balked at selling assets in a depressed market. One of them, Mrs Edna Adams, was eloquent in laying blame: 'The fault is that our amateur speculators tangled themselves up in these huge land purchases long after the wide boys had ceased to buy.'

She may have been right, but markets can go up as well as down, and hindsight also moves with the horizon. The property crash of 1973 held up and complicated things but the project went on to move into growing surpluses. By 1989 the profits had reached £10,400,000, with a 'residual land bank' worth 'between £6 million and £16 million'. Which end of the spectrum it would be depended upon the outcome of public inquiries:

... and the Secretary of State for the Environment's trump card, if he cares to use it, deciding emotive conservation dilemmas which were hardly given a second thought when the project started.

Redeveloping Canford Heath and taking its new road system across Alderney Heath to Wallisdown meant removing a number of Gypsy caravans and camps close to where their predecessors had been living for most of the century. Despite enabling

Poole Harbour and town, north-westwards from the lagoon on Brownsea Island with rafts of cormorants and oyster-catchers, to the towers of Sterte (left) *and Barclays House* (centre) *in 1984.*

legislation, before it could clear the land Poole Corporation had to create alternative sites. Suggested locations aroused antagonism from existing residents and were dropped. Although another proposal, for Mannings Heath, avoided the 'not in my back yard' response – there were no nearby houses – landowner Lord Wimborne had to be served with a compulsory purchase order before a permanent camp could be established in 1971. A total of 50 families were given replacement pitches on hard-standing there and in an 'authorised temporary camp' on Alderney Heath.

Cobb's Quay Marina (left centre) *in Holes Bay, Hamworthy Power Station* (centre) *and the Old Town* (upper left), *south-westwards to Sandbanks and Brownsea Island* (top right).

Her Majesty Queen Elizabeth II and the Duke of Edinburgh (far left) *meeting members of Bournemouth Symphony Orchestra on her visit to Poole Arts Centre in Kingland Road on 23 March 1979.*

The Guildhall (centre right) *and its setting, with the widest section of Market Street redeveloped as Guildhall Court* (left), *northwards across New Orchard to the Salvation Army hall and multi-storey car park* (right) *and Barclays House looming over the Conservative Club* (centre).

St Paul's at Okedale, Poole's newest church, in 1987.

Rest and relaxation beside the Jolly Sailor Inn on Poole Quay.

✦ CHAPTER 18 ✦

Port and Progress

The five divisions of Hamworthy Engineering became part of the Powell Duffryn Group in 1974. Former marshland and meadows around Fleet's Bridge saw an influx of major businesses, including B&Q Autocentre, Southern Toolmaking, Hunt's Motorists' Centre (a lesson in the use of the apostrophe), Marley Tiles and Palm Circuits.

Southern Ocean Supplies bought out R.A. Newman's boat yard in 1975 and set about production of the glass-fibre Ocean-75 sailing yacht. Costing £300,000 in 1977, it was superseded by the Ocean-90 at a modest £750,000.

From 1973 onwards, almost single-handed, Truckline and its generic offshoots around the Ferry Terminal at Hamworthy, did amazing things for 'the rejuvenation of Poole'. Commander Hank Mules, the 'buoyant and ebullient' chief executive of Poole Harbour Commissioners from 1970, received much of the credit 'for re-inventing Poole as a port and reorganising its dockers into a modern labour force'. With his penchant for statistics, Richard Blomfield put the slide-rule across the resultant successes and recorded that £12,992,950 of foreign trade in 1972 had risen to £213,647,887 in 1975. Truckline had achieved 'the most dramatic seaborne trade of Poole since the great Newfoundland fishery'.

From being the nation's 61st port in 1969, Poole jumped to 26th place in 1975, 'largely because we bring in 30,000 Citroëns a year', to quote Commander Mules. It was left to Richard Blomfield to spell out the underlying reason: 'And all because someone realised it was possible to design a ship of 3,000 tons and carrying over 1,000 tons of cargo which still only draws 11ft.'

The former Poole lifeboat *Thomas Kirk Wright* became a museum piece, in 1975, in the old boathouse at Fisherman's Dock on Poole Quay, decked out by the Royal National Lifeboat Institution as a typical lifeboat station of the mid-twentieth century. The newly created Maritime Museum, in the restored Town Cellars at the centre of the quay, became home to the first X-class yacht, dating from 1909.

It was in 1975 that the guardians of British culture chose to include Poole in their selection of towns to represent the nation in European Architectural Heritage Year. Given the demolition, on a scale approaching that of historic Chichester, this was seen by conservationists as particularly ironic, one commentator remarking that 'the event has achieved for architecture what the Eurovision Song Contest has for music'.

Barclays Bank International became operational from Poole on 27 January 1976, its building balanced, towards the harbour, by the square-cut lines of the headquarters of the Royal National Lifeboat Institution, also opened in 1976. Appropriately, its forward-thrusting windows, blessed with one of the best coastal panoramas in England, look down on workshops in the yards on the seaward side of West Street. The building was designed by Leslie Jones.

Poole Arts Centre, completed in 1978, faces the Arndale Centre – since renamed the Dolphin Centre – from the eastern side of the George Roundabout. Though the cost had escalated to £4,500,000, there were 'plenty of seats for the extra bucks'. A 1,500-seat concert hall adjoins the Towngate Theatre, which seats 600, while Wessex Hall provides a 'banqueting suite' for a similar number and a further few hundred can be absorbed in meetings and exhibitions staged in the Canford Room, Dorset Room and Longfleet Gallery. In-house catering for all this activity is provided from the Branksea Restaurant.

All ports have their off days. *Vechstoom* was hardly the first vessel to have a poor maiden voyage but her incoming cross-Channel crossing on 9 January 1978 came close to being alarmingly memorable. Having set off 'into the teeth of a winter storm' – with huge waves and winds gusting to 60 mile per hour – she lurched to 'the point of capsizing'. Lorries tipped on their sides 'and the decks were awash with claret'.

The significance of that anecdote is entirely dependent upon the direction in which the vessel is heading. Outward bound from Poole the cargo is likely to be little more interesting than chemicals, fish and meat. Incoming cargoes at that time were dominated by Zanussi washing-machines and other 'white goods', anonymous in their containers, between loads of car components and fruit and vegetables. Ships also arrived with separate cargoes, from those of historical vintage, such as grain and timber, through modern materials like fertilisers and steel, to the vital strategic substance of our times. A total of 300,000 tonnes of petroleum products were also passing through the port of Poole.

A snapshot of Poole-based trades is given by Richard Blomfield in *Poole Town and Harbour*. In 1978 he counted the number of firms in the following categories:

Engineering – 140
Electrical automation – 50
Yacht, boat-building and associated trades – 73

St Mary's Church (left), *Longfleet, and newly built Poole General Hospital* (right), *which was opened by Queen Elizabeth II on 11 July 1969.*

Seawards view from the windows and balconies of one of Britain's more desirable tower blocks, after redevelopment of Branksome Towers by Elliott Property in the 1970s.

Road haulage – 25
Printers, engravers and publishers – 32
Food and confectionery – 17
Timber and joinery – 30
Bricks, tiles, glass and concrete – 16

There were a hundred other 'miscellaneous companies', including such well-known names as Bluebird Caravans, Marley Tiles, Metal Box, Plessey, Remploy and Ryvita.

Poole as a playground was also booming. The harbour was now far busier than it had been in the 1930s, with 10,000 yachts and a dozen clubs for their owners, several with waiting-lists of prospective members. Poole Yachting Week attracted 479 entrants in 1977. This was organised by Parkstone Yacht Club with 2,000 members. Those at Poole Yacht Club looked much further afield, literally to the ocean waves, and organised long-distance cruises. Lilliput Sailing Club, founded in 1956 beside Parkstone Lagoon, pioneered the use of racing catamarans. Their social life was based on the Blue Lagoon Restaurant, while members of Poole Harbour Yacht Club contemplated their own communion with the water from the Salterns Way Club and Salterns Hotel.

Royston Pizey was running Lilliput Yacht Station, while the East Dorset Sailing Club, based below Evening Hill, had only 80 full members in the 1980s, according to Richard Blomfield, who pointed out, however, that it was unusual in having 'few facilities and no bar'. What made it desirable, for 100 additional 'pier members', was a pier across Whitley Lake giving easy access to the Main Channel. Across the shallows at Sandbanks, Blomfield's nearest neighbour, the North Haven Lake Association, attracted a new and much more active generation engaged in windsurfing and board-sailing, literally brightening the scene as 'they can be seen speeding in all directions like a flock of multi-coloured butterflies'.

Gravel pits and heathland at Broadstone, on the edge of advancing suburbia, in the 1970s.

The best view from Sandbanks is reserved for members of the prestigious Royal Motor Yacht Club which, dating from the beginning of the modern age, was founded by the Royal Automobile Club in 1905. Its 1,400 members, though mainly seen in motor cruisers, also pioneered X-craft sailing. Admiral of the Club, since his wife came to the throne in 1952, has been the Duke of Edinburgh.

Poole's Member of Parliament since 1964, Oscar Murton (born 1914) was created a life peer, choosing the title Baron Murton of Lindisfarne on his retirement as Deputy Speaker and Chairman of Ways and Means in 1979. Elected as a Conservative, he was returned to Parliament with healthy majorities from an electorate that had risen from 66,093 to 83,781. The surplus votes ranged from 8,282 in 1964 and 13,490 in 1970 to 11,425 in 1974. During this time the candidate in second place changed from Labour to Liberal.

In 1983 Poole's main lifeboat became a 33ft Brede-class vessel. Built in Rye on the Isle of Wight by Locklin Marine and sponsored by the women's section of Rotary International, it was named *Inner Wheel* in their honour. Harbour and inshore rescue

The Fairway Buoy from Poole Bay, plus anchors, retired to Holes Bay Roundabout on the A350 dual carriageway into the town.

Training ship Royalist, *berthed at Hennings Quay, beside Poole Aquarium* (right).

operations are carried out by two companion vessels, a high-speed semi-inflatable launch named *Atlantic*, and the 22ft Boston whaler *Outrage*.

Poole's boat-building capacity kept pace with its increasingly affluent customers during the 1980s, as John and Robert Braithwaite developed yards in West Quay Road into the production centre for a global enterprise which they named Sunseeker International. The business started in 1961, its Superyacht shipyard specialising in high-performance motor cruisers. By 1981 it was reported that even the cheapest models 'cost as much as a house', the very basic being priced at £30,000, 'and as for the upper limit that is somewhere in the sky for those who sail off into the sunset.' A boat, to borrow a saying heard in taverns on the quay, is 'a hole in the water into which one pours money.'

So, too, are most islands, although Furzey became the exception. Having been briefly owned by oil magnate Algy Cluff (born 1940), it was sold in 1983 to British Petroleum plc, who probed the northern extremities of their Wytch Farm oilfield from two sites drilled in the offshore pine woods. Some 10 acres of Furzey Island were dedicated as a nature reserve in 1999. The island comes into the jurisdiction of Corfe Castle Parish Council whose clerk, Stephen Yeoman, has urged that it should be kept for 'community and environmental benefit' rather than resuming its previous role as 'seaside gem', a hideaway or play-thing for entrepreneurs or celebrities.

In the late 1970s pollution in the harbour started to take insidious turns worthy of a science fiction plot. Strange things were happening here and in other places where yachts assemble in quantity and the sea manages only a half-hearted flush with the tide. The inch-long dog-whelk *Nucella lapillus* was once plentiful down to the low tide mark on the harbour side of Sandbanks peninsula. It is an attractive little snail with a pointed end to its whorled shell and multi-coloured variations ranging from white to orange, brown and black, with all kinds of banding between.

Marine biologists used to have no trouble sexing their dog-whelks – the males had a penis and the females, as is customary, did not. Then things began to change. Every dog-whelk had a penis, though some of them, on closer examination, were found to be female. These were the final kamikaze generation of dog-whelk, in which the penis, growing across the ovaries, left the female egg-bound.

Dog-whelks are carnivorous and therefore exist some way up the food chain. Their variable coloration gives some indication of food preference, the darker ones seeming to eat mussels and the lighter ones barnacles, the latter group being particularly susceptible. Disproportionately large numbers succumbed to this male-plight syndrome, and eventually a cause was suggested.

The blame came to rest upon a man-made substance specifically designed to discourage barnacles from growing on the bottom of boats. The use of the chemical tributyle tin as a highly effective anti-fouling agent had been widespread since the early 1970s. With traces found in mud and water a decade later it was taking the blame for killing the micro-algae of plankton at the start of the food chain. Further investigation revealed that it also caused the deformation of oysters and other shellfish, worrying amounts becoming concentrated in creatures significant to human gourmets. Scottish farmed salmon, on public sale, were found to contain 500 times more than the permitted amount – not that any amount is

Celtic Commander *being loaded with ball clay from Purbeck at the Ballast Quay in 2001.*

Sardinia *being loaded with ball clay, at the Ballast Quay, in 2001.*

Fishing vessel Nibbler *stuck on Hook Sands as the Poole Lifeboat attempted to refloat her.*

Nibbler *became a victim of Hook Sands in the 1990s.*

C.H. Horn, *the workhorse of Poole Harbour Commissioners, dredging the Quay Channel.*

A large Dutch dredger turning the Main Channel into what is now the Middle Ship Channel between Sandbanks and Poole.

Buoy maintenance, which includes replacing liquid petroleum gas tanks for 18A, 2001. This buoy marks the southern side of the inner entrance to the harbour at South Haven Point.

Navigation buoys are cleaned before being given a full service at Yard Quay in 2001.

Vigilant, *the Poole harbourmaster's launch, being lowered into the water at the start of the 2001 season.*

Russian ship at the Ballast Quay, 2001.

Harbourmaster on patrol, heading eastwards down the Quay Channel between Poole Quay and the Ballast Quay (background), *2000.*

The yacht Cabelle, *outward bound from the Quay Channel, passing a Truckline freighter and the eastern end of the container port, 2000.*

Brownsea ferry advertising Harvey's 'Islands cruise' and pleasure boat Purbeck Lady (right) *berthed at Poole Quay, 2000.*

Purbeck Lady *being prepared for a visit to Brownsea Island by the National Trust's Wessex region committee in 2000.*

Law enforcement corner of Poole Quay, with HM Customs launch (left) *and police boat* Alarm (right), *looking south-westwards to Poole Bridge* (centre) *and timber sheds* (top left) *at Hamworthy, 2000.*

Solent Scene (left) *and HM Customs and Excise cutter* Vigilant (right) *berthed at Poole Quay, 2000.*

Above: Vigilant *at Poole, in Navy grey but flying the blue ensign with the portcullis badge of the Customs service, and bristling with electronics and equipment.*

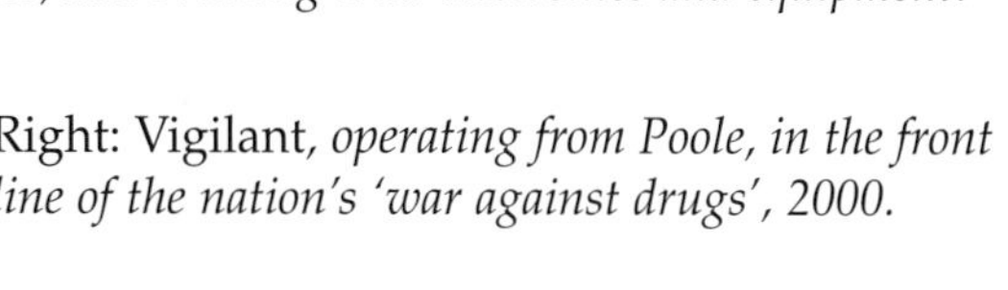

Right: Vigilant, *operating from Poole, in the front line of the nation's 'war against drugs', 2000.*

Beech Hurst (left), *1798-dated with flamboyant flourishes by first owner Samuel Rolles, and the classical rotunda of the Portman Building Society* (centre right), *with the bars of J.D. Wetherspoon* (right) *in the Borough Buildings, south-eastwards from the junction of High Street and North Street.*

Merchants House at Hunger Hill (left), *with a 15-storey building taking shape, south-westwards from Vanguard Road in 2003.*

known to be safe. As with radiation, all exposure to tributyle tin comes with a health warning. The story of the dog-whelk remains a cautionary tale that we ignore at our peril.

'A ban would be short-sighted,' was the comment from the Royal Yachting Association as Environment Minister William Waldegrave edged towards a ban. The chemical also had to be removed from the wood preservatives and other products with which a generation of do-it-yourself enthusiasts had sprayed themselves in the process of carrying out roof repairs.

What was convenient for yachtsmen in keeping their gin palaces spick and span was bad news for the commercial oyster industry. Fitch Lovell from London's Smithfield had introduced Pacific oysters to Poole Harbour in 1973. These grow twice as fast as the native species and do well as the climate of southern England – and this landlocked water in particular – edges towards Mediterranean values. The manager told Richard Blomfield of Sandbanks in 1978 that more of his oysters were being eaten in Blackpool than Poole. He was also having to contend with oil-spill pollution of the clams in Southampton Water, which were being brought to the purer waters of Poole Harbour and suspended from rafts for three weeks 'to cleanse them of hydrocarbon pollution', as Blomfield puts it in *Poole Town and Harbour*. The Southampton problem was also present, if to a lesser extent, in Poole Harbour. This and other difficulties led Fitch Lovell to sell the lease of the oyster-beds to Franklin's Fish Farms, but with over-fishing also being a problem, dredging of the native oyster – rather than its introduced cousin – was curtailed by the Harbour Commissioners in 1985.

The proudest moment for the Royal Marines in their time at Hamworthy came in 1985 as a 'thank you' for retaking the Antarctic island of South Georgia and undertaking hazardous landings on Argentine-occupied East Falkland. Margaret Thatcher arrived, on what was described as a 'personal' visit by the Prime Minister, to mark their battle honours in the South Atlantic campaign of 1982.

The logo, name and ownership of Truckline passed to Brittany Ferries in 1985 for what was then a cross-Channel journey of 4hr 30min. with a turn-around time of 2hr 30min., times achieved by Countances and Purbeck with 100 cars and 40 lorries. Their high-speed successors, starting with Condor, cut the times to such an extent that a day-trip to Cherbourg is now a practical alternative to an excursions into the Dorset countryside. Not for nothing is Cherbourg Poole's twin town. 'Ro-Ro' ('Roll on, roll off') was the road sign of the times.

Deverill plc, as it became, made its headquarters between West Street and West Quay Road in 1986. From 11,000sq.ft of offices at Itec House it advanced to the forefront of the micro-computer market. In addition to developing systems for blue-chip companies, the firm embarked on an extensive acquisitions programme, absorbing such businesses as Computer-store, Whymark Instruments, Solus Computers and ABS Business Systems.

Lady Wimborne's Bridge at Canford, over the A341, went the way of others along Lady Wimborne's Drive after Dorset County Council offered Canford School £2,163 towards the cost of its demolition in 1986. The concrete and iron structure was in good order apart from the fact that its 14ft 3in height restriction had been ignored by a number of vehicles, leaving the underside of its single span with a distinctly jagged profile. A similar bridge at Alderney had survived until the 1970s still carrying a prominent graffito from the 1930s urging 'No Arms for Nazis'.

The Swash Channel was dredged in 1988 for use by larger vessels and in the hope of improving 'flow

Poole Station, north towards Sterte Court (left), *with a Weymouth-bound train beside the down platform* (right).

Falkland Square and the Dolphin Centre (centre left) *northwards to the skyline presence of Marks & Spencer.*

Towngate Bridge (left) *and Barclays House* (centre) *above the shopping centre car park* (right) *at the heart of Poole.*

Phones 4u, being the mobile telephone company offering products 'For you', with W.H. Smith as the aged partner from another generation, fronting Falkland Square shopping centre (centre) *on the northern side of the tracks* (bottom left).

exchanges' between Poole Bay and Poole Harbour.

Thriller writer Ivan Ruff (born 1945) moved to Furze Hill Drive, Parkstone, in 1973. There he wrote *The Dark Red Star*, *Dead Reckoning* and *Blood Money*, the latter in 1988. He sent me a copy with the explanation that although it appears to be 'set in a mythical all-purpose England' it is actually set in Dorset and 'from first page to last the place is there'.

He paid me the compliment of borrowing a 'nuclear neighbour' phrase I coined in an old issue of *Dorset*, the county magazine, in reference to Winfrith, and was the only person to elevate that journal's haphazard publication schedule during my 20-year regime into a virtue by pronouncing 'the absence of date and irregular publication were in character with the timeless subject matter'. His own 'barely disguised Dorset bits' are sharply defined with the clarity and pace that only an accomplished crime writer can manage. The plot of *Blood Money* put an edge on the topography and it was nice to know that my jottings and ramblings had been of use.

At 6.15p.m. on 21 June 1988 a fire began in one of the chemical storage buildings of BDH (British Drug Houses) Ltd on their extensive industrial site beside West Quay Road. Prompt action by the emergency services prevented what could have been a far worse inferno. There was, however, damage to adjoining properties and because of the hazardous and toxic nature of the basic raw materials in the store the decision was taken to evacuate hundreds of nearby homes. People were not allowed back to their homes until the following morning which, the company said, was a precautionary measure, emphasising that there had been no injuries or disruption to its output:

> *Apart from the stores building on this site, there was no other damage within BDH. The major stores areas, production facilities, laboratories, administration and distribution facilities were all unaffected. Production is continuing normally and the computerised materials management system which we installed recently will ensure efficient replenishment of the lost materials.*

A crowded rush-hour train from Poole, Bournemouth and Southampton came to grief at Clapham on the morning of 12 December 1988. In the accident, in which an express train ploughed into

Victorian viaducts, with diesel locomotive 66187 crossing Surrey Road (centre), *in a view eastwards from Bourne Valley Road.*

South West Trains, with a passenger service (top right) *from Waterloo to Weymouth, passing under Towngate Bridge.*

Pedestrian crossing the cast-iron Victorian footbridge (centre) *in the High Street as trains bound for Waterloo* (left) *and Weymouth* (right) *pass through Poole.*

Railway footbridge (centre) *beside Omnibooks* (left) *in Falkland Square, as pedestrians reclaim their rights to the High Street.*

Heads in the crowd, capturing a sense of society in motion, with 'Food you can trust' being carried in a tide of pedestrians over the level crossing in Poole.

Level crossing in the High Street, as seen from the footbridge, after a train has rattled through the centre of Poole.

Mature oaks in Delph Woods between Dunyeat's Hill and Gravel Hill at Broadstone.

the back of a commuter train that had stopped at a malfunctioning signal outside Clapham Junction, 33 people were killed and 111 injured. There is a memorial to the victims at the top of the embankment from which rescue operations were carried out, beside the road across Spencer Park, London SW18.

Passageway stonework at Barbers Wharf incorporates commemorative bricks from 1753 and 1870, with a 1989-dated inscription below to record its rebuilding. The hot summer of 1989 was perfect for building work but highly stressful for such areas of Poole's relict heathland as the Corfe Hills public open space, which had also suffered in the droughts of 1975 and 1976. The 3-acre bog of sphagnum and tussock grass, lying in Rushcombe Bottom between the Corfe Hills, was designated a site of special scientific interest by the Nature Conservancy.

Despite fears for its future, and potentially devastating fires, the mire never lost its moisture in the drought years. Bird life includes Dartford warblers in the gorse scrub, though jays and woodpeckers are the usual and most conspicuous species in the older pines. Land at Barrow Hill and either side of Broadstone Golf Course is also managed as part of the nature reserve.

For devotees of Poole Speedway and its Poole Pirates team, formed in 1948, the 1989 and 1990 seasons were the best yet. As Alun Rossiter recalls, the team from the stadium in Wimborne Road were henceforth 'the Manchester United of the speedway world, with all the other clubs striving to match the achievements'. These included the National League Championship, for both years, as well as defeating Middlesbrough to win the Knock-Out Cup in 1990. The previous year Rossiter rode 'alongside the likes of Craig Boyce, Leigh Adams, Alastair Stevens, Gary Allan, Tony Langdon and Kevin Smart'. In 1990, to complete the 'glorious double', Adams, Smart and Stevens were replaced by Tom Knudsen, Ron Colquhoun and Gary Chessell.

C.H. Horn, workhorse vessel of Poole Harbour Commissioners, sometimes picks up more than has been anticipated. In 1990, while dredging off Town Quay, the trophy was an unexploded 1,100lb bomb. Steve Blundel, the scoop operator, summoned a bomb disposal team and eventually saw it blown up with a controlled explosion in Poole Bay. The blast shuddered through the hull even though it took place more than a mile away.

'An Island in the Bay?' was the title of 'a development concept for the oil reserves under Poole Bay' as promoted by BP Exploration in 1990. Its proposed location was a mile east of the Haven Hotel at Sandbanks, east of Hook Sands, in the vicinity of East Hook Buoy to the north of Studland Bay. Basing an oil rig above a 'sealed site' at sea, it was claimed, 'would enable almost 100 million barrels of oil to be recovered from the offshore extension of the Sherwood reservoir under Poole Bay'. In the event, the plan failed to win sufficient support, and the oil was reached by an unprecedented application of long-distance drilling from rigs on Goathorn peninsula in Poole Harbour.

The fishing boat *Nibbler* was claimed by the Hook Sands early in the 1990s. Having run aground, it rolled over and paid the price. Drums of diesel fuel recovered from the deck, from the pollution aspect, posed more of a threat to the environment than any hazards presented by the hull. This would be swallowed by the shifting sands, as is demonstrated by the occasional cars that have ceased waiting for the Sandbanks ferry at North Haven slipway and gone down the slope into the Swash Channel. 'The strength of the current is quite unbelievable there,' Kevin Nelson points out, with the result that vehicles disappear so quickly that divers fail to find any trace of them.

In March 1991, in an unprecedented move, the government took a stand on the loss of sites of Special Scientific Interest by blocking plans to extend Poole's newest suburb towards the skyline on Canford Heath. Michael Heseltine, Secretary of State for the Environment, announced that he was revoking planning permission for 200 houses – a victory for the conservationists who had fought a five-year campaign. The fragment of lowland heath was home to some of Britain's rarest species, from the sand lizard and smooth snake to the distinctive Dartford warbler.

Prior to the intervention – which had considerable compensation implications – the developers were winning, Poole Borough Council having successfully defeated an attempt to block the scheme in the High

Court. The Environment Minister said that the planning system was failing to protect such areas and that remaining undeveloped parts of Canford Heath had been nominated for the additional cachet of a 'special protection area' under European Community regulations. In the previous decade a third of Canford Heath had been lost to housing and roads.

Poole Pottery re-established itself as an independent company in October 1992, a £3/5 million buy-out led by Murray Johnstone freeing it from control by the Pilkington's Tile subsidiary of BTR. Roland Denning of Sock Shop became non-executive chairman while Peter Mills and Peter Henness, both from Dartington Crystal, became managing director and finance director respectively.

Portly rock star Greg Lake (born 1948) of the band Emerson, Lake and Palmer, came from Oakdale, Poole, as he reminded his audience at Bournemouth International Centre on what Jeremy Miles described as 'a nostalgia-soaked set that had ageing fans beside themselves with joy'. 'Back home again after all these years,' he yelled at the concert on 25 November 1992. Lake played guitar and provided the golden voice, with Keith Emerson at the keyboard of a beloved but battered Hammond organ and Carl Palmer on drums.

Ghost stories clustered around a block of modern maisonettes at Egmont Road, Turlin Moor, shortly before Christmas in 1992. The shadowy shape of a young soldier had been reported from several flats and poltergeist activity claimed in another. Cupboard doors had banged, church bells had rung and a spectral figure had 'even made love in one woman's bed', to quote the *Evening Echo*.

After its closure by National Power, Hamworthy Power Station and its pair of giant chimneys literally dropped from the landscape, at 10.15a.m. on 3 February 1993. Roads were closed and hundreds of people evacuated from 80 homes and numerous nearby businesses in the area around Hamworthy Station. Explosive charges brought down the chimneys, which fell almost as planned, just 15 minutes behind schedule, disturbing two seagulls as they collapsed towards Holes Bay.

A stretch of road near Heatherlands First School in Upper Parkstone had the first 20 miles per hour speed limit in Dorset. The 50th in England as a whole, it was declared operational by Roads Minister Kenneth Carlisle on 8 March 1993:

The momentum for these limits is growing. They have been very successful in stopping road accidents, reducing all casualties by well over half and child injuries by even more. Taming the motor car in areas like these gives streets back to the local people. Speed is the single most serious cause of accidents.

Following a £10,000 robbery in Poole on 4 April 1993, two police officers were taken to hospital with shotgun wounds after trying to stop a car. Two masked men, with Liverpool accents, had taken the cash from the Unigate Dairy. The shots came from a stolen black Ford Sierra driven by a third man. The blast, from 5 yards away, shattered both the passenger- and driver-side windows as the shell passed through the patrol car. The wounded officers, who had pellets removed from their arms and legs, were PC Charlie Dale (36) and PC Steve Hogarth (34).

By 1994 the Royal Marines base at Hamworthy was employing 600 service personnel, rising to a peak of 1,000 during training periods, plus 100 civilians. Then came the announcement of its closure, with the run-down to be completed in 1998, with the transfer of the Special Boat Squadron to Portsmouth. It was estimated that the closure would save £12 million over ten years and to free for sale a site worth £50 million. Defence Secretary Malcolm Rifkind announced:

The Royal Marines themselves suggested the move in order to reduce their support costs. They are therefore able to focus more of their resources on their fighting capability.

The Fairway Buoy from the safe side of the Main Channel was also pensioned off in the 1990s and retired to a traffic island beside Holes Bay.

As a 16-year-old, Gavin Eaton of Countess Close, Merley, began his stage and television career at the top in 1994, with an appearance at the London Palladium and a part in 'The Bill', in which his character found his ex-policeman grandfather dead at home:

When I appeared in 'The Bill' there was a lot of waiting around. It got a bit boring and frustrating sitting around in a van, but when we got down to the acting it was really good fun.

He also sang in the choir at Sadlers Wells Theatre and the Royal Albert Hall and took part in cabaret at the Grosvenor, the Mayfair Hotel and the Park Lane Hilton. Gavin beat a total of 300 applicants to win a scholarship to the Sylvia Young Stage School.

Canford School celebrated a windfall in the summer of 1994. Canford's unexpected millions came, literally, in the form of a relief. The carving of Ashurnasirpal II (King of Assyria, 883–859BC), which had looked down on the tuck shop for generations, having been among the Assyrian antiquities brought to Canford House by Sir Henry Layard, had always been regarded as a plaster copy rather than a stone original – in 1959 Sandy Martin of Sotheby's had found what turned out to be plaster repairs by probing with a pen-knife. Seven other panels were authenticated, however, and were sold at auction for a total of £13,485.

Instead of raising £2,000 at Sotheby's for Canford

Condor, *the flagship of Brittany Ferries, leaving Poole Harbour for Cherbourg in July 2005.*

School, in 1959, the panel sold at Christie's for £7,700,000 in 1994 to a buyer representing the Moa sect from Kyoto. Headmaster John Lever set about using the money to build a new theatre at Canford School, promising that 'an excellent' replica of Ashurnasirpal II would dominate the entrance.

John Lever answered critics by pointing out that Canford 'is not a museum but a school'. Those who had heard of Ashurnasirpal as a result of the publicity and reacted as if he was a patron of the arts, were reminded in *The Times* by Adrian Russell of Lytchett Matravers that Ashurnasirpal's progress from Thebes to Ninevah 'was marked by impalements, pyramids of human heads and other unspeakable savageries.' Christopher Godley suggested a new motto for the school: 'For this relief, much thanks.'

In the summer holiday of 1996 12 Gypsy families squeezed through a hedge to pitch camp at Canford School. Commander Michael Chamberlain, bursar of the 540-pupil public school which then charged £12,500 a year, sent in a mechanical digger to prevent others joining them and eventually negotiated a withdrawal under the Criminal Justice Act:

> *We are concerned about the security of our buildings and our young pupils. The police have been as helpful as they can be but are practically powerless in these sorts of situations. We are on good speaking terms with the Gypsies and we hope they will respect our courtesy and leave soon.*

In July 1997 national newspapers, starting with the *News of the World*, carried the story of Britain's youngest mother, 12-year-old Jenny Teague from Martin Kemp-Welch School in Poole, who had given birth that spring to a 7lb 6oz daughter, Sasha, by caesarean section. Given permission to speak publicly by her parents, Carol and Tom Teague, she told the press: 'My baby is gorgeous and I love her to bits. My mum and dad have been great but I wish I was 16. I'm too young to have a baby. My one big dream is to be older.'

Her headmaster, Keith Baddock, confirmed that Jenny was already pregnant when she started secondary education. He referred to it as a 'tragedy', adding that five other teenage girls at the school were also pregnant. Jenny had not realised she was expecting a baby until she complained of stomach aches when she was eight months pregnant. The headmaster said:

> *She must have been going through a nightmare. Her classmates have accepted her and she is a normal pupil. I don't know who the father is, or if he is at my school, but I understand that he is 13 years old.*

Vicar and councillor Revd Charles Meachin came to their support: 'These people are the salt of the earth. There is no better place to bring up a baby.'

'Morals campaigner' Victoria Gillick and Health Minister Tessa Jowell used the case to highlight under-age pregnancies and single motherhood as national problems. Ms Jowell blamed social inequalities:

> *It is all too likely to be a cause as well as a symptom of poor education, unemployment and social exclusion. If a healthy school can keep a child from following her mother by getting pregnant at seventeen she has a better chance of getting qualifications, getting a job, breaking out of the loop.*

The seals of Poole and Purbeck usually enjoy good public relations. They tend to arrive as individuals and develop personalities rather than reaching the pest proportions that threaten fisheries. Richard Blomfield, in *The Seal who Made Friends*, and Kevin Nelson in *Purbeck and Poole Magazine* described experiences reminiscent of *The Seal Summer* at Chapman's Pool as described by Langton Matravers author Nina Warner Hooke. Fishermen report that Sika deer have been known to swim across the channels of Poole Harbour. Other perennial favourites are the swans, particularly those that share human spaces or are unusually conspicuous, such as the pair that successfully brought up a brood of five young in 2001.

Despite suffering on an alarming scale as a fishing by-catch in the Bay of Biscay, Poole's emblem still puts in an occasional live appearance. Kevin Nelson has encountered dolphins on his 'working excursions' through the Swash Channel:

The brief sightings of these very intelligent and beautiful creatures always cause excitement and will forever remain in my memory. First, just a quick glimpse of that familiar dorsal fin, and then they are suddenly alongside the vessel looking up at you, as if they have come to investigate what you are doing in their environment. They swim along for only a few minutes and then they are away, satisfied that no harm is meant to them. They might re-appear again, once or twice on the surface, as they disappear into the distance and continue with their feeding or playing.

Dolphin Quay apartments and marina have replaced Poole Pottery to the east of Town Quay. Poole remains the operational heir to the Cinque Ports tradition. Now, as one of the last of Britain's so-called Trust Ports it is free of the perils of privatisation and the responsibilities of shareholder accountability. Both losses and profits stay in home waters. Fishing, leisure, navigation, shipping and transit have equal claims to the facilities. The idea of a people's port sounds trite but that is modern Poole.

A dolphin in the Swash Channel, heading towards the Bar Buoy (top left) *and Old Harry Rocks* (top right).

Bibliography

Admiralty, Hydrographic Department (1931), *Channel Pilot, Part 1*, London, 12th edn

Andrews, Ian, & Henson, Frank (2000), *Poole: the Second Selection*, Stroud

Bamford, Robert & Shailes (2004), *50 Greats: Poole Pirates*, Stroud

Beamish, Derek, with Bennett, Harold & Hillier, John (1980), *Poole and World War II*, Poole

Beamish, Derek, with Hillier, John and Johnstone, H.F.V. (1976), *Mansions and Merchants of Poole and Dorset*, Poole

Bell, Mrs Arthur (Nancy) (1916), *From Harbour to Harbour: Christchurch, Bournemouth and Poole*, London

Bennett, Alan R. (1979), *Horsewoman: The Extraordinary Mrs D.*, Milborne Port

Blake, George (1985), *Poole Past and Present*, Newbury

Blomfield, Richard (1974), *Harbour, Heath and Islands*, Milborne Port

Blomfield, Richard (1989), *Poole Town and Harbour*, Wincanton

Borough of Poole, The New Municipal Offices Souvenir (1932), Poole

Brannon, Philip (1875), *Guide to Poole and Bournemouth*, Poole and London

Butts, Mary (1937), *The Crystal Cabinet: My Childhood at Salterns*, London

Butts, Mary (1991), *With and Without Buttons*, London

Carter, Herbert S. (1933), *Captain Ben and the Almighty*, Poole

Carter, Herbert S. (1946), *Poole's My Port: Being some account of the small adventures of one who was fond of boats*, Poole

Carter, Herbert S. (1926), *What's ma'r wi' Poole?*, Poole, 2nd edn

Cochrane, C. (1970), *Poole Bay and Purbeck: 300BC–AD1660*, Dorchester

Cochrane, C. (1971), *Poole Bay and Purbeck (2): 1660–1920*, Dorchester

Cuthell, Lieutenant-Colonel T.G. (1893), *A Sailing Guide to the Solent and Poole Harbour*, London

Farr, Grahame (1971), *Wreck and Rescue on the Dorset Coast: the story of the Dorset Lifeboats*, Truro

Fox & Sons (1927), *Auction Sale of the Contents of the Mansion, Brownsea Castle, Brownsea Island, Dorset*, Bournemouth

Gilbert, Michael (1957), *The Claimant: The Tichborne Case Reviewed*, London

Guttridge, Roger (1987), *Dorset Smugglers*, Wincanton, 2nd edn

Hatts, Leigh and Marples (2000), *Marion Poole & Sandbanks*, Teffont

Haward, Samuel (1745), *Sermon Preach'd at Poole in Dorsetshire On Occasion of the Present Unnatural Rebelllion, December 1st, 1745*, London

Hawkes, Andrew (1995) *Lifeboatmen Never Turn Back: Poole Lifeboat Service from 1826* Poole

Hillier, John (1985), *Ebb-Tide at Poole*, Poole

Hillier, John (1992), *Poole After World War II: 1945–53*, Poole

Hillier, John and Blyth, Martin (1996), *Poole's Pride Regained*, Poole

Holroyd, Michael (1974), *Augustus John*, Vols 1 and 2, London

House of Commons (1836), *Report from the Select Committee on Poole Borough Municipal Election*, London

Hutchins, John (1774–1874), *History and Antiquities of the County of Dorset*, London, three editions

Kelly's Directories Ltd, *Kelly's Directory of Dorsetshire* London, editions for 1889, 1915, 1931, 1935 and 1939

Kennedy, Margaret (1924), *The Constant Nymph*, London

Kitchin, D.B. (1898), *The Solent Chart Book: between Selsea and Portland*, London

Legg, Rodney (1986) *Brownsea: Dorset's Fantasy Island* Wincanton

Legg, Rodney (2002), *Dorset Families*, Tiverton

Legg, Rodney (1986), *Literary Dorset*, Wincanton

Legg, Rodney (2004), *Dorset's War Diary: Battle of Britain to D-Day*, Wincanton

Legg, Rodney (1990), *Literary Dorset*, Wincanton

Legg, Rodney (1987), *Purbeck's Heath: claypits, nature and the oilfield*, Wincanton

Mills, A.D. (1980), *The Place-names of Dorset*, Part 2, London

Nash, Paul (1936), *Dorset Shell Guide*, London

Nelson, Kevin (2002), *Purbeck and Poole Magazine*, Issue no. 11. Tiverton

Pitfield, F.P. (1981), *Dorset Parish Churches, A-D*, Wincanton

Poole Pottery (1973), *The First 100 Years: of the story of Poole Pottery*, Poole

Royal Commission on Historical Monuments (1970), *Dorset*, Volume II, parts 2 and 3, London

Ruff, Ivan (1988), *Blood Country*, London

Ruff, Ivan (1987), *Dead Reckoning*, London

Short, Bernard C. (1927), *Early Days of Nonconformity in Poole*, Poole

Short, Bernard C. (1932), *Poole: The Romance of its Early History*, Poole

Short, Bernard C. (1932), *Poole: The Romance of its Later History*, Poole

Short, Bernard C. (1969), *Smugglers of Poole and Bournemouth*, Bournemouth

Short, Bernard C. (1927), *Smuggling in Poole, Bournemouth and Neighbourhood*, Poole

Smith, H.P. (1948–51), *The History of the Borough and County of the Town of Poole*, Volumes 1 and 2, Poole

Smith, Brother Harry P. (1937), *History of the Lodge of Amity, No. 137, Poole*, Poole

Sydenham, John (1839), *The History of the Town and County of Poole*, Poole and London

Sydenham, Guy (2000), *A Potter's Life: the Island Potters of Poole*, Tiverton

United States Navy Department (1942), *Sailing Directions for the South Coast of England*, Washington

van Raalte, Charles and Florence (1906), *Brownsea Island*, London

Wallace, Alfred Russel (1908), *My Life: A record of events and opinions*, London

Walmsley, Hugh Mulleneux (1872), *Branksome Dene: A Sea Tale*, three volumes, London

Wheway, Edna (1984), *Edna's Story*, Wimborne

Woodruff, Douglas (1957), *The Tichborne Claimant: A Victorian Mystery*, London

Sunset over Poole Harbour.

Subscribers

Gwendoline E. Allen, Poole, Dorset
Mrs Peggy Allgood, Poole, Dorset
Bryan R. Allner, Poole, Dorset
Phillip Anderton, Poole, Dorset
Violet M. Archer
Robert B. Baker, Poole, Dorset
Thelma Baker, Poole, Dorset
Raymond W. Bale, Poole, Dorset
John C. Barham Esq., Hamworthy, Poole
Iris Barnes, Parkstone, Poole, Dorset
Ivy and John Barnes CBE, Canford Cliffs
Mr G. Barnett
Hilary Barton, Poole
Martin Belford, Poole, Dorset
Jean E. Bennett, Alderney, Poole, Dorset
Anthony E. Bessant, Poole, Dorset
Mrs S. Bessant, Poole, Dorset
Charles Blair, Poole, Dorset
Terry and Joy Bowers, Parkstone, Poole
Mr Charles Derek Brobbin, Poole, Dorset
Mr Gordon H. Brown, Clarence Road, Parkstone, Dorset
Bernard J.K. Budden, Poole, Dorset
Kevin Burbidge, Poole, Dorset
Mark Burden, Oakdale, Poole, Dorset
William H. Burling
Andrew P. Burt, Parkstone, Poole
Mr and Mrs G.R. Caines, Poole
Mr and Mrs D. Challis, West End House, Poole
Sylvia Chappell (née Hayward), Poole, Dorset
Mrs E. Cheeseman, Poole, Dorset
Eric W. Cheeseman, Poole, Dorset
Eva Chisman, Poole, Dorset
Paul Christopher, Parkstone, Poole
Derek Churchill, Poole, Dorset
John and Mary Clark, Stenhurst Road, Oakdale, Poole, Dorset
Jonathan and Anne-Marie Clark, West Quay Road, Poole, Dorset
Elizabeth Clayton (née Pearce), Poole
Eric Cockwell, Poole, Dorset
Ivor R. Coleman, Poole, Dorset
John M. Cook, Poole, Dorset
Mrs Elizabeth Cooper, Upton, Poole
J. and M. Cooper, Poole
Mr and Mrs D.L. Cope, Hamworthy
Mark Cecil Copton, Poole, Dorset
Mr Christopher R. Corbin, Parkstone, Poole, Dorset
Mrs Pearl June Corbin, Poole, Dorset
Raymond K. Corbin, Parkstone, Poole, Dorset
A.V. Cox, Branksome, Poole, Dorset
Mr and Mrs D. Cox, Poole
Paul A. Cox, Upton, Poole
Michael D.P. Cox, Poole
Brian Dart, Poole, Dorset
Dai and Janet Davies, Poole
J.V. Davis, Poole, Dorset
Mr B. Dawson, Poole, Dorset
Janet S. Dennett, Poole, Dorset
Louise K. and Michael D. Dennis, Poole
Gordon L. Diffey, Poole
Peter W.J. Diffey, Christchurch, Dorset
Brian J. Dockery, Poole, Dorset
Mr Walter George Robert Dodd, Poole, Dorset
W.R.J. Downes, Poole
John G. Drake, Poole, Dorset
Christopher Durant, Poole, Dorset
David F. Eaton, Holton Heath, Poole, Dorset
Gerald and Lisa Edwards, Poole, Dorset
William and Patricia Edwards, Poole, Dorset
Patricia Ellis (née Christopher), ex-Market Street, Poole
Chris and Beth Farrier, Poole
Harold G. Farwell, Poole, Dorset
Brian Fisher, Wallisdown, Poole, Dorset
Colin Flooks, Bournemouth, Dorset
Sean and Jayne Frampton, Parkstone, Poole, Dorset
John and Ann Freeborn, Poole, Dorset
The Freeborns, Foundry Arms, Poole, Dorset
Graham and Janet Gale, Poole, Dorset
Philip J. Gillingham, Poole, Dorset
Mr Kenneth Gough, Poole, Dorset
Joan Green, Poole, Dorset
Mrs Pamela Greenslade, Poole, Dorset
Helen Griffiths, Parkstone, Poole, Dorset
Christine H. Hall, Poole, Dorset
Patricia Harris, Poole, Dorset
Mr R.R. Harris, Poole, Dorset
Anne M. Bevis Hatch, Parkstone, Poole, Dorset
Phyllis and Ted Hawes
Andrew Hawkes, High Street, Poole
Andrew Hayward, Poole, Dorset
Mark Hayward, Poole, Dorset
Michael E. Hayward, Poole, Dorset
Alan C. Heyward
Mr and Mrs Ronald G. Hibberd
Alfred J. Hicks, Poole, Dorset
J.W.G. Howes MBE, BEM, Parkstone, Poole, Dorset
Jean Hustler, Poole
Frederick G. James, Poole, Dorset

Mary M. Jamieson, Poole, Dorset
Mike and Sally Jeans, Poole, Dorset
Bruce, Viv and Family Jones, Parkstone, Poole
Mr Colin Jones, Poole, Dorset
Lynda Jones, Ipswich, Suffolk
Catherine Monica Kane, Motherwell, Scotland
Christopher James Keir, Talbot Village, Poole, Dorset
Mr Martin Addison King, Poole, Dorset
Edward D. Kitt, Wimborne, Dorset
James J. Kitt, Wimborne, Dorset
Robert A. Knight, Poole, Dorset
D. Lane, Poole, Dorset
Ann Lloyd, Ontario, Canada
Ken Longstreet, Poole
John Loosemore, Poole
Simon and Gilly Loveless, Poole
Roy and Brian Lovell, Poole, Dorset
Mr Barry W.D. Lyle, Poole, Dorset
Mr Keith Edward Marshallsay
Mrs B. Martin (née Harvey), Poole, Dorset
Keith John Matthews, Poole, Dorset
Reg and Maureen McLean, St Leonards-on-Sea, Sussex
Colin C. McLean, Poole, Dorset
Maureen Meaden, Poole, Dorset
Rob Meech, Parkstone, Poole, Dorset
W.F. Miles, Poole, Dorset
Mrs Beverley J. Miller, Poole
Mr Peter Moody, Poole, Dorset
James Moore, Poole, Dorset
Mrs Cora E. Moores
Roy Munford, Poole
Mr S.M. Munster, Poole, Dorset
Terence C. Musselwhite, Poole, Dorset
Iris A. Newbury, Poole, Dorset
Barry Nichol, Poole, Dorset
Phillip Noble, Poole, Dorset
Jock O'Pray, Upton, Poole
Ray Osborne, Poole, Dorset
Mr and Mrs G. Page, Poole
K.M. Pearce, Poole, Dorset
Harry A. Pethen, Poole, Dorset
Kathleen Phillips, Poole, Dorset
S.A. Poole, Dorset
Mr Roger David Potter, Poole, Dorset
Grace A. Pryor, Poole, Dorset
George W. Rand, Poole, Dorset
John and Rebecca Read, Broadstone, Dorset
Brian and Sheila Richards (née Foote), Parkstone, Poole, Dorset
Patrick A.C. Riggs, Parkstone, Poole, Dorset
Mrs A. Roberts, Parkstone, Poole
Anne and John Robinson, Coulsdon, Surrey
Richard H. Rumsby, Poole, Dorset
Mrs G. Ruston, Poole, Dorset
Sheila Sanders, Poole, Dorset
Paul Shee, The Water Garden Hotel, Bournemouth, Dorset
Mr Richard Sheppard, Bournemouth
John Sherwood, Poole, Dorset
Jessie Short, Poole, Dorset
Jim and Ruth Short, Poole, Dorset
Christopher M. Smith, Poole, Dorset
David R. Smith, son of Bertie and Ada, Poole, Dorset
David J. Spicer, Poole, Dorset
Terry Stewart, Canford Cliffs
David E. Stranks
D.E.N. Thompson, Poole, Dorset
D.J. Thoroughgood, Branksome, Poole, Dorset
Michael Tombs, Poole, Dorset
Brian E. Traves, Poole, Dorset
Phillip L. Traves, Portland, Dorset
Sara L. Tucker, Poole, Dorset
Gerald I. Vincent
John F.W. Walling, Newton Abbot, Devon
Jeremy D. Waters
Christine Wheatley, Weymouth, Dorset
Mr Edwin T. White, Poole, Dorset
Miss June S.P. White (born 1925), Poole
Julia M.E. Williams
Mr J. Williams, Poole, Dorset
Marion and John Williams, Parkstone, Poole, Dorset
Ian Charles, Chloe and Matthew Wilson, Poole, Dorset
Daphne B. Woodward, Poole, Dorset
Barrie and Tina Wootton, Parkstone, Poole
Julie Worthington, Branksome, Poole, Dorset
Ann S. Young, Poole, Dorset
Douglas S.G. Young, Poole, Dorset